Lecture Notes in Computer Science 4309

Commenced Publication in 1973
Founding and Former Series Editors:
Gerhard Goos, Juris Hartmanis, and Jan van Leeuwen

Paola Inverardi   Mehdi Jazayeri (Eds.)

Software Engineering Education in the Modern Age

Software Education and Training Sessions
at the International Conference
on Software Engineering, ICSE 2005
St. Louis, MO, USA, May 15-21, 2005
Revised Lectures

 Springer

Volume Editors

Paola Inverardi
University of L'Aquila
Computer Science Department
67010 L'Aquila, Italy
E-mail: inverard@di.univaq.it

Mehdi Jazayeri
University of Lugano
and Technical University of Vienna
E-mail: mehdi.jazayeri@unisi.ch

Library of Congress Control Number: 2006938014

CR Subject Classification (1998): K.3, K.4, D.2, J.1

LNCS Sublibrary: SL 2 – Programming and Software Engineering

ISSN   0302-9743
ISBN-10   3-540-68203-1 Springer Berlin Heidelberg New York
ISBN-13   978-3-540-68203-5 Springer Berlin Heidelberg New York

Springer is a part of Springer Science+Business Media

springer.com

© Springer-Verlag Berlin Heidelberg 2006
Printed in Germany

Typesetting: Camera-ready by author, data conversion by Scientific Publishing Services, Chennai, India
Printed on acid-free paper   SPIN: 11949374   06/3142   5 4 3 2 1 0

Preface

Software Engineering is a multifaceted and expanding topic. It aims to provide theories, methods and tools to tackle the complexity of software systems, from development to maintenance. Its complexity is made even more severe today by rapid advances in technology, the pervasiveness of software in all areas of society, and the globalization of software development. The continuous expansion of the field presents the problem of how to keep up for practitioners. For educators, the key questions are how should software engineers be educated and what are the core topics and key technologies?

Even looking only at the last decade, the tremendous changes that have taken place in the software engineering industry, and in the industrial world in general, raise many questions. What are the effects of: Outsourcing? Distributed software development? Open source? Standardization? Software patents? Model-driven development? How should these developments change the way we teach software engineering? Should textbooks be updated? Should software engineering play a different role in the computer science curriculum, for example, be more pervasive? How are instructors in universities handling these issues?

All these issues were discussed at the Software Education and Training sessions at the International Conference on Software Engineering (ICSE 2005) by leading researchers, educators, and practitioners in software engineering, who presented their—sometimes controversial—views and insights on software engineering education in the new millennium. In this volume we have collected some of the most representative and innovative approaches that were presented at the workshop. The authors revised their papers based on discussions at the conference and the comments they received from the reviews. Together, these papers show the state of the art and practice and the significant challenges facing our field in educating the next generation of software engineers.

The contributions are grouped in two parts. The first part discusses the present. It is introduced by two papers that discuss respectively the limits and the realities of today's software engineering education. The following four papers address the critical problem of teaching software modeling and design, that is, the problem of teaching at the same time, creativity and abstraction, rigorous specifications and easy formalization. The second part of the book deals with the future. In the two introductory papers, representatives from industry and academia, respectively, give their perspectives on the future. The last four papers address different challenges of future software engineering education. On-line education, in-context software engineering education, education to master outsourcing and other distributed software development, organizational software engineering are all concerned with widening the scope of interest of software engineers, intersecting with other disciplines and sciences.

This book provides a snapshot of the state of software engineering education at the beginning of the twenty-first century. It is a good starting point for software engineering researchers and educators alike. It is also a source of ideas for instructors who are looking to improve their software engineering courses.

This book is the result of the work of many people. Paola Inverardi and Mehdi Jazayeri organized the Software Engineering Education and Training Track at ICSE 2005. They requested contributions from the research and education community. The organizers selected the most appropriate contributions and invited the authors to present their positions at the conference. The presentations were followed by active discussions from the audience. In all, a few hundred people participated in the three days of meetings. After the meeting, we asked several of the participants to prepare papers on their contributions for this volume.

We would like to thank all the people who submitted their work to the conference, the people who participated in the sessions, and the authors of the present volume. We also would like to thank Catalin Roman, General Chair of ICSE 2005, who asked us to organize the track. Finally, we would like to thank Jochen Wuttke for helping us to prepare this volume.

September 2006

Paola Inverardi
Mehdi Jazayeri

Table of Contents

On Software Engineering Education

State of the Art and Practice: Creativity and Rigor

Challenges for Industries and Academia

Future Directions

Reflections on Software Engineering Education

Hans van Vliet

Vrije Universiteit, Amsterdam
hans@cs.vu.nl

Abstract. The "engineering" focus in software engineering education leaves instructors vulnerable to several traps. It also misleads students as to SE's essential human and social dimensions. In this paper we argue that there's more to SE than engineering. A major challenge is to reconcile the engineering dimension with the human and social dimension.

1 Introduction

In recent years, the SE community has focused on organizing our existing knowledge and finding ways to transform it into a curriculum. These efforts produced SWEBOK (the Guide to the Software Engineering Body of Knowledge; www.swebok.org) and Software Engineering 2004 (http://sites.computer.org/ccse). SWEBOK reflects a widely agreed-upon view of what a software engineer who has a bachelor's degree and four years' experience should know. SE 2004 offers curriculum guidelines for undergraduate SE degree programs. We can view SE 2004 as SWEBOK's education counterpart.

Both SE 2004 and SWEBOK are important milestones resulting from participants' extensive real-world experience and working-group discussions. Both heavily emphasize the 'engineering' in software engineering [1,2,3]. This focus influences the contents of a typical SE course as well as the students' understanding of what SE entails. However, SE has an important social dimension that's easily squeezed out by the omnipresent engineering attitude. Here, I discuss how this limited conception of SE contributes to five assumptions that can trap SE educators:

- An SE course needs an industrial project.
- SE is like other branches of engineering.
- Planning in SE is poorly done relative to other fields.
- The user interface is part of low-level design.
- SWEBOK represents the state of the practice.

The traps idea isn't highly original. Several authors have published similar articles on the myths of formal methods, requirements engineering, and SE programs [4]. In the latter case, the authors discuss whether the new SE degree programs are a silver bullet. The traps I discuss focus on a typical SE course's content and how it represents SE to beginning students. My aim is both to provoke discussion and to highlight the challenges these traps present to SE educators.

P. Inverardi and M. Jazayeri (Eds.): ICSE 2005 Education Track, LNCS 4309, pp. 1–10, 2006.

2   Context

My teaching situation partly determines and bounds the traps I discuss. Typically, Dutch universities don't offer separate computer science (CS) and SE degrees. They have a three-year bachelor's program and a two-year master's program in CS. Most students enroll in the bachelor's program right after high school. The program doesn't have much specialization and usually has one general SE course. Typically, this course includes theory and project work. The master's program generally contains a series of more specialized SE courses.

The Vrije Universiteit rates its SE course's theoretical and practical parts at 4 and 8 ECTS credits, respectively. (In the European Credit Transfer System, 1 ECTS amounts to approximately 28 study hours; a full year is 60 ECTS.) The course lasts 12 weeks. Students are scheduled to take it in the second year of their bachelor's program, which means they have little maturity in CS or SE when they enroll. The course is compulsory for students in CS, AI, and information science. Typically, 150 to 200 students enroll each year.

In terms of SE 2004, we follow a CS-first approach: students aren't introduced to SE in a serious way until the second year. Our course's content strongly resembles that of SE 2004's proposed SE201 course, presenting SE's basic principles and concepts.

3   Software Education Traps

At one time or another, I've fallen into most of the traps discussed here, as have many colleagues with whom I've discussed SE education over the years.

Trap 1: An SE course needs an industrial project
The idea behind this assumption is that we should prepare students for "the real world," which is complex, full of inconsistencies, and ever changing. The real world also involves participants from different domains and has political and cultural aspects. To meet this challenge, we might base projects on real industry examples [5] or introduce obstacles and dirty tricks into student exercises [6]. The question is, how helpful is this?

Student overload. Prior to their second year, students usually have taken courses on programming, data structures, computer organization, and so on. In such courses, instructors typically structure the work clearly and give students unambiguous problems. And too often, the problems have only one right answer. In the SE course, students are suddenly overwhelmed with many new topics. Of course, it might be possible to gently introduce some SE principles in other introductory courses. In practice, this isn't easy in a CS environment.

So, at the start of our SE course, students aren't familiar with requirements engineering (RE) and don't know how to

- write unambiguous requirements or elicit them from stakeholders from other
   domains,

- prioritize requirements,
- relate requirements to effort (to them, all requirements are equal, regardless of their content), or
- document requirements.

Last but not least, students don't (yet) appreciate RE's value. For example, only a few years ago, I asked students to write a requirements document as their first task. In response, one student complained, "How can I possibly write down what the system does when I haven't programmed the damned thing yet?"

The problem isn't limited to RE. Design, testing, configuration management, quality assurance, and so on all face the same issues. Combining an introduction to all these topics with a real-life case simply asks for too much. Additionally, the students aren't mature enough to appreciate the importance of many SE topics. On one hand, many issues sound obvious: pay attention to documentation, apply configuration control, test thoroughly, and so on. On the other hand, our students have difficulty appreciating issues—such as team organization and cost estimation—that software professionals know from the trenches.

Simplify (when possible). In my SE textbook [7], I use a swimming-lessons analogy. Around 1900, Amsterdam schoolchildren typically learned to swim on the school playground, practicing proper movements while lying on wooden benches. In contrast, my father grew up in the countryside and learned to swim the hard way. His father simply tied a rope around his middle, threw him into the river, and shouted: "Swim." Nowadays, swimming lessons start off gently, in a toddler pool with Mama and plenty of flotation devices. Gradually, the amount of floating material is reduced and the pool gets deeper.

I favor a similar approach. In my SE course, I view my students as toddlers on the SE playground. I concentrate on (at most) a few issues in an orchestrated environment. While I cover all the requisite course topics—and tell my favorite anecdotes—the class project highlights only a few targeted issues. In later years and other courses, students will confront additional real-life aspects. I've often noticed that students' appreciation for my initial SE course comes only years after they've suffered through it.

Design is one key SE issue that instructors can address in an orchestrated way—and that's also a major hurdle for most students. Design is "wicked" [8] because of the following:

- *It has no definite formulation.* We can't neatly separate the design process from the preceding or subsequent phases because they all overlap and influence each other.
- *There is no stopping rule.* No criterion exists to tell us when we've reached the solution.
- *Solutions aren't true or false.* Design involves trade-offs between potentially conflicting concerns. Stakeholders in the design process might define different acceptable solutions rather than one best solution.

The latter point, in particular, opens up interesting project possibilities. An instructor might ask different student groups to design the same system but with different priorities (with respect to quality requirements or requirements priorities, for example). The groups might later collectively study and discuss the different designs. (My colleague and I have reported on experiences with this approach at the software architecture level [9].)

An interesting and often-applied option is to have a dual program, in which students spend, say, half a year in industry and half a year at school. This reduces the pressure on the university to include "real-life" course elements while also increasing the likelihood that students will appreciate typical SE topics. Unfortunately, that's not an option for all instructors (yours truly included), mainly because of university systems that target full-time students who enter the university right after high school.

Trap 2: SE is like other branches of engineering

All SE texts discuss the similarities between SE and other engineering branches—as well, of course, as the differences (interesting examples compare SE with bridge design [10] and high-pressure steam engines [11]). The overall message, however, is that the similarities prevail.

Engineering's limits. Although the engineering metaphor is useful, there's a downside to it. Our field uses numerous engineering words: building software, requirements, specification, process, maintenance, and so on. Altogether, this induces a model of how we view the software development practice; the engineering metaphor plays an active role in our thought processes [12]. For example, we generally characterize the RE process as follows:

- Information (the requirements) flows from A (the user) to B (the software engineer).
- Good communication doesn't involve any frictions or blockages.
- Good reception of the information involves only extraction.

The underlying model is that requirements exist somewhere; we just have to capture them. Thus, it's a *documentation* issue. If we run into problems, there must be a blockage or breakdown in the communication channel: "Why can't the users express their real demands?"

But there are other options, such as viewing RE as an *understanding* issue. It then becomes a dialog between parties, with the requirements engineer acting as a kind of midwife. The requirements aren't something immutable "out there," but rather, they're constructs of the human mind [13].

Social dimensions. Numerous approaches—such as participatory design, rapid application design, joint application design, facilitated workshops, early user involvement, and so on—try to overcome the traditional, functionalist view's disadvantages with respect to RE. Given the clear assignments students are accustomed to from earlier courses, they often perceive the more open attitude toward RE as confusing. One student spoke for many others in labeling it "a badly organized educational exercise."

At a larger scale, a similar tension exists between the heavyweight, document- and planning-driven life-cycle models from SE's engineering realm and the various lightweight approaches that emphasize software development's human aspects. Combining the virtues of both is a major challenge. This is true for the state of the practice and even more so for the educational environment, where students are entrenched in the engineering view of the software development world and are not mature enough to perceive the limits of that view.

The latter became apparent recently when several students majoring in multimedia and culture took our SE course. These students clashed with the regular CS students, who held a rather one-sided, traditional view and failed to see and appreciate the nontechnical issues involved.

Today, engineers from all disciplines need social competences, including communication, organization, and conflict-resolution skills. Also, technological possibility is no longer the only driving force behind success. Increasingly, engineers must weigh competing values such as those related to economics, quality of life, and the social and economic impact of job eliminations [14]. We must prepare our students for this future.

Trap 3: Planning in SE is poorly done relative to other fields
Many papers on SE and SE education have quotes like "Approximately 75 percent of all software projects are either late or cancelled." [15] In his wonderful book, *Death March*, Edward Yourdon quotes the Standish Group and gurus such as Capers Jones and Howard Rubin, stating that, "The *average* project is likely to be 6 to 12 months behind schedule and 50 to 100 percent over budget." And "the grim reality is that you should expect that your project will operate under conditions that will almost certainly lead to some degree of death march behavior on the part of the project manager and his or her technical staff." [16] The sometimes explicit, sometimes implicit message is this: A better software education will help, and might eventually even do away with most runaway projects. I question this connection between SE education level and planning accuracy.

Findings on other fields' infrastructure projects. Looking to other fields can be instructive here. Engineers are currently building an expensive high-speed railway connection to carry freight from Rotterdam's harbor to Germany (and beyond). In 1992, officials estimated total costs at 2.3 billion euro; by 2000, they raised the estimate to 4.7 billion euro. Over the same period, the connection's freight estimates continuously dropped. Many people think the connection will never make money.

In 2005, the Dutch parliament launched an inquiry into the project. It first interviewed Danish economist Bent Flyvbjerg and his coauthors Nils Bruzelius and Werner Rothengatter, who studied over 250 international infrastructure projects [17]. They found that nine out of 10 projects underestimate costs, and almost all projects overestimate revenues. The combination makes projects look good and helps ensure decision makers' approval. Now, people naturally overestimate the good and underestimate the bad, particularly in cases of uncertainty. If you ask people whether they think more people die of cancer or diabetes, they'll most likely say cancer. In fact, it's diabetes, which most people consider to be the less dangerous disease. But there are other explanations as well.

Flyvbjerg, Bruzelius, and Rothengatter cite several well-known projects with spectacular overruns:

- Suez Canal (1869): 1,900 percent over budget
- Sydney Opera House (1973): 1,400 percent over budget
- Concorde (first flight in 1969): 1,100 percent over budget
- Panama Canal (1913): 200 percent over budget
- Brooklyn Bridge (1883): 100 percent over budget

On railway projects, they found that the average project overrun is 45 percent. Next come bridges and tunnels, which have an average overrun of 34 percent.

The authors dismiss technical explanations for such project overruns. If it were simply a matter of technology, then statistically, they would have also found projects with cost underruns. They didn't. Likewise, they dismiss psychological explanations related to estimators' natural optimism. If that were true, we could assume that estimators don't learn from past mistakes. The conclusion? Estimators intentionally underestimate project costs for political reasons: the pressure is high, the parties involved have already made a deal, the project "must be done," and so on.

Software analogue. Many of the arguments that hold for infrastructure project cost and schedule overruns are also valid for software development projects. Educating future software engineers to better count function points, engineer requirements, and approach other key tasks won't on its own resolve overrun issues. As Tom DeMarco put it in 1982, "One chief villain is the policy that estimates shall be used to create incentives." [18] This is as true today as it was then.

In one interesting software cost-estimation experiment [19], the authors studied the "winner's curse," which has the following characteristics:

- Software providers differ in their estimate optimism: some are overly optimistic, some are realistic, and some are pessimistic.
- Software providers with overly optimistic estimates tend to have the lowest bids.
- Software clients require a fixed-price contract.
- Software clients tend to select a provider with a low bid.

The resulting contract often delivers low or negative profits to the bidder; it can also be risky for the client. In one experiment [19], for example, Magne Jørgensen and Stein Gromstad asked 35 companies for bids on a certain requirements specification. They then asked four companies to implement the system. They found that the companies with the lowest bids incurred the greatest risks.

Both Flyvbjerg and Jørgensen emphasize the need for careful risk management. As one experienced project manager told me, "Risk management is project management for adults." Risk management definitely deserves a front seat in a full-fledged SE curriculum.

Trap 4: The user interface is part of low-level design

We can't worry about these user interface issues now. We haven't even gotten this thing to work yet!—R. Mulligan et al. [20]

A system's user interface is important: In an interactive system, about half the code is devoted to the user interface. In a recent study, researchers found that 60 percent of software defects arose from usability errors, while only 15 percent related to functionality [21]. In addition, adequate attention to user interface quality can increase sales of e-commerce sites by 100 percent [22]. For Web-based systems, usability goals are business goals. To improve the state of the practice, we should integrate appropriate user interface design techniques into our software development process. The place to start this practice is SE education.

Ignoring human factors. Is the SE community integrating user interface design techniques into the development process? SWEBOK and SE 2004 offer the most relevant answers here. SWEBOK lists human-computer interface (HCI) as a "related discipline" of SE, concerned with understanding the interactions among humans and other system elements. SE 2004 takes a similar position, describing an HCI course in which user interface design concerns topics such as "use of modes" and "response time and feedback."

Both organizations reflect Mulligan and colleagues' limited view of the user interface. This view totally ignores the fact that many current and future software development projects will aim to develop systems in which human use and related human factors are decisive elements of product quality.

A broader view. Interface design and functionality design go hand in hand. We might even say that the user interface *is* the system. There are two main reasons to take this broader view of the user interface. First, the system—and hence its interface—should help users perform certain tasks. The user interface should therefore reflect the task domain's structure. The design of tasks and their corresponding user interfaces influence each other and should be part of the same iterative refinement process. Like quality, the user interface isn't a supplement. Second, dialog and representation alone don't provide users with sufficient information. To work with a system, users sometimes need to know "what's going on behind the screen."

Various studies corroborate the need to better attend to HCI in SE and CS curricula. Timothy Lethbridge [23], for example, addresses the question of what software professionals need to know. He found that HCI is one of the topics with the widest educational knowledge gap. As Lethbridge reports, practitioners called HCI an important topic but one they'd learned little about in school. Nigel Bevan [24] shows that we must expand the traditional quality assurance approach—which emphasizes software's static and dynamic properties—to incorporate quality-in-use aspects that address broader ergonomic issues.

Proponents of traditional SE see user interface design as a separate activity and don't include it in the mainstream software development process model. We need a more eclectic approach in which we attend to user interface issues from the start. If, as I believe, the user interface is the system, then software developers must have a basic understanding of HCI issues. SE or CS curricula must therefore offer at least an introductory HCI course [25].

Trap 5: SWEBOK represents the state of the practice
In my opinion, SWEBOK and SE 2004 lag behind the state of the practice in some areas and run ahead of the herd in others.

Outpacing reality. As an example of SWEBOK's running ahead of practice, consider data from MOOSE (Software Engineering Methodologies for Embedded Systems; www.mooseproject.org), a recent European research project. MOOSE researchers created a Web repository with 100 entries describing participating companies' industrial experiences. Of the companies' products, researchers found that

- 50 percent were developed without an RE method,
- 75 percent were developed without an RE tool,
- 25 percent were designed without a design method,
- 50 percent were designed using a generic drawing tool or no tool at all,
- 33 percent were tested manually, and
- 90 percent were developed using some configuration management tool.

Clearly, the state-of-the-practice is still quite a bit removed from SWEBOK and the average SE textbook. Fresh graduates are likely to enter environments characterized by the practices this data reflects, which will probably further increase the perceived distance between universities and industry. Although there's some room for improvement, industry prefers evolution over revolution.

Lagging behind. SWEBOK lags behind the state of the practice because the SE field changes rapidly. New approaches—such as model-driven development and service-oriented architecture—have made a considerable impact on both research and practice, but SWEBOK and SE 2004 have yet to mention them. The same holds for my favorite topic: software architecture.

Admittedly, SWEBOK and SE 2004 discuss software architecture, but in a rather shallow way. By and large, these documents view architecture as global design. The now-prevalent view of software architecture is that it involves balancing quality and functional requirements [26]. So, architecture design doesn't follow RE, it's intertwined with it.

Many architectural decisions involve tradeoffs because they affect multiple quality attributes. For example, the choice of communication protocol can have implications for both performance and security. Through architecture design, developers make these trade-offs, communicate them and their consequences to stakeholders, and document them in architectural views. Software architecture is therefore about documenting and sharing important design decisions rather than the components and connectors that result [27].

Heterogeneity. SE is becoming increasingly heterogeneous, as recent developments show:

- Distributed development, involving teams from different cultures, affects work processes [28].

- For many organizations, combining inhouse software developed with COTS with open source and other externally acquired software is now policy—if not a necessity—rather than an unfortunate event.
- To get the best of both worlds, organizations combine traditional, document-driven development approaches with the more recent, people-driven agile development approaches.

In their basic structure, SWEBOK and SE 2004 largely follow a traditional view. Although both periodically stress evolution's importance, the documents' surface structure suggests a greenfield situation, in which software is developed from scratch. Although unintentional, this structure is nonetheless likely to influence student attitudes. Because SE's emergent heterogeneity further complicates industrial practice, it should have some counterpart in education.

4 Conclusion

There's more to SE than engineering. A major challenge is to reconcile the engineering dimension with the human and social dimension in SE. Practitioners know from the trenches that both are important. Students are easily misguided if we only stress the engineering part.

Acknowledgments

I'm grateful for discussions about the SE traps with Philippe Kruchten, Patricia Lago, and Chris Verhoef (of course, they don't agree with all of them). An extended abstract of this article was published in Proceedings of the 26th International Conference on Software Engineering (IEEE CS Press, 2005, pp. 621–622).

References

1. Kruchten, P.: Putting the "engineering" into "software engineering". In Strooper, P., ed.: Australian Software Engineering Conference (ASWEC 2004), Melbourne, Australia, IEEE Computer Society (2004) 2–8
2. Parnas, D.: Software Engineering Programs Are Not Computer Science Programs. IEEE Software 16(6) (1999) 19–30
3. Shaw, M.: Prospects for an Engineering Discipline of Software. IEEE Software 7(6) (1990) 15–24
4. Saiedian, H., Bagert, D., Mead, N.: Software Engineering Programs: Dispelling the Myths and Misconceptions. IEEE Software 19(5) (2002) 35–41
5. Dawson, R., Newsham, R.: Introducing Software Engineers to the Real World. IEEE Software 14(6) (1997) 37–43
6. Dawson, R.: Twenty Dirty Tricks to Train Software Engineers. In: Proceedings 22nd International Conference on Software Engineering (ICSE22), IEEE (2000) 209–218

7. Vliet, H.v.: Software Engineering, Principles and Practice. Second edn. John Wiley & Sons (2000)
8. Budgen, D.: Software Design. Second edn. Addison-Wesley (2003)
9. Lago, P., van Vliet, H.: Teaching a Course on Software Architecture. In: Proceedings Eighteenth Conference on Software Engineering Education & Training, IEEE Computer Society (2005) 35–42
10. Spector, A., Gifford, D.: A Computer Science Perspective of Bridge Design. Communications of the ACM **29**(4) (1986) 267–283
11. Leveson, N.: High-Pressure Steam Engines and Computer Software. In: Proceedings 14th International Conference on Software Engineering (ICSE14). IEEE (1992) 2–14
12. Bryant, A.: Metaphor, myth and mimicry: The bases of software engineering. Annals of Software Engineering **10** (2000) 273–292
13. Hirschheim, R., Klein, H.: Four Paradigms of Information Systems Development. Communications of the ACM **32**(10) (1989) 1199–1216
14. Lewerentz, C., Rust, H.: Are software engineers true engineers? Annals of Software Engineering **10** (2000) 311–328
15. Hilburn, T., Humphrey, W.: The Impending Changes in Software Education. IEEE Software **19**(5) (2002) 22–24
16. Yourdon, E.: Death March, The Complete Software Developer's Guide to Surviving "Mission Impossible" Projects. Prentice Hall (1997)
17. Flyvbjerg, B., Bruzelius, N., Rothengatter, W.: Megaprojects and Risk: An Anatomy of Ambition. Cambridge University Press (2003)
18. DeMarco, T.: Controlling Software Projects. Yourdon Press (1982)
19. Jørgensen, M., Grimstad, S.: Over-optimism in Software Development Projects: "The winner's curse". Improve, Software Process Improvement Newsletter (4) (2004)
20. Mulligan, R., Altom, M., Simkin, D.: User Interface Design in the Trenches: Some Tips on Shooting from the Hip. In: Proceedings CHI'91, ACM (1991) 232–236
21. Vinter, O., Poulsen, P., Lauesen, S.: Experience Driven Software Process Improvement. In: Software Process Improvement, Brighton (1996)
22. Nielsen, J.: Web Resarch: Believe the Data. Alertbox (11 July 1999; www.useit.com/alertbox/990711.html) (2000)
23. Lethbridge, T.: What Knowledge Is Important to a Software Professional? IEEE Computer **33**(5) (2000) 44–50
24. Bevan, N.: Quality in Use: Meeting User Needs for Quality. Journal of Systems and Software **49**(1) (1999) 89–96
25. van der Veer, G., van Vliet, H.: A Plea for a Poor Man's HCI Component in Software Engineering and Computer Science Curricula. Computer Science Education **13**(3 (Special Issue: Human-Computer Interaction)) (2003) 207–226
26. Bass, L., Clements, P., Kazman, R.: Software Architecture in Practice. Second edn. Addison-Wesley (2003)
27. Bosch, J.: Software architecture: The next step. In: Proceedings European Workshop on Software Architecture, Springer Verlag, LNCS 3047 (2004) 194–199
28. Borchers, G.: The Software Engineering Impacts of Cultural Factors on Multicultural Software Development Teams. In: Proceedings 25th International Conference on Software Engineering (ICSE25). IEEE (2003) 540–545

Reflections on Software Engineering 2004, the ACM/IEEE-CS Guidelines for Undergraduate Programs in Software Engineering

Joanne M. Atlee[1,*], Richard J. LeBlanc Jr.[2], Timothy C. Lethbridge[3], Ann Sobel[4], and J. Barrie Thompson[5]

[1] University of Waterloo, Canada
jmatlee@se.uwaterloo.ca
[2] Georgia Institute of Technology, USA
rich@cc.gatech.edu
[3] University of Ottawa, Canada
tcl@site.uottawa,ca
[4] Miami University, USA
sobelae@muohio.edu
[5] University of Sunderland, United Kingdom
Barrie.Thompson@sunderland.ac.uk

Abstract. This paper is a collection of reflections on some of the curricular decisions made in "Software Engineering 2004," the Software Engineering volume of the Computing Curricula 2001 project. We briefly describe the contents of the Volume and the process used in developing the Volume's guidelines. We then look in more detail at the rationale behind some of the more controversial decisions made. We conclude with how we expect the Volume to be used in practice.

1 Introduction

In autumn 1998, the IEEE Computer Society (IEEE-CS) and the Association of Computing Machinery (ACM) established a joint task force to produce a new version of their curricular guidelines for undergraduate programs in computing. The project was named Computing Curricula 2001 (CC2001) [2] and led to the production of five volumes of curricula guidelines, one of which is devoted to Software Engineering (SE). Work on the SE curricula evolved from the Software Engineering Education Project (SWEEP), which was set up by the ACM and IEEE-CS, to address education issues relevant to software engineering. In late 2001, SWEEP was replaced by the ACM/IEEE-CS joint project group titled Computing Curricula – Software Engineering (CCSE). In summer 2004, the final draft of the software-engineering volume, titled *Software Engineering 2004* (SE2004 Volume), was approved by ACM Education Board and the IEEE-CS Education Advisory Board.

---

[*] On behalf of the SE2004 Steering Committee (see Appendix A).

P. Inverardi and M. Jazayeri (Eds.): ICSE 2005 Education Track, LNCS 4309, pp. 11–27, 2006.

The SE2004 Volume contains a wealth of information for educators who seek advice on how to design and implement an undergraduate degree program in software engineering. The Volume includes curricular requirements, in the form of a core body of software-engineering education knowledge (the SEEK). The SEEK specifies not only what topics should be covered in any software-engineering degree curriculum, but also the minimum depth to which each topic should be covered. The Volume also includes patterns on how to package the SEEK requirements into courses and curricula for a wide variety of contexts, and offers general guidance on how to implement and deliver a software-engineering degree program.

This paper looks at some of the more controversial decisions surrounding the contents of the SE2004 Volume – in particular, the contents of the SEEK. The goal of the SE2004 project was to provide guidelines on undergraduate curricula. There was an attempt to be as comprehensive as possible, and include not only the teaching and practicing of software-engineering knowledge, but also cover prerequisite material and leave sufficient free space in the curriculum for non-SEEK degree requirements and for specialization. At the same time, decisions about the SEEK's contents were heavily constrained by what curricular outcomes could be reasonably achieved within the framework of an undergraduate degree program. In general, the philosophy used to make decisions about the SEEK was to emphasize the fundamentals and the concepts that are best learned in a formal education setting, and to require only overviews of the other topics. As a result, the SEEK does not purport to be complete. Rather, it captures practices and principles that are applicable to most software products, provide some assurance of quality, and can be covered adequately in an undergraduate program.

The rest of this paper is organized as follows. We first provide a brief overview of the SE2004 Volume, its development, and its contents. We then look at issues that were considered in some of the more controversial decisions made about the SEEK – in particular, the coverage of software quality, software process, human-computer interactions, and professional practice. We conclude with some views on the Volume's expected use by educators and researchers.

2   Overview of the SE2004 Volume

Work on the Software Engineering Volume (SE2004 Volume) [5] started in 1998 with the Software Engineering Education Project (SWEEP), but did not begin in earnest until late 2001, with the formation of the SE2004 Steering Committee (see Appendix A) and the Advisory Board. The work progressed in three stages. The first stage focused on a set of desired curriculum outcomes, describing what every SE graduate ought to know. The second stage produced a core body of software-engineering education knowledge (the SEEK), specifying the minimum curriculum of any SE degree program. The third stage produced a set of curriculum recommendations, advising how to design and deliver an SE degree program in the context of various university settings.

A number of tactics were employed to encourage members of the SE academic, research, and industrial communities to participate in each stage of the Volume's development:

- Open meetings and workshops were held at major conferences (e.g., ICSE[1,2], CSEE&T[3]), to solicit early views on SE education, to provide feedback on work in progress, and to evaluate sections of the Volume via active reviews.
- An invitation-only workshop, funded partly by the National Science Foundation, was held, during which leading SE educators and practitioners helped to identify the set of SE concepts and techniques that would constitute a core body of knowledge for SE undergraduate curricula.
- More than a hundred volunteers from the international SE-education community were recruited to develop drafts of the SEEK and drafts of pedagogical guidelines for using the SEEK to create undergraduate programs in SE.
- Multiple rounds of public reviews were held via the Internet, to attain feedback on the proposed SEEK and on drafts of the Volume. Reviewers' comments and responses to comments can be found on the project Web site [4].
- Recognized experts in academia, research, and industry were approached individually to provide in-depth reviews of drafts of the SEEK and the Volume.
- Presentations at major conferences (e.g., ICSE, FSE, CSEE&T) were held to keep the community informed.
- Articles appeared in community publications, such as FASE and ACM SIG-SOFT Software Engineering Notes (e.g., [9,10]), to inform the community and to solicit participation in public reviews.

In its annual report, the ACM Education Board commended the SE2004's development, saying that it "sets a new standard for international involvement in the development and sponsorship of curriculum guidelines" and "sets a new standard for acquiring and responding to public comment" [1].

2.1   The SEEK

The SEEK comprises the essential and desirable knowledge and skills that any software-engineering program should try to include in its curriculum. This body of knowledge includes knowledge from related disciplines (e.g., mathematics, computer science, engineering, economics) as well as software-engineering knowledge. Table 1 shows a summary of the SEEK's contents. The highlighted rows show the 10 knowledge areas and the recommended minimum number of lecture hours to devote to each knowledge area. The unhighlighted rows show how each knowledge area is decomposed into knowledge units, and show the recommended

---

[1] International Summit on Software Engineering Education (SSEE), co-located with the 24th IEEE-CS/ACM International Conference on Software Engineering (ICSE2002), May 2002.

[2] Second International Summit on Software Engineering Education (SSEE II), co-located with the 25th IEEE-CS/ACM International Conference on Software Engineering (ICSE2003), May 2003.

[3] Workshop on Developing Software Engineering Courses using CC2001 Documentation, 15th Conference on Software Engineering Education & Training (CSEE&T2002), February, 2002.

KA/KU	Title	hrs	KA/KU	Title	hrs
CMP	**Computing Essentials**	**172**	**VAV**	**Software V&V**	**42**
CMP.cf	Computer Science foundations	140	VAV.fnd	V&V terminology and foundations	5
CMP.ct	Construction technologies	20	VAV.rev	Reviews	6
CMP.tl	Construction tools	4	VAV.tst	Testing	21
CMP.fm	Formal construction methods	8	VAV.hct	Human computer UI testing and evaluation	6
			VAV.par	Problem analysis and reporting	4
FND	**Mathematical & Engineering Fundamentals**	**89**	**EVO**	**Software Evolution**	**10**
FND.mf	Mathematical foundations	56	EVO.pro	Evolution processes	6
FND.ef	Engineering foundations for software	23	EVO.ac	Evolution activities	4
FND.ec	Engineering economics for software	10			
PRF	**Professional Practice**	**35**	**PRO**	**Software Process**	**13**
PRF.psy	Group dynamics / psychology	5	PRO.con	Process concepts	3
PRF.com	Communication skills (specific to SE)	10	PRO.imp	Process implementation	10
PRF.pr	Professionalism	20			
MAA	**Software Modeling & Analysis**	**53**	**QUA**	**Software Quality**	**16**
MAA.md	Modeling foundations	19	QUA.cc	Software quality concepts and culture	2
MAA.tm	Types of models	12	QUA.std	Software quality standards	2
MAA.af	Analysis fundamentals	6	QUA.pro	Software quality processes	4
MAA.rfd	Requirements fundamentals	3	QUA.pca	Process assurance	4
MAA.er	Eliciting requirements	4	QUA.pda	Product assurance	4
MAA.rsd	Requirements specification & documentation	6			
MAA.rv	Requirements validation	3			
DES	**Software Design**	**45**	**MGT**	**Software Management**	**19**
DES.con	Design concepts	3	MGT.con	Management concepts	2
DES.str	Design strategies	6	MGT.pp	Project planning	6
DES.ar	Architectural design	9	MGT.per	Project personnel and organization	2
DES.hci	Human computer interface design	12	MGT.ctl	Project control	4
DES.dd	Detailed design	12	MGT.cm	Software configuration management	5
DES.ste	Design support tools and evaluation	3			

Table 1. SEEK Knowledge Areas and Knowledge Units [5]

Table 2. Partial Modeling and Analysis SEEK (adapted from [5])

	k,c,a	E,D,O	Hours
Software Modeling and Analysis			53
Modeling Foundations			19
Modeling principles (decomposition, abstraction, generaliza-tion, projection/views, explicitness, use of formal approaches, etc.)	a	E	
Pre & postconditions, invariants	c	E	
Introduction to mathematical models and specification languages (Z, VDM, etc.)	c	E	
Properties of modeling languages	k	E	
Syntax vs. semantics (understanding model representations)	c	E	
Explicitness (make no assumptions, or state all assumptions)	k	E	
...	...	...	...

minimum number of lecture hours to devote to each knowledge unit. There was a concerted effort to keep the SEEK small, so that any SE curriculum based on SEEK would have enough room and flexibility for customization, either in the form of program-specific requirements or unconstrained electives. Thus, the total number of lecture hours required for SEEK topics is less than half the hours available in a four-year honours program.

Note that over half of the SEEK lecture time is devoted to the Computing Essentials and the Mathematical & Engineering Fundamentals knowledge areas. As such, the SEEK inherits significantly from Computing, Engineering, and Mathematics. But by itself, the SEEK does not satisfy the curriculum requirements for either a Computer Science program or an Engineering program. As will be seen, other sections of the SE2004 Volume show how to embed the SEEK into the degree requirements of various contexts, including those of a Computer Science or an Engineering Department.

Table 2 shows part of the SEEK's Software Modeling and Analysis knowledge area: it shows the Modeling Foundations knowledge unit, the set of topics that make up that unit, and the degree to which each topic is assessed as being essential (E), desirable (D), or optional (O) in any SE curriculum. Each topic is also annotated with the degree to which a graduate is expected to master the topic. Bloom's taxonomy of educational outcomes [6] is used to indicate these capability levels:

- Knowledge (k): To be able to recall the knowledge
- Comprehension (c): To be able to adapt the knowledge to new contexts
- Application (a): To be able to apply the knowledge to solving problems

The SEEK differs from the Software Engineering Body of Knowledge (SWE-BOK) [7] in that the SEEK focuses on knowledge for an undergraduate curriculum, whereas SWEBOK focuses on knowledge used by a practicing software-engineer. To be precise, SWEBOK is aimed at specifying the knowledge that a practitioner ought to have acquired from a combination of academics and four years of work experience; one of the goals of SWEBOK is to scope the knowledge to be tested in advanced professional-engineering examinations, which tend to be taken four years after graduation. Moreover, unlike SEEK, SWEBOK specifies SE knowledge only and does not consider required knowledge from related disciplines, such as computing, engineering, or mathematics.

2.2 Curricular Guidelines

For educators who are designing an SE program from scratch, the most useful part of the SE2004 Volume may be the set of guidelines on SE curriculum and pedagogy. The guidelines provide advice on curriculum philosophy, curriculum design, strategies for SE pedagogy, and expectations for faculty background and skills. Example guidelines include [5].

Guideline 7: Software engineering must be taught in ways that recognize that it is both a computing discipline and an engineering discipline.

Guideline 4: Many SE concepts, principles, and issues should be taught as recurring themes throughout the curriculum.

Guideline 5: Concepts requiring maturity should be taught late in the curriculum.

Guideline 6: Students must learn some application domain(s).

Guideline 14: The curriculum should have a significant real-world basis (case studies, practical assignments, course projects, experience in an industrial work setting).

Guideline 18: Curriculum designers should strive for important efficiencies and synergies by combining the delivery of related types of knowledge.

There are 18 guidelines in all, and each of the guidelines is expanded to provide further advice on its application and on warnings, where appropriate, about where problems could occur.

2.3 Example Curricula

The SE2004 Volume provides a number of example curricula showing how the SEEK can be taught according to the Volume's guidelines on curriculum and pedagogy. There are comprehensive course patterns, with mappings from course content to topics in the SEEK. There are also a number of curriculum patterns, showing how courses can be combined into degree programs in various contexts, such as international contexts, computer-science vs. engineering contexts, and reduced course-load contexts.

Table 3 shows the pattern for a North American engineering-style program. The shaded boxes identify SE courses. The courses whose names are expressed in roman font are courses that cover SEEK requirements, both SE and non-SE requirements. The courses whose names are in italic font are non-SEEK courses that are required as part of an engineering education. *Gen Ed* courses are required nontechnical courses, such as communications or humanities courses, that help to develop the student's understanding of society and its needs. As another

Table 3. Engineering-style curricular pattern (adapted from [5])

Year 1		Year 2		Year 3		Year 4	
Sem 1A	**Sem 1B**	**Sem 2A**	**Sem 2B**	**Sem 3A**	**Sem 3B**	**Sem 4A**	**Sem 4B**
Prog Fund	OO Paradigm	Data Str & Alg	Comp Arch	OS & Networks	Database	Capstone Proj	Capstone Proj
Calc 1	*Calc 2*	*Calc 3*	Software Construct	Statistics	Soft Arch & Design	Proj Mgmt	*Tech Elective*
Physics 1	*Physics 2*	Intro to SE	HCI	Quality Assurance	Req Anal	*Tech Elective*	*Tech Elective*
Chemistry	Discrete Math 1	Discrete Math 2	*Linear Algebra*	Prof Practice	*Tech Elective*	*Tech Elective*	*Tech Elective*
Tech Writing	*Engineering*	Eng Econ	*Gen Ed*	*Gen Ed*	*Gen Ed*	*Gen Ed*	*Gen Ed*

Table 4. Three-year curricular pattern (adapted from [5])

Year 1		Year 2		Year 3	
Sem 1A	**Sem 1B**	**Sem 2A**	**Sem 2B**	**Sem 3A**	**Sem 3B**
Prog Fund	OO Paradigm	Data Str & Alg	Software Systems	Capstone Proj	Capstone Proj
Discrete Math 1	Discrete Math 2	Statistics	Software Design	Formal Methods	*Tech Elective*
Tech Writing	Intro to SE	Software Architecture	Soft Process & Management	*Tech Elective*	*Tech Elective*
Eng Econ	Prof Practice	Software Testing	HCI	*Tech Elective*	*Tech Elective*
–	–	–	–	–	–

example, Table 4 shows the pattern for a three-year program in which, such as in the U.K., many of the SEEK's fundamental math, science, and humanities requirements are satisfied by a student's secondary-school education. As before, the shaded boxes identify SE courses, the courses whose names are expressed in roman font are SEEK-related courses, and the courses whose names are in italic font are non-SEEK courses that satisfy degree requirements imposed by the context (department, college, university) in which the degree is offered. A table entry containing a dash "–" represents an unconstrained elective course. The names of the SE courses in the two examples differ, because they use different decisions to package SE-related SEEK topics into SE courses; both packages are described in the SE2004 Volume.

In addition to example curricula, the SE2004 Volume discusses considerations in adapting curricula to alternative teaching environments (e.g., distance education), to institutional environments (e.g., coordination with other university programs), and to alternative degree formats (e.g., associate-degree programs in the U.S.).

3   The Boundaries of the SEEK

Probably the hardest and most controversial decisions made about the contents the SE 2004 Volume were those that define the boundaries of the SEEK, with respect to both the breadth and depth of knowledge units. The discipline of Software Engineering encompasses a wide range of knowledge and skills. It requires a solid foundation in mathematics and statistics, computers, computer science, engineering, and project management. On top of this background material, it introduces SE-specific philosophies, principles, paradigms, practices, processes, patterns, and technologies. From this expanse, it is challenging to carve out a core body of knowledge that the SE community can agree on, and that can be taught within the confines of an undergraduate degree program.

The SE2004 Steering Committee used the following criteria in deciding what to include in the SEEK and in deciding to what depth a software-engineering undergraduate student should master SEEK topics:

1. The SEEK should comprise a *core* body of software-engineering knowledge that a graduate of any undergraduate software-engineering program ought to know. This core should be small enough to accommodate additional degree requirements that could be imposed by the program's host department and institution (e.g., a liberal arts university may have rules that require students to take courses in a variety of subjects). The SEEK should also provide enough room and flexibility to allow a program to customize its curriculum (e.g., allow a program to specialize in particular areas of software engineering, or allow a student to study one or more application domains).

2. SEEK topics should focus on knowledge and practices that are deemed to be both effective and practical. Such knowledge should include essential problems that are encountered in developing software, and should highlight practices that are not only useful in solving these problems but are also economical to apply. (Note that "economy" is context dependent, in that an expensive method may be considered affordable when developing a critical product [8].) As such, the SEEK includes practices that are more rigorous (e.g., specification and design documentation) than those commonly applied in commerical software development, and excludes many promising practices whose effectiveness or feasibility have not yet been demonstrated.

3. The SEEK should be limited to knowledge that can be delivered to students who have an undergraduate background in computing and software engineering. That is, the SEEK should avoid, or recommend shallow treatment of, concepts and technologies that are too difficult for students of average ability; such topics should be deferred to graduate studies or research. The SEEK should also preclude any technology, such as program analysis or control theory, that depends on significant non-software-engineering background knowledge. The time taken to cover such a technology, along with all of its prerequisites, would likely be better spent on other concepts that are more essential to software engineering. Because of this criterion, the SEEK excludes or limits exposure to some practices (e.g., program analysis, reverse engineering) that are effective and practical, but whose proficiency is too resource-intensive to ask of all software-engineering undergraduates.

4. Application-level coverage of SEEK topics should be limited to knowledge and practices that are best learned in a university setting. In particular,

several software-engineering tasks and technologies, such as traceability, problem tracking, and design patterns, can be learned without significant practice. Other activities are best experienced in a real-world setting with real project data, such as process improvement or management of changing requirements. A software-engineering curriculum ought to include exposure to these concepts, so that the student is aware of his or her responsibilities and of the resources (e.g., patterns repositories, standards documents) that are available. However, lessons need not include hands-on experience with all design patterns, standards, and industrially relevant activities.

The rest of this section discusses in more detail the types of discussions that the SE2004 Steering Committee members and the Volume's reviewers had, with respect to both what topics to include in the SEEK and what level of proficiency to ask of SE graduates.

3.1   Software Quality

Software Quality is a cross-cutting concern that touches all aspects and phases of software engineering. In this respect, it is tempting to treat quality as an implicit attribute of other SEEK topics (e.g., quality requirements specification, quality product assurance, quality process assurance). However, the SE2004 Steering Committee felt that an emphasis on quality is one of the key attributes that distinguishes software engineering from general software development. In the end, the Committee decided not only to list, explicitly, quality-related concepts and activities as SEEK topics, but to elevate Software Quality to be one of the SEEK's top-level knowledge areas. The rationale behind this latter decision was to help ensure that software-quality topics would not be neglected, in curriculum development or in course delivery, as being obvious or being second class to more technical topics.

The Software Quality knowledge area comprises process assurance, product assurance, quality standards, and the need to establish a culture of being quality oriented. The goal of this knowledge area is to emphasize that quality assurance is not limited to testing the product; rather, quality assurance must be employed throughout a product's development to be successful. The knowledge unit lists various processes and techniques (quality attributes, standards, processes, metrics, etc.) for measuring, controlling, or improving the quality of a software product or development process. Coverage of most of these topics is limited to being able to recall information about quality assurance or being able to adapt this knowledge to new contexts. This minimal level of proficiency ensures that all students are at least aware of quality-assurance processes and standards. The student who needs more advanced knowledge in this area can readily acquire this knowledge on the job.

In contrast, most of the SEEK's technical methods (reviews, inspections, testing, debugging, problem tracking, etc.) for evaluating software artifacts are to be covered in enough detail that students learn how to apply them. It is partly for this reason that the SEEK's recommended minimum number of lecture hours for covering Software Verification and Validation (V&V) knowledge is almost three times the recommended minimum number of hours for covering Software Quality knowledge. However, allocating more lecture time to V&V, and teaching V&V topics to greater depth than teaching Quality topics, does not mean that V&V is considered to be more important than Quality. Rather, to be mastered properly, the V&V topics tend to require more course-based instruction and hands-on practice than the Quality topics do. This need is especially true of the testing material, such as test-case design, testing at different levels of abstraction, coverage analysis, and testing tools, which together constitute half of the recommended V&V lecture time.

Software quality also includes a software product's quality attributes, such as usability, reliability, safety, security, maintainability, portability, efficiency, performance, and availability. Techniques for ensuring that a product meets its specified quality attributes are distributed throughout the SEEK. For example, the Modeling and Analysis knowledge area includes analyzing quality attributes (e.g., safety analysis, security analysis, performance analysis); the Software Design area includes designing for quality attributes (e.g., design tactics that improve usability, maintainability, performance, security, fault tolerance); and the Software Verification and Validation area includes testing of quality attributes and metrics for measuring quality attributes in a software product. The degree to which these topics should be covered, as specified by the SEEK, varies – primarily by the degree to which we know how to teach this material to an undergraduate audience.

For example, we know how to express quality-attribute requirements so that they are testable, and we know how to test such requirements. We know a number of specialized analysis techniques for modeling a software design and assessing the quality attributes of that model. We know how to use and develop code libraries to facilitate code reuse, and we know how to use exception handling to encapsulate and manage exceptional behaviour. These topics are expected to be taught to sufficient depth that students learn how to apply these techniques and solve these problems.

In contrast, knowledge about designing for specific quality attributes is less mature, and there is less undergraduate-level material available for use as course texts. The exception to this is human-computer interface design, whose concepts have been packaged for an undergraduate audience. Thus, designing for quality attributes is expected, at a minimum, to be taught at a conceptual level; individual degree programs may choose to require more extensive coverage of this topic, either in general or with respect to specific quality attributes.

3.2   Software Process and Formal Methods

Some participants in SEEK development, particularly those who attended the NSF-funded development workshop, were adamant that software engineering is primarily about process. At first glance, it might appear that their views were taken to heart: In the final SEEK, there is a Software Process knowledge area, and there are also several other knowledge areas that are substantially about process, such as Software Management, Software Quality, and Software Evolution. Taken together, these knowledge areas require 58 hours. In addition, process topics appear in other knowledge areas.

The process advocates were nevertheless disappointed with the amount of process coverage: in particular, that the Software Process knowledge area itself was cut back to 13 required hours. Ultimately, the foundational knowledge areas, along with design, modeling, and V&V, were given more prominence from the perspective of educating an undergraduate. The main rationale for this was twofold: 1) process is believed to be not well appreciated by undergraduates until they have experience with larger and longer-term projects, and 2) the topics given more prominence are more readily taught in a university context than process topics are (e.g., we can teach design concepts and give students small and medium-scale tasks that apply the design concepts).

Another group of advocates strongly argued that software-engineering practice should be rooted in mathematical approaches commonly called *formal methods*, and that there should be extensive coverage of these in the SEEK. The core of their arguments is that other branches of engineering matured only after the underlying physics and mathematics matured, enabling design decisions to be made by applying the appropriate mathematical analysis to each problem. Because of this maturity, undergraduate education for the other branches of engineering focuses on a well-understood set of science, mathematics, and engineering-analysis topics. Formal-methods advocates argue that software engineering has similarly matured – that enough is already known about how to develop software formally – and that we ought to educate software-engineering undergraduates with a formal mindset, so that they can transfer formal technologies into industrial practice when they graduate.

Interestingly, it seemed that the process advocates and the formal-methods advocates had completely distinct visions of software engineering: It was as though there were two separate disciplines. Ultimately, the steering committee opted to balance the two perspectives. By doing so, we mirror the other branches of engineering, which do have engineers, called *industrial engineers*, who focus on process. Moreover, our knowledge of formal methods currently focuses on software correctness, reliability, and safety; this technology is not so helpful in achieving other quality attributes, like maintainability, usability, and economy. By balancing the two perspectives, the steering committee decided that the SEEK should reflect the broad nature of software engineering, which inherits ideas from analytical engineering and industrial engineering, as well as from heuristics-oriented engineering.

The final coverage of formal methods in SEEK is as follows. There is a unit in the Computing Essentials knowledge area called Formal Construction Methods (8 hours). There is also coverage of formal approaches in the Modeling and Analysis knowledge area: topics cover formal modeling principles, formal analysis, formal specification languages, and formal requirements analysis. The Design knowledge unit includes topics on formal design analysis; the Verification and Validation knowledge area has a topic on formal hypothesis testing; and the

Management knowledge area has a topic on formal communication. Formality is therefore treated as a cross-cutting concern, like process and quality.

3.3   Human-Computer Interaction

The Steering Committee of the SE2004 Volume encountered many different opinions about how to incorporate what we will here refer to as human-computer interaction (HCI). HCI includes all issues related to developing software systems with an understanding of their human end-users. The terms 'human factors', 'usability engineering', 'user-centred design' (UCD), and 'user interface (UI) design' are among the other terms often used to describe aspects of this domain.

SWEBOK was used as one of the key inputs to the early development of the SEEK. Its developers made the decision to consider HCI to be a related discipline, not part of software engineering. Some of the contributors who attended workshops for the development of SE2004 or who reviewed drafts agreed with this view. Part of their argument for excluding HCI from the SEEK was that there is a well-established community of professionals specializing in HCI who generally do not consider themselves to be software engineers. These contributors also tended to have a vision of software engineering that focused on either the more mathematical aspects of the field (e.g. formal methods) or the more managerial aspects (e.g. process and quality).

Other contributors, however, disagreed and argued that software engineers need to know enough about HCI design and implementation to create suitable user interfaces in simple cases and to interact with HCI professionals when developing more complicated user interfaces. Some of the rationale for incorporating HCI more deeply into SEEK are

- Almost all software systems have user interfaces so software engineers will inevitably be faced with development of UIs at some point.
- A high percentage of project failures and cost overruns can be attributed to poor knowledge of HCI.
- Although there are specialists in HCI, there are also specialists in many other areas considered part of software engineering, such as software architecture and testing.
- Research has shown that HCI is the computing topic with the widest knowledge gap – that is, the largest difference between the perceived importance of a topic and the amount that practitioners actually know about that topic [11].

Ultimately, this was the view adopted by the steering committee. The final version of SEEK thus has considerable coverage of HCI topics. There was some argument in favour of creating an entire knowledge area for HCI. In the final version of SE2004, however, HCI topics are split among several units and topics. The most prominent of these is Human-Computer Interface Design – a unit of the Design Knowledge Area, with seven essential topics devoted to HCI. These topics include HCI principles, use of modes, navigation, visual design techniques, interaction styles, localization, internationalization, and HCI design methods.

The importance that the steering committee placed on HCI can be seen by the fact that this unit has 12 dedicated hours, versus 9 for Architectural Design, 8 for Design Strategies, 3 for Design Concepts, and 3 for Design Tools and Evaluation. Detailed Design is the only other design unit with 12 hours.

HCI-related topics also appear in several other knowledge areas. For example, four knowledge areas cover usability as a quality attribute: Modeling and Analysis, Verification and Validation, Quality, and Design (in its 'concepts' unit). The Modeling and Analysis knowledge area also explicitly refers to human-centered design in the context of requirements and systems engineering. The Professional Practice knowlwedge area covers topics such as interacting with stakeholders and individual cognition, both of which are foundational for HCI. Finally, there is a 6-hour unit on human-computer interface testing and evaluation in the Verification and Validation knowledge area.

Some of the final reviewers of SEEK and the SE2004 Volume as a whole complained about the amount of coverage of HCI. However, the complaints were about equally balanced among those who thought there was too much and those who thought there was too little. The steering committee felt, therefore, that the balance was probably about right.

3.4   Professional Practice

The Computing Curricula 2004 Overview Report [2] highlights that Software Engineering, as a discipline, has evolved in response to the increased importance of software in safety-critical applications and to the growing impact of large, complex software systems on society as a whole. This increased importance of software places heavy responsibilities on practicing software engineers, as made clear in the preamble to the Software Engineering Code of Ethics and Professional Practice [3]: "Because of their roles in developing software systems, software engineers have significant opportunities to do good or cause harm, to enable others to do good or cause harm, or to influence others to do good or cause harm. To ensure, as much as possible, that their efforts will be used for good, software engineers must commit themselves to making software engineering a beneficial and respected profession."

Professional Practice is concerned with the knowledge, skills, and attitudes that Software Engineers must possess to practice Software Engineering in a professional, responsible, and ethical manner. The first draft of the SEEK followed very closely the technical subject divisions of the SWEBOK [7], and had no area explicitly devoted to Professional Practice. However, at a National Science Foundation funded workshop held in the Summer of 2002, there was an impassioned request made on behalf of Don Gotterbarn, who led the effort which produced the Software Engineering Code of Ethics and Professional Practice, for such an area to be included in SEEK. Following this advice, a knowledge area devoted to Professional Practice was developed for inclusion in the first public review of the SE2004 Volume.

The Professional Practice knowledge area is subdivided into three units: group dynamics and psychology, communication skills that are specific to Software

Engineering, and professionalism. The ratio of times needed to cover these three units is 1:2:4. The three units are broken down into topics that include dynamics of working in teams, dealing with uncertainty and ambiguity, group communication, presentation skills, codes of ethics and professional conduct, roles of technical standards, and the economic impact of software.

This emphasis on professionalism within Software Engineering is also represented in the Volume's Guiding Principles, which formed the basis for many of the decisions regarding guidelines on curricular design and delivery. In particular, Principle 10 states

> SE2004 must include exposure to aspects of professional practice as an integral component of the undergraduate curriculum. The professional practice of software engineering encompasses a wide range of issues and activities, including problem solving, management, ethical and legal concerns, written and oral communication, working as part of a team, and remaining current in a rapidly changing discipline [5].

In addition, Principle 3 emphasizes the role of professional associations in ensuring that there is an ongoing review process for the curricula and that there is promotion of effective external assessment and accreditation of Software Engineering programs because of the professional nature of the discipline.

The SE2004 Volume also provides specific guidelines on how to deliver some of the professionalism topics. For example, it is recommended that at least part of the teaching be supported using presentations by guest speakers; that students be encouraged to read and discuss articles from the popular, trade, and academic press; that students be involved in debates on ethical issues; and that students be encouraged to explore areas such as licensing/certification of professionals and the patenting of software. It is also important that students engage in discussions on current issues relevant to professionalism. A variety of pedagogical approaches that support consideration of ethical issues have been outlined at recent conferences devoted to Software Engineering Education and Training [13,14].

Analysis of reviews from three public reviews of the Volume shows a very positive reaction to the Professional Practice knowledge area and to the associated supporting sections within the Volume.

3.5 Evidence-Based Education

A final point worth making is that there was considerable discussion among steering committee members about ensuring that whatever is taught at an undergraduate level is based on solid research backed by evidence. This discussion arose from the concern that much of what is taught in software engineering is just what some professor or textbook author feels is good practice. Many of the arguments about process, formal methods, and other controversial topics were not, in fact, backed up by research. The jury is still out, for example, on the extent to which industrial practice would actually benefit from people trained in certain processes or formal methods. Given that this is the case, some participants argued that stronger weight should be given to topics where there is more supportive research. Furthermore, the steering committee was urged to include references to the research in the final report.

In the end, the committee included many references to educational research, and some of these references do provide concrete evidence about which topics are most important in practice. Backing up all of the committee's detailed decisions with scientific research was, however, considered infeasible. Instead, the steering committee opted for a rigorous multi-step review and editing process to incorporate and balance as many opinions of experts as possible. Although perhaps suboptimal, this approach does seem to be the standard for most respected curriculum-development efforts.

4   Conclusion

Because the discipline of software engineering is so vast, and because different sectors of the SE community (researchers, practitioners, and educators) have different opinions as to what constitutes core software-engineering knowledge, it is impossible to reach unanimous agreement on the SEEK. Moreover, we have to be realistic in what outcomes we can expect from an undergraduate degree program. In particular, our expectations must be tempered by the limited amount of time, within a three- or four-year program, for covering topics and practicing skill sets, and by the limited amount of real experience that students get from course projects.

The philosophy used in making decisions about the SEEK was to emphasize the fundamentals and the concepts best learned in a formal education setting, and to require overviews of the other topics. As such, we expect that graduates of a software-engineering program that is based on the SEEK and the other SE2004 Volume guidelines to be able to function in an SE environment, but not to know everything there is to know about software engineering. This philosophy is in keeping with at least some practitioners' expectations: Steve McConnell recommends hiring graduates who know the fundamentals of software engineering, with the belief that software practitioners develop most of their SE skills in on-the-job learning and work experiences – that, in fact, some skills cannot be learned in a university setting [12].

In this sense, the SEEK reveals a number of open research problems, the foremost being simplifying practical SE techniques, so that they become teachable to undergraduate students. Any SEEK topic that is technical in nature and that has a Bloom capability level of "knowledge (k)" or "comprehension (c)" is a candidate SE technique that might be taught at the "application (a)" level if the technique were easier to use or easier to teach. Researchers can search the SEEK for omitted SE knowledge, as indicators of open problems, of knowledge that has not been proven effective, or of techniques that need to be simplified for an undergraduate audience.

References

1. ACM Education Board, "Annual Report FY 2004", December, 2004; http://www.acm.org/about_acm/commreports/fiscal_year_2004/ed_board_FY2004.pdf.
2. ACM/AIS/IEEE-CS Joint Task Force for Computing Curricula 2004, "Computing Curricula 2004, Overview Report," 22 November 2004 Draft, May 2005; www.tech.purdue.edu/Cpt/ IAB/Files/Overview_Draft_11-22-04.pdf.
3. ACM/IEEE-CS Joint Task Force on Software Engineering Ethics and Professional Practices, "Software Engineering Code of Ethics and Professional Practice," Version 5.2, May 2005; http://www.acm.org/serving/se/code.htm.
4. ACM/IEEE-CS Software Engineering 2004 Web site, May 2005; http://sites.computer.org/ccse.
5. ACM/IEEE-CS Task Force on Computing Curricula, "Software Engineering 2004: Curriculum Guidelines for Undergraduate Degree Programs in Software Engineering", May 2005; http://sites.computer.org/ccse/SE2004Volume.pdf.
6. Bloom, B., M. Englehart, E. Furst, W. Hill, and D. Krathwohl, *Taxonomy of Educational Objectives: The Classification of Education Goals: Handbook I, Cognitive Domain*, Longmans, Green, 1956.
7. Bourque, P. and R. Dupuis, eds.," "Guide to the Software Engineering Body of Knowledge," IEEE CS Press, 2001.
8. Denert, E., D. Hoffman, J. Ludewig, and D. Parnas, "Software Engineering Research and Education: Seeking a New Agenda", Dagstuhl Seminar 99071, February 14-19, 1999.
9. Henderson, P., "Software Engineering Education (SEEd)" column, in ACM SIG-SOFT Software Engineering Notes, May 2003.
10. Hilburn, T., "Computing Curriculum 2001 – Software Engineering". FASE, Volume 12, Number 04 (Issue 147), April 15 2002.
11. Lethbridge, T.C., "What Knowledge is Important to a Software Professional", *IEEE Computer*, Vol. 33, No. 5 (May 2000), pp. 44-50.
12. McConnell, S., "After the Gold Rush: Establishing a True Profession of Software Engineering", keynote talk at the Conference on Software Engineering Education and Training (CSEE&T'01), February 2001.
13. Towell, E., "Teaching Ethics in the Software Engineering Curriculum", Proceedings of the *Sixteenth Conference on Software Engineering Education & Training*, (CSEE&T 2003), March, 2003.
14. Towell, E. and Thompson J.B., "A Further Exploration of Teaching Ethics in the Software Engineering Curriculum," Proceedings of the 17th Conference on Software Engineering Education & Training (CSEE&T2004), March 2004.

Appendix A SE2004 Steering Committee

- Co-chairs
    - Rich LeBlanc, ACM, Georgia Institute of Technology, USA
    - Ann Sobel, IEEE-CS, Miami University, USA
    2002: Susan Mengel, Texas Tech University, USA
- Knowledge Area Chair
    - Ann Sobel, Miami University, USA
- Pedagogy Focus Group Co-Chairs
    - Mordechai Ben-Menachem, Ben-Gurion University, Israel
    - Timothy C. Lethbridge, University of Ottawa, Canada

- Co-Editors
  - Jorge L. Daz-Herrera, Rochester Institute of Technology, USA
  - Thomas B. Hilburn, Embry-Riddle Aeronautical University, USA
- Organizational Representatives
  - ACM
    * Andrew McGettrick, University of Strathclyde, United Kingdom
  - ACM SIGSOFT
    * Joanne M. Atlee, University of Waterloo, Canada
    * Spring - Summer 2002: Prem Devanbu, University of California at Davis, USA
  - ACM Two-Year College Committee
    * Elizabeth Hawthorne, Union County College, USA
  - Australian Computer Society
    * John Leaney, University of Technology Sydney, Australia
  - British Computer Society
    * David Budgen, Keele University, United Kingdom
  - Information Processing Society of Japan
    * Yoshihiro Matsumoto, Musashi Institute of Technology, Japan
  - IEEE Computer Technical Committee on Software Engineering
    * Barrie Thompson, University of Sunderland, United Kingdom

Deciding What to Design:
Closing a Gap in Software Engineering Education

Mary Shaw[1], Jim Herbsleb[1], Ipek Ozkaya[2], and Dave Root[1]

[1] Institute for Software Research
School of Computer Science
Carnegie Mellon University
Pittsburgh PA 15213
{mary.shaw, jdh, droot}@cs.cmu.edu
[2] Software Engineering Institute
Carnegie Mellon University
Pittsburgh PA 15213
ozkaya@sei.cmu.edu

Abstract. Software has jumped "out of the box" – it controls critical systems, pervades business and commerce, and infuses entertainment, communication, and other everyday activities. These applications are constrained not only by traditional capability and performance considerations but also by economic, business, market and policy issues and the context of intended use. The diversity of applications requires adaptability in responding to client needs, and the diversity of clients and contexts requires the ability to discriminate among criteria for success. As a result, software designers must also get out of their boxes: in addition to mastering classical software development skills, they must master the contextual issues that discriminate good solutions from merely competent ones. Current software engineering education, however, remains largely "in the box": it neglects the rich fabric of issues that lie between the client's problem and actual software development. At Carnegie Mellon we address this major shortcoming by teaching students to understand both the capabilities required by the client and the constraints imposed by the client's context.

1 The Changing Face of Software

Software intensive systems have become essential to everyday activity and business in the global economy. Not only is public dependence on software increasing, but in addition the character of the software itself is changing – and with it the demands on the software developers. The quality of this software depends on an adequate supply of software developers who are proficient in the full spectrum of concepts and skills required to respond to emerging types of software as well as the classical types.

1.1 Current Forces of Software Development

The prevailing model of software development, on which most educational programs are based, involves a team of professional software developers in a single institution

P. Inverardi and M. Jazayeri (Eds.): ICSE 2005 Education Track, LNCS 4309, pp. 28–58, 2006.

working under a well-defined process and product cycle to produce software for a known client or market and deliver it on a known schedule. This *closed-shop software development model* is increasingly at odds with actual practice. Some of the discrepancies between the closed-shop development model and the needs of modern software development include:

♦ System requirements emerge as the clients understand better both the technology and the opportunities in their own settings. This often requires software development to be carried out concurrently with business re-engineering.
♦ The pervasive integration of information technology with business operations and products requires software design to comply with market, regulatory, and policy requirements that typically are not evident in the project-specific requirements elicited from the client.
♦ Products of interest are often distributed and embedded hardware/software systems, not pure software. Classical software development methods focus tightly on functionality, performance, and technical quality requirements; they are not well suited to respond to constraints arising from the context of the application rather than its specific requirements.
♦ Mobile wireless applications that run on handheld devices with limited resources in dynamically changing environments impose new requirements for dynamic reconfiguration and interoperability. They also revitalize old needs for efficiency and usability.
♦ Software, especially system-level software, is now being developed by communities of cooperating volunteers. In open-source software, for example, code is published freely and interested users critique it and propose changes. Quality arises through an intense, highly parallel social process with rapid feedback rather than a carefully managed process.
♦ Software development often involves globally distributed teams. Accommodating geographic and organizational separation of developers within projects imposes substantial constraints on product architecture, processes, tools, and communication regimes.
♦ Applications are often created by harnessing coalitions of existing resources that are not under control of the software developer. The resources include calculation, communication, control, information, and services; they are often distributed, dynamic, autonomous, and independently managed. They may be modified or decommissioned without notice to users.
♦ Software development is increasingly disintermediated – software is adapted, tailored, composed, or created by its end users rather than by professional software developers. Placing enormous computational power in the hands of end users raises the stakes for making software-intensive products dependable, understandable, and usable. These end users need to understand software development in their own terms, not the terms familiar to professional programmers; they particularly need ways to decide how much faith to have in their creations. Current software products do not support these users very well.

These new aspects of software development often require an *open-shop development model* that is a major departure from the usual closed-shop model, and the uncertainties associated with external policy constraints and externally-managed resources require correspondingly more sophisticated analysis.

Most educational programs underplay the significance of these changes from software development of a decade ago. For example, developers trained to deliver well-defined products to specific clients or discrete products for the open market are ill-equipped to deal with the shifting needs of opportunistic web-based integration and the expanding involvement of end users.

In either the traditional or the emerging setting, the point of greatest leverage on overall software quality is early in design, before the usual software development methods can be applied. Early decisions often commit resources that will incur costs throughout the project. Boehm and Basili report that "finding and fixing a software problem after delivery is often 100 times more expensive than finding and fixing it during the requirements and design phase" and also that the uncertainty in cost predictions is largest during early design [5,6]. Most software development methods, however, are largely linear processes that refine an initial design. These methods pay only passing attention to evaluating a variety of design alternatives early in development, and they place scant emphasis on understanding the market, business, economic, and policy context that limits the space of acceptable solutions.

The essential challenges are world-wide problems. Although we describe these challenges in terms of specific examples from the United States, the overall implications are global.

1.2 Resulting Forces on Software Engineering Education

To respond to these forces, we must prepare software engineers to construct and analyze systems that are heavily constrained by contextual considerations in addition to the usual technical requirements. These issues can affect the design in profound ways, such as by requiring or limiting essential functionality (e.g., audit trails) or pervading the implementation (e.g., security requirements) or limiting the architectural options (e.g., structuring databases for privacy). Contextual requirements are much easier to deal with as integral parts of the requirement than as add-ons to an existing design. However, to incorporate contextual requirements from the outset, developers must understand and respect these requirements as much as they do the requirements elicited directly from the client.

Currently, most software developers are educated principally in tools and methods for writing, analyzing, and managing software. For example, the ACM/IEEE Software Engineering 2004 curriculum design [23] devotes over 50% of its material to basic programming and analysis, about 25% to correctness and quality, 10-15% to process and management, and less than 10% to design. "Design" for this curriculum means implementing software to conform to requirements. The ACM/IEEE curriculum includes as guiding principles [23],

> Reconcile conflicting project objectives, finding acceptable compromises within limitations of cost, time, knowledge, existing systems, and organizations. Students should engage in exercises that expose them to conflicting, and even changing, requirements. There should be a strong element of the real world present in such cases to ensure that the experience is realistic. Curriculum units should address these issues, with the aim of ensuring high quality requirements and a feasible software design.

and

> Design appropriate solutions in one or more application domains using software engineering approaches that integrate ethical, social, legal, and economic concerns. Throughout their study, students need to be exposed to a variety of appropriate approaches to engineering design in the general sense, and to specific problem solving in various kinds of applications domains for software. They need to be able to understand the strengths and the weaknesses of the various options available and the implications of the selection of appropriate approaches for a given situation. Their proposed design solutions must be made within the context of ethical, social, legal, security, and economic concerns.

The curriculum itself, however, gives scant attention to these topics: about 3% for traditional requirements topics and 1-2% for contextual concerns in design.

1.3 Carnegie Mellon's Response

We believe that the greatest opportunity to improve software engineering education lies in improving students' ability to bridge the gap between traditional client-focused requirement elicitation and the capability-focused processes of software development – that is, in teaching them how to decide what to design. We created a new course to address these issues. Carnegie Mellon's software engineering tradition is strongly technical; compared to most software engineering programs, we place greater emphasis on engineering of the software product than on the development process. In addition. Our educational tradition emphasizes the enduring value of the content as well as the skills of immediate, possibly short-term, use. Details of both technical and nontechnical aspects of software engineering change with time, so we teach the enduring principles that support current practice as well as the current practice itself. This paper describes an innovative course in early design analysis rooted in the context of the Carnegie Mellon software engineering educational philosophy. We interleave sections from our statement of philosophy [38] with sections that describe our new course and show how it satisfies the principles.

Section 2 describes Carnegie Mellon's view on the content of software engineering. Section 3 presents our new course in the context of Section 2. Section 4 describes Carnegie Mellon's pedagogical philosophy, and Section 5 explains how the course satisfies that philosophy. Section 6 discusses experience with several course formats, and Section 7 suggests ways to adapt the course to other settings. Section 8 reflects on the role of this course in a modern software engineering curriculum.

2 The Carnegie Mellon Approach to Software Engineering

This section articulates Carnegie Mellon's core academic values for the discipline of software engineering. Curriculum design must reconcile academic values with the objectives of numerous other stakeholders; this is the case for the academic values stakeholder. This characterization of software engineering is informed by other software engineering and computer science curriculum designs, such as the ACM/IEEE guidelines [23], the IEEE SWEBOK [21], and the Carnegie Mellon Undergraduate Curriculum of 1985 [36], but it is independent of them.

2.1 Definition

Software engineering is the branch of computer science that creates practical, cost-effective solutions to computation and information processing problems, preferentially by applying scientific knowledge, developing[1] software systems in the service of mankind. Software engineering entails making decisions under constraints of limited time, knowledge, and resources. The distinctive character of software raises special issues about its engineering. These include:

---

[1] "Develop" -- Software engineering lacks a verb that covers all the activities associated with a software product, from conception through client negotiation, design, implementation, validation, operation, evolution, and other maintenance. Here, "develop" refers inclusively to all those activities. This is less than wholly satisfactory, but it isn't as bad as listing several verbs at every occurrence.

- Software is design-intensive; production costs are but a small component of product costs.
- Software is symbolic, abstract, and more constrained by intellectual complexity than by fundamental physical laws.

Software engineering is often confused with mere programming or with software management. Both comparisons are inappropriate, as the responsibilities of an engineer include the deliberate, collaborative creation and evolution of software-intensive systems that satisfy a wide range of technical, business, and regulatory requirements. Software engineering is not simply the implementation of application functionality, nor is it simply the ability to manage a project in an orderly, predictable fashion.

2.2 Core Principles

Software engineering rests on three principal intellectual foundations. The technical foundation is a body of *core computer science* concepts relating to data structures, algorithms, programming languages and their semantics, analysis, computability, computational models, etc.; this is the core content of the discipline. This technical knowledge is applied through a body of *engineering knowledge* related to architecture, the process of engineering, tradeoffs and costs, conventionalization and standards, quality and assurance, etc.; this provides the approach to design and problem solving that respects the pragmatic issues of the applications. These are complemented by the *social and economic context* of the engineering effort, which includes the process of creating and evolving artifacts, as well as issues related to policy, markets, usability, and socio-economic impacts; this provides a basis for shaping the engineered artifacts to be fit for their intended use.

These are the fundamental, pervasive, integrative principles that transcend specific details and characterize the field. They are core beliefs that shape our values about what things are important and how we as a faculty approach problems. These principles characterize the distinctive Carnegie Mellon approach to software engineering.

Physicists often approach problems (not just physical problems) by trying to identify masses and forces. Mathematicians often approach problems (even the same problems) by trying to identify functional elements and relations. Engineers often approach problems by trying to identify the linearly independent underlying components that can be composed to solve a problem. Programmers often view them operationally, looking for state, sequence, and processes. Here we try to capture the characteristic mindset of a software engineer.

2.2.1 Computer Science Fundamentals

The core body of systematic technical knowledge that supports software engineering is the algorithmic, representational, symbol-processing knowledge of computer science, together with specific knowledge about software and hardware systems. Major computer science principles include:

Abstraction enables the control of complexity. Abstraction allows selective control of detail and consequently separation of concerns and crisp focus on design decisions. It leads to models and simulations that are selective about the respects in which they are faithful to reality. It permits design and analysis in a problem-oriented frame rather than an implementation-oriented frame. Some levels of design abstraction, characterized by common phenomena, notations, and concerns, occur repeatedly and independently of underlying technology.

Imposing structure on problems often makes them more tractable, and a number of common structures are available. Designing systems as related sets of independent components allows separation of independent concerns; hierarchy and other organizing principles help explain the relations among the components. In practice, independence is impractical, so issues of cohesion and coupling affect the results. Moreover, recognizing common problem and solution structures allows reuse of prior knowledge rather than reinvention. Software systems are sufficiently complex that they exhibit emergent properties that do not derive in obvious ways from the properties of the components.

Symbolic representations are necessary and sufficient for solving information-based problems. Control and data are represented symbolically, and this enables their duality. Notations for symbolic description of control and data enable the definition of software. These representations allow the description of algorithms and data structures, the bread and butter of software implementation.

Precise models support analysis and prediction. These models may be formal or empirical; formal and empirical models are subject to different standards of proof and provide different levels of assurance in their results. The results support software design by providing predictions of properties of a system early in the system design. Careful documentation and codification of informal knowledge provides immediate guidance for developers and a precursor for more precise, validated models.

Common problem structures lead to canonical solutions. Recognizing common problem and solution structures allows reuse of prior knowledge rather than reinvention.

2.2.2 Engineering Fundamentals

The systematic method and attention to pragmatic solutions that shapes software engineering practice is the practical, goal-directed method of engineering, together with specific knowledge about design and evaluation techniques. Major engineering principles include:

Engineering quality resides in engineering judgment. Tools, techniques, methods, models, and processes are means that support this end. They can enhance sound judgment, they can provide a basis for evaluating designs, and they can make activities more accurate and efficient, but they cannot replace sound judgment.

Quality of the software product depends on the engineer's faithfulness to the engineered artifact. This quality is achieved through commitment to understanding the client's needs; it is evaluated by assessing the properties of the artifact that are important to the client. This is the basis for ethical practice.

Engineering requires reconciling conflicting constraints. These constraints arise both from requirements and from implementation considerations. They typically over-constrain the system, so the engineer must find reasonable compromises that reflect the client's priorities. Engineers generate and compare alternative designs and refine the most promising; they prefer quantitative evaluations and predictions. Finding sufficiently good cost-effective solutions is usually preferable to optimization.

Engineering skills improve as a result of careful systematic reflection on experience. A normal part of any project should be critical evaluation of the work. Critical evaluation of prior and competing work is also important, especially as it informs current design decisions.

2.2.3 Social and Economic Fundamentals

The concern with usability and the business and political context that guides software engineering sensibilities is organizational and cognitive knowledge about human and social institutions. This is supported by specific knowledge about human-computer interaction techniques. Major socio-economic principles include:

Costs and time constraints matter, not just capability. The costs include costs of ownership as well as costs of creation. Time constraints include calendar (e.g., market window) as well as staffing constraints. These factors affect the system design as well as the project organization.

Technology improves exponentially, but human capability does not. Computing and information processing capability should be delivered to end users in a form that those users can understand and control. Systems should adapt to the users, not users to the systems, and the computing activities should fit well with users' other activities.

Successful software development depends on teamwork by creative people. Software developers must reconcile business objectives, client needs, and the factors that make creative people effective; they must communicate effectively with clients. Modern projects are too complex for individuals to handle alone.

Business and policy objectives constrain software design and development decisions as much as technical considerations do. Long-range objectives, competitive market position, and risk management affect the business case for a software development. Public policy and regulation add requirements that the client may not be aware of. These objectives should have equal standing with other objectives, such as technical and usability objectives, in the development process.

Software functionality is often so deeply embedded in institutional, social, and organizational arrangements that observational methods with roots in anthropology, sociology, psychology, and other disciplines are required. It is often relatively easy to capture the obvious functionality and constraints, but the subtle ones often go unnoticed and cause projects to fail or to incompletely satisfy users.

Customers and users usually don't know precisely what they want, and it is the developer's responsibility to facilitate the discovery of the requirements. Developers need to use appropriate techniques to help the customers and users explore the design space, and understand the relevant alternatives, constraints, and tradeoffs. This requires knowledge both of the technology and the context of use. Since most customers and users are unlikely to acquire substantial technical knowledge, developers must take the initiative to bridge the gap by working to acquire more than a superficial knowledge of the context of use.

2.3 Core Competencies

The fundamental material informs and pervades the curriculum. More visibly, the curriculum includes content, both mature and immature, that develops software engineering capability on the three foundations of core computer science, engineering, and the social and economic context. To describe the content, we develop a rough classification that allows us to plan curricula, to assess students' skills, and to identify intellectual gaps.

Software engineers should master a set of core competencies. These are abstract capabilities (e.g. "ability to reason in a formal system") not specific skills (e.g., any particular choice among CSP, Z, Larch, etc), and especially not skills in using particular products. It follows that different students may satisfy the capability requirements in different ways. So degree programs could be described with coverage requirements that refer to these capabilities. We might say, for example, that each masters student should demonstrate proficiency in reasoning with symbolic systems by using two such systems at some point during the masters program; this might be in a class, in a major project of the program, as part of an independent study project, etc. This model becomes increasingly important as the flexibility in the programs and the diversity of student activity increases. To support this, we envision a mapping from our educational offerings (courses, projects, etc) to these capabilities. Software engineers should:

- Be able to discover client needs and translate them to software and system requirements
- Reconcile conflicting objectives, finding acceptable compromises within limitations of cost, time, knowledge; understand the nature of unstructured, open-ended (sometimes known as "wicked") problems
- Design appropriate solutions, using responsible engineering approaches
- Evaluate designs and products
- Understand and apply theories and models that provide a basis for software design
- Work effectively in interdisciplinary contexts, in particular to bridge the gap between computing technology and the client's technology and to interpret and respect extra-technical constraints
- Work effectively within existing systems, both software artifacts and organizations
- Understand and apply current technical solution elements, including specific components, tools, frameworks, and also abstract elements such as algorithms and architectures
- Program effectively, including code creation, component use, and integration of multiple subsystems
- Apply design and development techniques as appropriate to realize solutions
- Organize and lead development teams, including team-building and negotiation
- Communicate effectively, both verbally and in writing
- Learn new models, techniques, and technologies as they emerge; integrate knowledge from multiple sources to solve problems; serve as a change agent for adopting new technology

For programs organized around courses, traceability from competencies to content could be performed for each course. For a self-paced project-based curriculum, the selection of specific topics may be driven by individual projects; in this case the traceability could be done for each student as a means for determining whether each student has satisfied the overall requirements of the program.

3 Course Content: Deciding What to Design

Section 1 identified the ability to bridge the chasm between client needs and the beginning of software development[2] as a gap in most software engineering curricula, in the capabilities of most software developers and, indeed, in the product design capabilities of most organizations that produce software. We developed a course to close this gap by teaching students how to handle the engineering design responsibilities that precede traditional software design – that is, we address the design tasks that move from requirements to set the stage for selecting a software architecture and applying a software development method. This section describes the course, "Methods: Deciding What to Design", and shows how it was shaped by the principles of Section 2.

Our course brings together a variety of methods for understanding the problem the client wants to solve, various factors that constrain the possible solutions, and approaches to deciding among alternatives. The course is principally intended for students in our professional masters' program in software engineering (MSE) [11]. The students are not expected to have previous knowledge in any of the topics covered in the course, but there is a prerequisite of having minimum three months hands-on software development experience in industry. The course lasts one full semester, 15 weeks, and is designed as a 12 unit course. This corresponds to approximately 12 hours of effort per week for students, including the time spent in class. The class size has been between 25-30 students. This program is built around a substantial ongoing project, the MSE Studio, in which students develop a software subsystem for a real client. The students take our course during their first semester on campus, at precisely the point when they receive the first, inevitably vague, statement of what the customers for the ongoing project want. As a result, we expect the students to find immediate uses for the course material.

As noted above, software development depends on bridging the gap between a vague statement of a problem and decisions about the specific components that make up a working software system. The challenge for software engineers is often bridging from the system-specific requirements and unspoken constraints from the operating environment to the high-level design of the system. This has been a persistent challenge for our students.

Most software engineering curricula have some courses that focus on requirements and other courses, for example about software architecture or object-oriented design that focus on the high-level software system design. These independent courses usually fail to address the nuances of recognizing tradeoffs, generating and comparing alternatives, identifying the implicit constraints that arise from the context of the project, and ensuring that the software product will be usable by its intended audience. Our course explicitly covers these contextual issues, and it requires students to apply their understanding of this material to the MSE Studio projects.

The overarching objectives of this course are for the students to be able to explain the major forces, both technical and contextual, that shape and constrain the solutions

---

[2] In our view, the ideas covered in this course correspond to the design phase of an engineering project. However, software engineering uses the word "design" to refer to the activities that begin with choosing implementation strategies such as software architecture.

to their clients' problems, to evaluate and address the ways these forces constrain the software implementation, and to select and apply appropriate techniques for resolving the constraints and selecting a preliminary design. Students should learn to handle easy cases themselves, and they should be prepared to interact constructively with domain experts such as business or usability experts for more difficult cases. Students should come to understand that good solutions come not from applying processes by the book but from genuinely understanding the client's real needs, then selecting and applying whatever techniques are appropriate to solving the client's problem.

In practice, the course is organized around five core competencies: identifying types of problems and their structures; eliciting technical needs; matching the design to user needs; understanding and analyzing business, economic, and policy constraints; and adopting an engineering approach to software systems. The course requires students to apply these competencies in the context of the MSE Studio project. We address each of these competencies in turn, describing the material in the most recent offering of the course. We have also taught the course with the order of Sections 3.1 and 3.2 reversed. We find, probably because of the coordination with the MSE studio project, that students respond better to the order presented here. Section 7 discusses alternative topics that could be substituted to make a comparable course suited for somewhat different audiences.

3.1 Identifying Types of Problems and Their Structures

In this section of the course, students learn to identify types of computing and information processing problems and their structures by studying a vocabulary of common problem types. We use Jackson's Problem Frames [22] approach as a way to identify the elements of a client's problem, identify pertinent properties of these elements, and recognize classes of similar problems whose well-established solutions can provide guidance for the problem at hand. Students learn to identify distinct concerns, or domains, of the problem and determine the characteristics of each domain – for example whether it is under the control of the software developer, whether it is physical or symbolic, whether it operates autonomously or only through external control. After analyzing the problem domains, students identify common problem templates (called frames), such as device control, information display, or data transformation, that appear in the client's problem. Finally they formulate the criterion for demonstrating that the software they're designing in fact solves the problem. The problem frames describe phenomena in the problem space, but they are common problems for which solution strategies, and hence software design alternatives, are well known.

Problem frame analysis of problems demonstrates several design principles:

♦ Good designers draw on a rich vocabulary of well-understood design fragments. This allows them to map new problems to systems of known problem types.
♦ Common problem structures appear regularly, even across application areas. Recognizing them allows the software designer to apply existing knowledge about solutions (and pitfalls), which is usually more effective than developing new solutions from scratch.
♦ Precise, often formal, analyses provide insight into problem characteristics, and analysis techniques should be selected opportunistically to match the problem.
♦ Problem analysis should enhance the designer's understanding of the client's needs and yield a plan for showing that the problem, and each subproblem, has been solved correctly.

♦ Idealized templates provide good guidance, but they must be adapted in each case to handle the details of the problem at hand.

Problem frames provide students with a way to sharpen their own understanding of the client, to impose structure that will lead to solutions, and to map the new problem into more familiar territory. This is a relatively short unit, and we do not use supplemental materials.

The project requires students to perform a problem frame analysis for their ongoing projects. This assignment comes early in the semester, so we emphasize understanding the major domains of the client's problem and the types of the main problem and a few principal subproblems.

3.2 Eliciting Technical Needs

In this section of the course, students learn ways to discover what the system should actually do in order to address the users' evolving needs. Use case modeling and contextual design methods address these concerns.

3.2.1 Use Case Modeling

Use case modeling [2] provides techniques for identifying an appropriate system boundary, understanding the interactions of external entities with the system, developing the capabilities the system should provide, and understanding the domain the software problem is situated in. This provides an effective starting point for matching users' expectations with what the system should actually do. A significant advantage of use case modeling is that it allows the students to formulate alternative usage interactions at a goal level rather than a mere functionality level. Our approach emphasizes use case modeling as an elicitation technique that can be used early in the software design to develop an understanding of the problem at hand.

Use case modeling allows us to demonstrate principles of:

♦ Software should be designed around the expected benefits to the users. Use case modeling accomplishes this by capturing the goals of users, not just the system functionality.
♦ The full complexity of the users' domain needs to be captured. Use case modeling requires identification of the various classes of roles and external entities that need to interact with the system.
♦ Identifying anticipated interactions with the system helps to identify implicit requirements. Specifying needs in general terms often glosses over complex and subtle user needs.

Supplemental readings help to broaden the students' understanding of the context of use. In particular, Carroll provides an alternative view to use case modeling by showing how the use of scenarios can transform information systems design. Scenario-based design uses concretization; scenarios are concrete stories about use [13].

Through individual exercises the students experiment with reverse engineering a product for a partial use case model and developing a domain understanding of the system they are designing. The project requires them, with their team, to develop an initial use case model and reflect on parts of the problem that they were not able to capture with techniques provided in use case modeling.

3.2.2 Contextual Design

Contextual design provides a particular example of a method for discovering subtle user requirements, translating them into an initial design, and iterating with prototypes and customer feedback in order to validate and refine the design. The method sets out techniques for conducting interviews with potential users, generating models that describe how the work is actually done and the context of that work, and consolidating the work models and organizing functionality in a way that conforms with the ways users actually work [4].

Contextual design is firmly grounded in the tradition of social science methods for discovering social, institutional, and organizational phenomena. It prescribes a modeling discipline that resonates with software engineering students and helps to make the social science techniques accessible to them. Finally, it provides a coherent and comprehensive set of techniques that go from initial conception to a prototype solution. We present contextual design as an illustration of several general, enduring principles that guide early design:

♦ Representing the context of use requires appropriate techniques. Assumptions and prejudices about how users will interact with the system are an unsound foundation for design.

♦ Interactions with users in the design process should be carefully planned, and the interactions should center on concrete instances of the user's work. Simply talking to users, or just asking them what they want is unlikely to yield satisfactory results.

♦ Users are experts at their tasks, and system design must allow them to exploit their expertise.

♦ Good design usually results from informed exploration of alternatives, not from simply adopting the first solution that presents itself.

♦ Design of interactive software generally implies a redesign of how users work, with attendant risks to the user's ability to work effectively. These risks must be recognized and managed.

Supplemental readings bring a number of related points into the discussion. Suchman [44] discusses the difficulty of embedding a plan-based model of the user in the system as a means of guiding interactions in the context of copying machines. She emphasizes the need to help the user understand the state of the machine in order to interact with it. Moody [28] and Kidder [24] provide inside views of the often chaotic and turbulent design process in real organizations and of the push and pull of business and social forces. Christensen [14] introduces the notion of disruptive innovations. He makes the case that the designer's attention should not be limited to what the clients are asking for at the moment, but rather it should extend to understanding the business and technical contexts deeply enough to anticipate the client's longer-term needs and to place intelligent technology bets. This is complemented by von Hippel's analysis of the evolutionary nature of development [46].

The project requires students to conduct actual data collection by identifying at least two potential users of the system they are designing, planning and conducting contextual interviews, constructing work models, and specifying the organization of functionality from a user's perspective – the "user environment design" in contextual design terminology.

3.3 Matching the Design to User Needs

In this section of the course, students learn to evaluate solution alternatives from a user's point of view. The section begins with a continuation of contextual design, focusing here on constructing prototypes and interacting with users in order to evaluate them. Norman [29] expands on the theme of usability, exposing the students to a classical discussion of user-centered design principles and a wide-ranging collection of examples.

The course uses current examples of design as material to which the principles can be applied. Recently, for example, the class focused on the BMW iDrive system that uses a control knob and menus to access over 700 of the automobile's non-critical functions. This interface provides a wealth of material for analysis of affordances, focus of attention, mappings, design for error, and mental models. This example also sets the stage for understanding the significance of business drivers – the initial version of the system was extraordinarily difficult to use and expensive to correct.

These materials provide students with concrete examples of techniques that embody several principles:

♦ Designing for users is an iterative process where interaction between user and designer focuses on meaningful, concrete representations of the designed system, presented to the user in context.
♦ Determining an appropriate level of prototype fidelity is a tradeoff between the cost of the prototype and the accuracy and precision of the feedback. For many purposes, low fidelity prototypes, such as paper and pencil mockups, are most appropriate.
♦ Software design requires simultaneously learning from codified experience and deeply understanding the unique subtleties of each particular design problem.
♦ The key to usability is creating a design in which the user correctly, continuously, and effortlessly maps the perceptual experience of the system to the user's mental model and the user's preferred way of working.

Supplemental material enriches the discussion with additional points of view. Brown and Duguid [8] offer an analysis of the difficulties inherent in separating knowledge from people and the inherently social nature of information, ideas that are critical for effective information system design. CSTB [15] offers a variety of ideas and research directions that focus on making computing available to a broader group of users. Winograd [48] shows how classical design knowledge applies to software, and Waldrop [47] provides a history of the creative thinking that transformed computers from remote mainframes used by specialists to ubiquitous tools in "human-computer symbiosis" with their users, connected intimately to daily work. Finally, Snyder [43] provides a comprehensive look at paper prototyping and its many applications in early design.

The project for this section requires students to construct at least two different prototypes for two focus areas of the user environment design that was the final product of a previous project. They then evaluate these alternatives, applying Norman's principles [29] and explanatory concepts in a process based on cognitive walkthroughs. If we had sufficient time available from project clients, we would prefer to have the students evaluate these prototypes with interviews conducted in the users' context.

3.4 Understanding and Analyzing Business, Economic, and Policy Constraints

In this section of the course students learn about the contextual forces that arise from the economic and business settings of software development projects. This section reviews elementary financial concepts and discusses the ways business considerations can dominate factors in software design decisions. It covers ways to predict the value – benefit net of cost – of a software system by analyzing early design representations. The course exploits an example of current interest, such as privacy or internationalization, as a setting for understanding legal and policy constraints.

By treating software development as a value-creating activity, the course provides a framework to relate technical and contextual factors in software design decisions. On the one hand, students see how economic models such as utility theory can guide software design selection. On the other hand, they see how business, economic, and political requirements affect the kinds of solutions that will be acceptable. For example, international differences in privacy regulations should be anticipated at the point of database design, so that information that is regulated differently in different countries can be tagged or isolated. No textbook is available to cover all this material. We use Shapiro and Varian [35] to show students how economic concepts show up in the software market, but we must rely on a selection of papers for the rest of the material [19, 25, 27, 32, 33, 34, 39].

The material supports these principles:

♦ The objective of software design and development should be value to the company or client, not merely functionality. This requires analyzing both lifetime costs and benefits
♦ Analysis of value must take into consideration risk and time value of resources.
♦ Early, careful evaluation of designs makes software development more efficient.
♦ Many contextual requirements affect software design in fundamental ways; they should be addressed early in design.
♦ Decision models used in economics and social science can be useful for software design.

Supplemental material elaborates several aspects of this section. Shapiro and Varian [35] and Cusumano and Yoffie [18] show how market and competition shape strategic design questions. Two CSTB studies [16, 17] explore social and international issues in access to computing. Lessig [26] examines the tension between the original concept of the Internet as a commons for ideas and the use of the Internet as a commercial marketplace.

The project for this section requires students to identify one design issue for which the designer must consider business or economic constraints in order to get a good outcome for the client. They must identify two feasible solutions or approaches and compare the values of these alternatives, *as the client will see them*, applying topics of this unit as appropriate.

3.5 Adopting an Engineering Approach to Software Systems

In this section of the course students compare software engineering to traditional engineering disciplines to gain perspective on engineering practice, especially the need to reconcile conflicting constraints with limited time, knowledge, and resources. They study the nature of software systems, including the difference between program and product, issues of embedding, and the responsibilities of engineers. A discussion of the engineering approach to solving problems, both in software systems and in engineered systems more generally, complements this view.

By reading Brooks [9], students are reminded of recurring characteristics of software engineering projects such as manpower, scheduling, and second system effect. They also see how other engineering disciplines draw on codified knowledge whenever possible.

The core principles we develop in this unit are already well recognized in other engineering disciplines. For example, design for scalability, situated design reuse, evaluation of designs in adapted contexts, attribute dependency and codifying design knowledge are common engineering techniques. The key principles we study are:

♦ Engineering entails making decisions with limited time, knowledge, and resources. However, problems often recur. Recognizing the recurring patterns and extracting knowledge from a codified knowledge base are typical of an engineering approach.

♦ Using a codified engineering base effectively is only possible when engineers understand the implications of changing scale and problem context on designs.

♦ Collection of relevant science and empirical results occur over time and experience. The use of these resources help engineers craft solutions to routine problems. Software engineering is now mature enough to start accumulating such resources. Recognizing the repeating routine problems in software engineering and driving the core knowledge from them is essential for the establishment of the software as an engineering discipline.

♦ Engineers must evaluate the complexity of their designs when they are put to use. They must recognize the dependencies between different components of their designs and evaluate their outcomes for human aspects.

We rely on supplemental material to provide concrete examples of engineering principles. We begin with material from computer science. Hoffman and Weiss [20] review Parnas' fundamental contributions to software engineering through topics as relational and tabular documentation, information hiding as the basis for modular program construction, abstract interfaces that provide services without revealing implementation, and program families for the efficient development of multiple software versions. Simon [41] explores design as a science; in particular he helps establish how software does admit to the same sorts of science as the natural world.

We complement this with reflections on older engineering disciplines, including aspects from civil, architectural, chemical, aeronautical, and mechanical engineering. Petroski [31] offers case studies showing the importance of understanding the context a design will operate in. He emphasizes the criticality of recognizing why and how errors occur in advancing the engineering methods for creating innovative solutions to problems. Vincenti [45] explains how engineering knowledge accumulates and describes how engineers use this knowledge in problem solving. Akin [1] shows how the architectural design process can be formalized and codified; he shows how expert civil architects go about solving their problems. Perrow [30] helps expose the social aspects of engineering design, especially in dealing with high-risk technologies. He presents complexity, especially tight coupling of subsystems, as a source of unpredictable cascading failures.

Students are expected to recognize the fundamental engineering principle discussed in the material and apply it to software engineering with examples either from their projects, past experience, or other units of the course.

4 Pedagogical Principles

The course we describe is a core course in a professional masters program. Many topics compete for attention in the curriculum, and many activities compete for faculty and student time. The Carnegie Mellon software engineering faculty regards education as an investment from which students should reap benefits for decades. These pedagogical principles guide our curriculum and course implementations [38].

University education must provide knowledge of enduring value together with immediate competency. Universities walk a careful line between education in enduring principles and training in vocational skills. The Carnegie Mellon faculty believe both that a graduate should have certain competencies and that the investment in education should continue to pay off over a long period of time, and accordingly we ask our courses to serve both ends. There is ample evidence that the two are compatible, because students typically learn the principles best by working out examples that apply those principles.

In engineering, tools and skills cannot replace judgment. Engineering requires finding cost-effective solutions from among many and diverse alternatives. Methods, tools, processes, skills, heuristics, and other tools and techniques can help to organize the solution search to concentrate on good candidate solutions. These engineering tools and techniques remind you to consider possibilities that you might otherwise ignore. They can help a good (or even adequate) engineer find better solutions more effectively. They are not – and cannot be – a substitute for actually understanding the problem and making sound judgments about solutions. An intrinsic characteristic of engineering is the requirement to strike appropriate balances among conflicting goals. So pursuing one tool or technique to the exclusion of all others is only very rarely, if ever, appropriate. Above all, we should teach our students engineering judgment and the commitment to use it; all the specifics support this end. In particular, as students in our class apply their newly-acquired knowledge to the studio projects, faculty and other students facilitate reflection by providing constructive critique of their efforts.

The Carnegie Plan provides excellent guidance about engineering education. Each student should learn not only specific content, but also the principles and mindset of the profession, the ability to learn new material independently, and the perspective and judgment to be a responsible adult. In particular, graduates should be able to assume responsibility for their own continued professional development. Therefore, they should learn not only today's methods and technologies, but also the underlying principles and critical abilities that will allow them to select and master new methods and technologies as they emerge. This idea is captured in the Carnegie Plan, which Carnegie Mellon established half a century ago as part of a major restructuring of engineering education, both at Carnegie Mellon and throughout North America (see Appendix). Carnegie Plan carries institutional memory for our university. It is also an enduring statement that provides guidance for blending theoretical understanding and practically focused experience into durable skills and the ability to learn new material.

Hands-on, attentive time on task is critical to learning. Simon showed us that the strongest correlation between demonstrable learning and any of the student and instructor activities is with the student's engaged, attentive time practicing with whatever was being learned/taught: "Learning has to occur in the students. You can do anything you like in the classroom or elsewhere – you can stand on your head – and it doesn't make a whit of difference unless it causes a change in behavior of your students" [42]. He also told us that experts have indexed memory of 50,000 to

100,000 chunks in the area of expertise, taking 10 years to acquire this expertise. So a reasonable aspiration for a university course is to get a good start on the 50-100,000 chunks by providing the student with a conceptual roadmap, lots of hands-on practice in various parts of the domain, and the ability to fill in more of the chunks.

Curriculum design is at heart a resource allocation problem. The scarce resource is student attention, measured however imperfectly by courses, hours spent, pages of reading, numbers of projects. To provide the greatest value, we must require each course to contribute to both enduring value and immediate competency. This favors content backed by good theory, because good theories compress lots of content into tidy packages; however, this leverage should not be allowed to drive out important (but partially codified) content in favor of pure theory. On the other hand, extensive exercises in a process that is likely to be obsolete in a couple of years can (usually) only be justified to the extent that they support long-term knowledge. It is easy to identify "important" content that more than fills the space in the program -- whether space is measured as class time, student attention, hours of work, or something else. It is much harder to set the priorities that lead to a curriculum that strikes the right balance of coverage and depth.

Sampling is sufficient; it is not necessary to cover everything. For students of the high quality that we admit, thorough mastery of a few exemplars coupled with principled overviews should provide a sufficient basis for learning other related material. We must take care, though, to provide sufficient coverage. This is a reasonable choice because curriculum space is a scarce resource and, per the Carnegie Plan, our students can assume responsibility for their own professional development.

Admissions should be selective, and we should make every effort to help admitted students succeed. The overall quality of students in a class affects the level at which the class functions, especially in interactive settings. When, as in many of our activities, students work in teams, the quality of each student's experience depends on the quality of the other students. Further, failure of some students affects the whole community of students. It follows that we should attempt to admit students with a good chance of success and commit to making them successful.

The educational setting should enable students to learn effectively. Learning depends chiefly on the active engagement of students, who make a substantial investment of time and resources. We should provide opportunities and resources that allow students to do this effectively. While providing sufficient resources, we should at the same time provide a realistic development setting

5 Course Organization: Engaging Students Actively

Our "Methods: Deciding What to Design" course is a core course in the MSE program at Carnegie Mellon. This is a terminal degree program for students with several years of software development experience; its objective is to enable its graduates to practice software engineering at a very high level of proficiency and to serve as technical leaders and agents of change in their companies. In implementing this course, we considered the type of students who enter our professional masters programs and the principles of Section 4. We also considered other courses in our curriculum and ways the full suite of courses plus the Studio complement each other.

This course emphasizes mastering the material for use in practice. It won't serve the MSE program or the broader pedagogical principles if it is taught as a set of facts and skills. It can only work if it engages students in thinking hard about real – not textbook – problems. To that end, we teach the course by engaging students with real problems in as close to a real-world setting as we can arrange.

In terms of the Bloom taxonomy[3], we are principally interested in mastery at the higher (analysis, synthesis, and evaluation) levels. It follows that the objectives for our courses include a combination of "understands" verbs and "can-do" verbs. Further, the "doing" parts of the course must support the "understanding" parts. We probably all agree that courses in which students can hack their way to apparent success aren't serving their ends. It also follows that reflection and interpretation are more important than extensive routine drilling, comprehension more important than highly technology-specific skills.

The course takes advantage of a key feature of the MSE program – the MSE Studio. The entire program emphasizes application of course material in a practical hands-on experience, and the MSE Studio is built around projects for real, paying clients who expect actual deliverables. These year-long Studio projects provide students with a real software development setting where they must overcome technical challenges, understand new problem domains, manage team dynamics and client interactions, formulate problems, and – in the end – deliver software products to their clients. The course described here relies on the MSE Studio for real (not simply realistic) examples, and observations about how they apply course material to the Studio provides valuable course feedback. The use of real projects allows students to develop immediate competency to critique and apply the techniques they have learned rather than only acquiring textbook knowledge. Section 7 discusses ways to teach a course such as this in the absence of a Studio.

5.1 Homework

We emphasize applying and interpreting the readings, not simply doing small-scale exercises. Homework assignments for each of the readings help students focus on the aspects of the reading that are important to the course. Moreover, students do the homework based on the reading material and the class is used for discussion and interpretation, in contrast to the traditional format of presenting material in class as a basis for the homework assignment. Some of the homework questions ask students to answer questions on the day's reading; others ask them to apply class material to a problem or to their Studio project. The recurring objective verbs in our assignments are "understanding", "applying", "assessing", "discriminating", and "identifying". By

---

[3] The attributes of the Bloom taxonomy [7] are:
- Knowledge: remembering previously learned material.
- Comprehension–: understanding the meaning of material.
- Application: using learned material in new and concrete situations.
- Analysis: breaking down material into component parts to understand its structure.
- Synthesis: putting parts together to form new wholes.
- Evaluation: judging the value of material.

clearly explaining the objectives of the assignments, we both focus the students' efforts in answering the assignments and remind them of the enduring values to take away from the course [40]. We use sampling as a technique to balance coverage with providing enough hands-on experience for understanding the topics. By limiting their answers to a page or two in length, we try to help them focus on the most important aspects of the topics. Students find this more challenging, but we see them engaging the material at higher levels of the Bloom taxonomy, especially in class discussions. When an assignment asks for answers based on the Studio project, students work with their project groups on that assignment. However, they must answer the daily homework assignments individually to show their own understanding of both the project and the class material. The homework assignments provide individual hands-on attentive time on tasks for students. It also provides the team with multiple points of view of the same approach, allowing them to evaluate alternatives against each other when they need to apply the same technique to their project as a team.

5.2 Real-Life Projects

In each unit of the course, the project groups apply ideas of the unit to their MSE Studio projects and report the result to the class. Reporting to the class includes making a short 8-minute presentation of the main points, leading class discussion, and providing a 2-3-page summary of the major ideas. Students start working with the clients for their Studio projects the first week of the class. The projects help the students develop preliminary results with their clients; they can subsequently build on these results as part of the Studio. This allows the students to rapidly evaluate the effectiveness of the methods they learn in class for their project. We expect them to reflect on their experience, which also provides them an opportunity to recognize the core competencies set out in Section 2.

Each unit runs between two and three weeks. Through project assignments we address curriculum resource allocation and sampling, in addition to providing further opportunities for hands-on practice. Students get an opportunity to immediately apply what they learned to a selected part of their project. This first experience does not make students experts in the area of the assignment, but this exposure provides a basic understanding they can build on later, in accordance with the Carnegie Plan.

5.3 Communication Skills

The MSE program places a strong emphasis on communication skills. In designing the Methods course to include significant numbers of student presentations in class, we are both relying on the communication skills the students have already developed and providing more opportunities to exercise and further develop their skills. Each student presentation uses almost 1% of the class time in the course, and we depend on each student to contribute comparable value through his or her presentations. Since the purpose of each presentation is to explain to the class what the main idea of the topic is and how that idea should affect software design, we expect clear presentations that make the connection between the background material and the class projects. These criteria remind students not only to master the material presented in class, but also bring in their own experience and critical insight to the class.

5.4 Independent Interpretation

Most of the supplemental materials are books. We incorporate them in the course by assigning each book to a project group. The group is responsible for reading the book and reporting on how ideas from the book are related to the course. The reports on the books do not attempt to cover the entire book, but rather to identify and explain the most important points relevant to the course and software engineering in general. Similar to the projects, each report consists of an 8-minute presentation followed by discussion and a short written report from the group, 2-3 pages in length.

These independent interpretations provide another opportunity to combine the pedagogical principles of sampling and curriculum resource allocation. The supplemental readings and reports not only enrich the units, they also provide further sampling of techniques to which students can return when applicable. This activity also highlights the value of engineering judgment because we emphasize critical evaluation of the key take away of the books and application of the ideas to their Studio projects rather than a summary of the topic.

To help students prepare for the presentation and to focus the report, we ask them to provide a short abstract (approximately 50-75 words) of the viewpoint in advance. The purpose of the statement is not simply to identify the topic the author writes about -- it requires the students to identify what the author "says" about the topic. For example the statement should not be of the form "*the authors talk about the business of software...*" but "*the authors refute arguments that we need new economic models for software by arguing that the old models work, just with radically different parameters. They support this with discussions of adoption curves, lockin, ... For our studio project this implies, for example, ...*" We describe this as a statement that will help people remember what the book might offer them, so that they'll remember enough to find the book when they discover sometime later that they need it.

We expect critical analysis and independent interpretation of the selected books. Sometimes students have to try several times before they are able to explain how the reading applies to the course instead of just giving a book report. In the process they develop their engineering judgment skills as they have to think about how to report their conclusions to the rest of the class most effectively.

This exercise helps students learn to recognize outside material relevant to the course. It not only introduces them with a broader set of concepts, but it also gives them experience with evaluating techniques on their own. In addition, it allows them to recognize how to use different techniques together for the principles introduced in the course. For example for their projects students have in the past opted to use paper prototyping [43] in conjunction with either use case modeling [2] or scenario-based design [44] and evaluated their results through Norman's design principles [29]. The students are able to arrive at such rich combinations that cross over multiple units as a result of the variety of activities they engage in during the course.

5.5 Critical Evaluation

We expect students not only to learn the material they study, but also to apply it spontaneously to practical problems. In this way we require the students to evaluate which techniques work well, which techniques may work with improvement, and which techniques may not be suitable for the task at hand. Reflective practice is entirely consistent with the Carnegie Plan's combination of education grounded in enduring principles, skills in applying these principles and continual improvement, and experience grounded in the real world.

The opportunities we provide for students to develop critical evaluation skills extend to all the activities of the class. Our evaluation criteria emphasize that we value insights combined with a student's experience over only reporting back what the lectures or readings already covered. In project reports we expect teams to evaluate how they have applied the methods to the specific project domain they are working in. We conduct the class meetings by providing ample opportunities for students to not only ask questions, but also contribute with their experience obtained either from other classes or from industry experience (simply repeating material from the reading without adding insight does not count as valuable discussion).

6   Experience and Evaluation

Our evaluation of this course is based on our own reflection, on the progress we and other faculty observe in the Studio projects after the students finish the course, and on the feedback we receive from the students (both while they are still in the program and after they graduate).

6.1   Our Evaluation

We have offered this course in lecture format four times. The third time we concurrently prepared the course for distance delivery, and the second distance offering is underway as this paper is under preparation [10]. After each offering we have reflected on student performance and participation and revised the course accordingly. Our own reaction is that the course addresses the concerns we had when we designed the course. This provides an element of face validity.

The faculty mentors of the MSE Studio report that since we have started connecting class assignments directly to the Studio projects, the students' performance in applying course material to the Studio has substantially increased. Changing the order to present problem frames first has enhanced this effect.

When real projects are introduced to the curriculum, the closed-shop software development model no longer holds even in the educational environment. The concerns we identified in Section 1.1 are challenges that software engineers need to learn to deal with in school as well. Our students have to live through the challenges of evolving system requirements as the clients understand both the technologies and the opportunities available to them. The contextual design, use case modeling, making the result useful, and problem frame analysis methods we introduce in the course provide opportunities to help the teams to help their clients understand their needs. This year all three projects that are assigned to our on-campus teams have requirements where the end product needs to be adapted or tailored even after it is delivered. Open source development and globally distributed teams is no longer a myth, but a reality. The business and economic considerations and problem frames analysis topic assist in surfacing challenges, consideration the teams must pay attention to.

6.2 Responses from MSE Program

The responses from the MSE program focus on improvements in how students get engaged with solving the problems for their Studio projects early on using the techniques introduced in the Methods course. Several teams opt to continue using the methods that they are only introduced to in the course in their Studio projects. The teams continue using these methods as a driver for their software development efforts in a longer term and larger context. They report that the techniques help them bridge the gaps between the client, the team and the technical challenges.

♦ A team of four students from the 2003-2004 academic year with members ranging from 2 to 10 years of experience, report that using paper prototyping, a technique they learned from independent interpretation of supplemental material, helped them scope a problem context that would otherwise have been hard to manage. This allowed them develop a technically competent solution in a short amount of time. Their success led other teams to try out the technique in subsequent years.
♦ All the teams each year employ advanced use case modeling as a problem understanding and requirement specification technique. The distance education students, who tend to have more industry experience than the on campus students, report advanced use case modeling as a strong technique to employ directly in industry, especially when coupled with contextual design – provided that economic resources are available.
♦ Two out of the three on-campus teams of 2004-2005 used problem frame analysis successfully to understand and refine the scope of their problem. Teams used this technique internally rather than sharing it with their clients, so they report their application as "informal". In the semester following this course, one team that was been struggling with representing the intrinsic details of their system with use case modeling revisited their problem frame analysis. They used problem frames together with use cases to identify different subsystems and discover which subsystems acting on other subsystems. They report that using problem frames to identify subproblems and their relations with each other helped them understand why their use cases were being criticized as trivial.
♦ One on-campus team of 2004-2005, after studying industrialization and versioning as part of the business and economic considerations unit, decided to address this and to their surprise discovered that this was one of their client's concerns, though it was not mentioned in client discussions before the students brought it up.
♦ One 2005-2006 team used cost/benefit analysis comparing an open source tool to a $60,000 commercial one They showed better long term return with the commercial tool. The customer bought the commercial tool because of this analysis. Discussions with the team members revealed that they were resigned to using the far less capable open source one, until they did the analysis as part of their class work.

6.3 Student Responses

Students with little industrial experience find it challenging to be asked to apply the material to an actual project, with all the ambiguity and hidden constraints that are typical of real projects. As they get more experience with the material, either by applying it to the Studio project or applying it on the job after they graduate, they find it very valuable. Students in the distance offerings also report that the course is both challenging and worthwhile. Distance students are usually working at the time they are taking the course, and they often report applying the material in their current projects. The feedback we get from students relate to several areas of the course organization.

Collaborating with other professionals. The revelation that a professional has to be able to collaborate with people with complementary skills comes as a surprise to students with little industry experience.

♦ Two students from Fall 2004 report that dealing with a team member who was more experienced than themselves in the problem domain was challenging. This even influenced how they perceived the applicability of the methods introduced; however, it also gave them an understanding of how they should have relied on using the methods in dealing with the experience gap.

Critical thinking. The course format comes as the biggest surprise to some students. Going from memorize-and-recite-back courses to critical application of content, learning to make public presentations, and learning to contribute to discussions is challenging at first. However, students start realizing the benefits as they are encouraged to conduct these activities regularly. We expect not only substantive results, but also communication and organization skills. We provide immediate feedback so that students can work on their weak skills before they have to deal with similar tasks again. Admittedly, this course is fast paced and does at points stretch the students if they come with insufficient background. On the other hand, students start seeing the benefits as early as a few weeks into the course. The benefits of frequent individual homework assignments with specific hands-on tasks -- at times frustrating due to time constraints -- are appreciated.

♦ One student from Fall 2004 reports, "In my undergrad, we had only final semester exams and we were graded based on that exams' performance. We would never get our answers back and hence never understood what mistakes we committed! The way it is done here is very beneficial and I really appreciate the way you put comments on each and every one's answers. This has been a new experience for me, and I am benefiting a lot."
♦ One student from Spring 2003 reports "Honestly, after my first presentation, at first I did not even understand why I did not do so well. Your feedback on my presentation was really valuable for me, not only for grade improvement, but also for my communication skills."

Formal exposure to known techniques. Students with longer industry experience are encouraged by seeing what they had to deal with in industry presented in a structured manner, and they also appreciate new techniques for dealing with familiar problems.

♦ A student from Fall 2004 with 5 years of experience reports that although he had to design and prototype many software products he never was introduced to approaching them with principles covered for making the result useful unit. He emphasizes that this exposure helped him evaluate how it can be done more effectively.
♦ A student from Fall 2003 with 10 years of software architecture development experience reports that he was very happy to have been introduced to Brook's [9] principles after he graduated because there have been several incidents where he had to be reminded of the relationship between adding complexity and scheduling.
♦ A student from Spring 2005 offering who is taking the distance education version of the course reports he will take back contextual design to the rest of his company to use as a part of their software development process because it will help them identify product visions that are more in line with user needs. He also adds that they will first need to look very carefully into cost-benefit analysis of resource allocation.
♦ A student from the Spring 2006 distance offering reported, "Despite all of the moaning about problem frames, I think I 'like' it most of the three approaches so far. (Does this make me ill in the head?) It is more applicable to my work than Use Cases and Contextual Design. At [my company], I work with embedded systems that by nature interact with other

systems. There is no human actor, no user centric context. While use cases can have system actors, that isn't really strong suit. Contextual design is almost entirely focused on the user environment which doesn't exist in my systems. So consider this a vote in favor of problem frames. My only gripes really are that I believe it can be boiled down to a science and Jackson is almost there. He has 90% of the concepts down at 70% clarity."

- The distance education students of Spring 2005 and 2006 offering also had to deal with challenges of not being collocated. These students were current industry professionals who were attending the program while they continue to work. They embraced the challenges of the distance environment as a learning opportunity and report that this allowed them to evaluate how they can apply the techniques in an outsourced and distributed environment. The distance education students readily embraced problem frames, which students with less practical experience find one of the most challenging techniques. They report this technique could be very useful to bridge communication gaps when parts of a project are outsourced.

- Many students with extensive experience come into the course having applied, or at least having heard of use case modeling. A student from Spring 2005 distance education offering reports going through the process in a different way than the one employed in his company allowed him to improve his use of the technique.

7 Adapting the Course for Other Settings

This course is organized around the particular educational setting at Carnegie Mellon. In this section, we discuss our assumptions about the setting and about ways to adapt the course when these assumptions do not hold.

7.1 Selection of Topics

One major practical advantage of the sampling principle is that the contents of various sections of the course can be varied substantially while achieving the same educational objectives. There may often be good reason to choose example techniques to illustrate the important principles other than those mentioned here. Techniques may be changed because of their immediate applicability to a project or because a change complements the content of other courses.

We have taught this course four times as a lecture course and twice as a distance course. We have varied the specific techniques several times. For example, in the Eliciting Technical Needs section, we have taught task analysis rather than contextual design; in the Business, Economics, and Policy section, we have covered privacy and security in place of internationalization, and we have sometimes covered QFD [3]; in the Making the Results Actually Useful section, we have covered cognitive walkthroughs rather than paper prototyping. This kind of flexibility has allowed us to experiment with new content that we think will build immediate competency and to take advantage of available expertise in our environment.

7.2 Student Presentations

Our time budget for class meetings is heavily influenced by the need to schedule two presentations by each student. Typically, each student will make formal presentations of one independent interpretation and one project report during the semester. As a team member, each student will work on about five written project reports and five written independent interpretation reports. As mentioned above, we consider the presentation part of the course as a key skill-building element as well as a way of bringing diverse content into the class discussions.

This approach does not scale well, of course. We typically have 25 or so students in the class, and adding significantly to this number would require cutting back on student presentations in order to allow sufficient time for other course content. One solution would be to have recitation sections for student presentations and discussion. Large classes could be divided into a sufficient number of recitation sections to introduce concurrency into the student presentation component. This depends, of course, on the availability of sufficient faculty and teaching assistant resources.

Similarly, very small classes with students fewer than 12-15 students would pose challenges as well. Small classes could lose from the content, especially with reduction of the independent interpretations from students.

A more challenging situation is presented by a distance education version of the course. Several approaches are possible here, given the availability of appropriate technology. In situations where students meet regularly with a distance education instructor, presentations can proceed more or less as usual. If there are no, or very few, face-to-face meetings, presentations could be done using some form of conferencing technology. To the extent that students have reasonable equipment available, this could be an effective option. The most critical pieces are good audio quality and a way of sharing presentation slides. For the Spring 2005 and 2006 distance education offerings of the course we used a web-based collaboration technology which allowed us to speak using voice over IP and share presentations via desktop sharing. With a class size of 10-13 this technology worked smoothly; however, for larger classes it would pose challenges in providing students enough opportunities to participate and present in this kind of an environment. Another option would be to digitally record a student's presentation using some local resource, and providing the audio, slides, and perhaps video to other students online. Discussion could proceed by means of a discussion board (if students observe at different times) or chat session (if students observe simultaneously) in which the students (including the presenter) and instructor participate.

7.3 Student Prior Experience

Our students typically have a year or more of industry experience, and we have found that this experience is critical for success in the course. Less experienced students often struggle because they don't have the same level of intuitive understanding of the problems of large projects with real customers. This need for experience has been reinforced in observing the distance offerings of the course. The distance students have, by comparison, an average of over 5 years experience and did not have any of the problems associated with some of the minimally experienced students on campus. Additionally the discussions, albeit asynchronous through a discussion board tended to be more robust and insightful. While part of this is undoubtedly due to asynchronous discussions providing more time to ponder questions and formulate responses, the impact of higher levels of experience can't be overlooked.

For classes where students have not had such experience, we strongly recommend that this course not be the first course in which students encounter a team-based project. For such students it would be very helpful for this course to follow one or more courses that include a team-oriented project with a real customer, using versioning and change management tools. Otherwise, students are likely to thrash, struggling to learn too many things at once.

7.4 Availability of a Studio Project

We depend heavily on a substantial, year-long project with a real client. Such projects are richer and deeper than textbook projects, and the students have realistic interactions with clients, with all of the ambiguity, frustration, and need for diplomacy that such encounters require. Unfortunately, not all contexts in which this course might be taught will have access to such a project.

We have developed one alternative for our distance education version of the course. During the semester when the class sessions were recorded, we planned carefully to capture as much as possible of the contextual material for one of the studio projects. We have materials such as a videotaped initial presentation by the client of what they want, and both documentation and code from the client from the application of which the project will become a part. The goal is to provide enough material for the distance education instructor to act as a realistic surrogate client, answering questions and posing convincingly as an interviewee for contextual design.

One company that uses our distance offerings would like to use its own in-house project as a basis for student assignments. This would be a natural fit for this course, which would provide a different set of techniques from the company's usual process. We would need to be careful to avoid conflicts of interest between the course and the project goals, and we, by policy, do not offer course credit for work done on the job.

Another scenario for handling the lack of a real project is to create a mock-up project with sufficient problem complexity. This project can serve as a resource for typical issues that the students would encounter in a real project. The challenge of this approach is being able to introduce multiple real world constraints to the problem such as conflicting requirements, possible scenarios of integration with existing products, business and economic consideration, and non-trivial design issues. In addition, this approach requires the creation of substantial supplemental material that will be instrumental in introducing the project to the students. In this scenario the instructor needs to serve as the client as well, creating realistic challenges that may not necessarily happen in a course setting, but could occur in a real project. Carnegie Mellon West uses this approach in their Management of Software Systems Development program, where they have crafted a project in which they conduct the activities of the program as a series of mock-up client-employee interactions [12].

An alternative that would require a significant investment, but promises very broad and substantial benefits, would be to create a national resource in the form of one or more sample full records of software development projects. In addition to all versions of the code, maintained in a version control system, the resource should include a complete change history, records of design discussions, and inputs from customers and users. Although this idea has been discussed several times in the past, it has always stumbled on the question of acquiring a code base that can be made public. With the advent of open source, this problem has largely disappeared. Open source projects could provide the foundation for the resource we have in mind.

In order to create the sort of sample project records we have in mind, an open source project should be augmented with materials such as requirements and design documentation, contextual interviews with users, competitive analyses with other products, and training materials that instructors and teaching assistants can use to become convincing surrogate customers and users. The full project record could become the baseline in a version control system; each course could create its own code branch, allowing students to implement changes without burdening the open source project and without forcing students to cope with a code base that is changing underneath them (unless this serves an educational objective for a particular course).

In addition to serving as a resource for this particular class, such a resource would serve a variety of educational and research objectives. Researchers could, for example, directly compare the ability of various formal approaches such as model checking to detect significant bugs. Various ways of approaching important tasks such as refactoring could be directly compared. Visualization techniques could be tried out to see what they reveal about the code base that is relevant for various tasks. More generally, it would provide a very realistic example for many educational purposes, since our students are much more likely to spend their professional careers dealing with existing code bases rather than green field development.

8 Conclusion

The core problems of software engineering have evolved dramatically over the last decade or so, and we need to respond to these changes in order to equip our students with the skills and knowledge they need to excel in this new environment. The particular challenge for educators is that the need for the skills we taught ten or twenty years ago has not gone away. Students who find themselves working on embedded software, for example, still need to understand how to optimize for space and/or time, how to efficiently use machine-level instruction sets, memory overlays, and all the other skills that were important in the early days of computing. All our students still need to understand how to structure programs, how to handle exceptional conditions and errors, and how to organize the code so that anticipated changes can be localized. The need for basic skills in the design and construction of software, knowledge of how to make appropriate uses of abstraction and formality, have not gone away – in fact, as systems get larger, more critical, and more complex, the skills we have taught for the last 10 or 20 years are increasingly important.

Nevertheless, we believe that the technical, social, and business context of current developments provide additional challenges for which our traditional courses do not adequately prepare our students. Further, we believe that these additional challenges are sufficiently important to justify space in the curriculum. The course we describe in this paper represents our attempt to respond to the contemporary environment in a way that reinforces principles that underlie traditional teachings, and prepares our students to continue to learn, while providing skills they can apply immediately. The challenge to us as educators is to solve the curriculum design problem in a way that allocates the students' scarce attention to tasks that serve multiple goals at once. In an environment that imposes new challenges without relinquishing the old, that represents our only real hope of keeping up.

Acknowledgements

Thanks to colleagues, especially members of Carnegie Mellon's Institute for Software Research, International (ISRI) and its Master of Software Engineering (MSE) program, who have taught us about education, showed us new alternatives, and otherwise stimulated our appreciation of the problems and opportunities in software engineering education. Thanks especially to In-Young Ko, and Ho-Jin Choi for working with us on course development, and to all the students of the first four offerings of the course who helped us work out the ideas and the wrinkles of implementation. Sections 2 and 4 are derived from an ISRI working paper on curriculum design [38], and we particularly thank Jonathan Aldrich, Ray Bareiss, Shawn Butler, Lynn Carter, Owen Cheng, Steve Cross, Jamie Dinkelacker, Dave Farber, David Garlan, John Grasso, Martin Griss, Tim Halloran, Carol Hoover, Lisa Jacinto, Mark Klein, Deniz Lanyi, Beth Latronico, Jim Morris, Priya Narasimhan, Joe Newcomer, Linda Northrup, Mark Paulk, Mel Rosso-Llopart, Walt Shearer, Bill Scherlis, Todd Sedano, Gil Taran, Jim Tomayko, and Tony Wasserman for their contributions. Portions of Section 1 are derived from Shaw's education roadmap [37]. Carnegie Mellon does not have a definitive statement of the Carnegie Plan. Minor revisions are regularly made for different settings; the version presented here is a close variant of versions that have appeared in University publications over the years.

References

1. Omer Akin. *The Psychology of Architectural Design.* Pion, 1987.
2. Frank Armour and Granville Miller: *Advanced Use Case Modeling: Software Systems.* Addison-Wesley, 2001.
3. Toru Asada, Roy F. Swonger, Nadine Bounds, and Paul Duerig. The Quantified Design Space. In Mary Shaw and David Garlan, *Software Architecture: Perspectives on an Emerging Discipline*, Prentice-Hall 1996, Sec 5.2, pp 116-128.
4. Hugh Beyer and Karen Holtzblatt. *Contextual Design: Defining Customer-Centered Systems.* Morgan Kaufman, 1998.
5. Barry W. Boehm et al. *Software Cost Estimation with COCOMO II.* Prentice Hall 2000.
6. Barry W. Boehm and Victor R. Basili. Software defect reduction top 10 list. *IEEE Computer,* January 2001, pp. 2-4.
7. Benjamin S. Bloom and David R. Krathwohl (ed). *Taxonomy of educational objectives: The classification of educational goals. Handbook I, cognitive domain.* Longmans, Green, 1956.
8. John Seely Brown and Paul Duguid. *The Social Life of Information.* Harvard Business School Press, 2000.
9. Frederick P. Brooks. *The Mythical Man-Month: Essays on Software Engineering.* 20th Anniversary Edition, Addison-Wesley Professional, 1995.
10. Carnegie Mellon University. Distance Education in Software Engineering. Degree program description, Carnegie Mellon University, http://www.distance.cmu.edu/
11. Carnegie Mellon University. *Master of Software Engineering.* Degree program description, Carnegie Mellon University, February 2005, http://www.mse.cs.cmu.edu/

12. Carnegie Mellon West. *Management of Software Systems Development.* Degree program description, Carnegie Mellon University, February 2005,
13. John M. Carrol. *Making Use: Scenario-Based Design of Human-Computer Interactions.* MIT Press, 2000.
14. Clayton Christensen. *The Innovator's Dilemma.* Harper Business, 2000.
15. Computer Science and Telecommunications Board, National Research Council. *More than Screen Deep: Toward Every-Citizen Interfaces to the National Information Infrastructure.* National Academy Press, 1997.
16. Computer Science and Telecommunications Board, National Research Council. *The Digital Dilemma. Intellectual Property in the Information Age.* National Academy Press, 2000.
17. Computer Science and Telecommunications Board, National Research Council. *Global Networks and Local Values.* National Academy Press, 2001.
18. Michael Cusumano and David Yoffie. *Competing on Internet Time: Lessons from Netscape and its Battle with Microsoft.* Touchstone, 1998.
19. Thomas H. Davenport. The case of the soft software proposal. *Harvard Business Review,* May-June 1989.
20. Daniel M. Hoffman and David M. Weiss (eds.). *Software Fundamentals: Collected Papers by David L. Parnas.* Addison-Wesley, 2001.
21. IEEE Computer Society Professional Practices Committee. *SWEBOK: Guide to the Software Engineering Body of Knowledge, 2004 version.* IEEE Computer Society, 2004.
22. Michael Jackson. *Problem Frames.* Addison-Wesley, 2001.
23. Joint Task Force on Computing Curricula. *Software Engineering 2004: Curriculum Guidelines for Undergraduate Degree Programs in Software Engineering.* A Volume of the Computing Curricula Series. ACM and IEEE Computer Society, August 2004.
24. Tracy Kidder. *Soul of a New Machine.* Back Bay Books, 2000.
25. L. Korba and S. Kenny. Towards Meeting the Privacy Challenge: Adapting DRM. *ACM Workshop on Digital Rights Management,* Washington, DC, November 2002.
26. Lawrence Lessig. *The Future of Ideas.* Random House, 2001.
27. The Localization Industry Standards Association (LISA). *The Localization Industry Primer,* 2nd edition. LISA, 2003.
28. Fred Moody. *I Sing the Body Electronic: A Year with Microsoft on the Multimedia Frontier.* Penguin Books, 1995.
29. Donald Norman. *The Design of Everyday Things.* Currency/Doubleday, 1990.
30. Charles Perrow. *Normal Accidents.* Princeton University Press, 1999 (updated edition).
31. Henry Petroski. *Design Paradigms: Case Histories of Error and Judgment in Engineering.* Cambridge University Press, 1994.
32. Vahe Poladian, David Garlan, and Mary Shaw. Software Selection and Configuration in Mobile Environments: A Utility-Based Approach. *Position paper for the Fourth Workshop on Economics-Driven Software Engineering Research (EDSER-4),* affiliated with the 24th International Conference on Software Engineering (ICSE'02), May 2002.
33. Vahe Poladian, Shawn A. Butler, Mary Shaw, David Garlan. Time is Not Money: The Case for Multi-dimensional Accounting in Value-based Software Engineering. Position paper for the *Fifth Workshop on Economics-Driven Software Research (EDSER-5),* affiliated with the 25th International Conference on Software Engineering (ICSE'03), May 2003.
34. Reidenberg, J.R. Resolving conflicting international data privacy rules in cyberspace. *Stanford Law Review* 52 (2000), pp. 1315-1376.

35. Carl Shapiro and Hal R. Varian. *Information Rules: A strategic guide to the network economy.* Harvard Business School Press, 1998.
36. Mary Shaw (ed). *The Carnegie-Mellon Curriculum for Undergraduate Computer Science.* Springer-Verlag, 1985, 198 pp.
37. Mary Shaw. Software Engineering Education: A Roadmap. In A. Finkelstein (ed), *The Future of Software Engineering*, pp. 371-380), ACM Press, 2000.
38. Mary Shaw (cd). Software Engineering for the 21st Century; a basis for rethinking the curriculum. *Technical Report CMU-ISRI-05-108*, Institute for Software Research International, Carnegie Mellon University, March 2005.
39. Mary Shaw, Ashish Arora, Shawn Butler, and Chirs Scaffidi. *In search of a unified theory for early predictive design evaluation.* Working paper, 2004.
40. Mary Shaw, Jim Herbsleb and Ipek Ozkaya. *Methods: Deciding What to Design.* Course home page. Sept. 2005- December 2005. School of Computer Science, Carnegie-Mellon University. http://spoke.compose.cs.cmu.edu/method-fall-05/
41. Herbert Simon. *The Sciences of the Artificial.* MIT Press, 1996 (3rd edition).
42. Herbert A. Simon. What we know about learning. *Journal of Engineering Education*, vol 87 no 4, Oct 1998, pp. 343-348. Cached at http://www.ic.polyu.edu.hk/esh/KB/good-practices/GTP9016.pdf
43. Carolyn Snyder. *Paper Prototyping.* Morgan Kaufman, 2003.
44. Lucy Suchman. *Plans and Situated Actions: The Problem of Human-Machine Communication.* Cambridge University Press, 1987.
45. Walter Vincenti. *What Engineers Know and How They Know It.* Johns Hopkins University Press, 1990.
46. Eric von Hippel. *The Sources of Innovation.* Oxford University Press, 1994.
47. M. Mitchell Waldrop. *The Dream Machine: J.C.R. Licklider and the Revolution that Made Computing Personal.* Penguin Books, 2001.
48. Terry Winograd (ed). *Bringing Design to Software.* Addison-Wesley, 1996.

Appendix. The Carnegie Plan for Engineering Education

A Carnegie Mellon education aims to prepare students for life and leadership. In a continually changing world, the most important qualities we can help our students develop are the ability to think independently and critically, the ability to learn, and the ability to change and grow. As future leaders they must have courage to act, be sensitive to the needs and feelings of others, understand and value diversity, and honor the responsibilities that come with specialized knowledge and power.

Carnegie Mellon's educational programs are designed to help students acquire:

- *Depth of knowledge* in their chosen areas of specialization and *genuine intellectual breadth* in other fields.
- *Creativity and intellectual playfulness*, moving beyond established knowledge and practice to create imaginative ideas and artifacts.
- *Skilled thoughtfulness and critical judgment*, which allow them to evaluate new ideas; identify and solve or explore problems; and appreciate a variety of different forms of analysis and thought.
- *Skills of independent learning*, which enable them to grow in wisdom and keep abreast of changing knowledge and problems in their profession and the world.
- *A considered set of values*, including commitment to personal excellence and intellectual adventure, a concern for the freedoms and dignity of others, and sensitivity to the special professional and social responsibilities that come with advanced learning and positions of leadership.
- *The self-confidence and resourcefulness* necessary to take action and get things done.
- The *ability to communicate with others* on topics both within and outside their chosen field of specialization.

Most instruction at Carnegie Mellon is focused on fundamentals useful in later learning, rather than on particulars of knowledge and techniques, which may soon become obsolete. Advanced courses provide students with the opportunity to refine their skills by applying and exercising the fundamentals they have acquired in earlier courses and by exploring new analytical and creative directions. We are committed to bring together the traditions of liberal and professional education. In a world which has sometimes placed too little emphasis on "skill," we take pride in educating students who display excellence in application, students who can do useful things with their learning.

Values, including a sensitivity to the feelings, needs, and rights of others, are learned in part through example. To this end, the faculty and staff of Carnegie Mellon work to provide a supportive and caring environment that values and respects intellectual, philosophical, personal, and cultural diversity. The faculty strive to identify and discuss with their students, both in formal classroom settings and in a variety of informal contexts, their responsibilities as professionals, citizens and human beings, and to teach through example.

The educational programs at Carnegie Mellon are designed to help our students become accomplished professionals who are broadly educated, independent, and humane leaders.

A Pedagogical View on Software Modeling and Graph-Structured Diagrams

Tetsuo Tamai

The University of Tokyo, Tokyo, Japan
tamai@acm.org

Abstract. Software modeling plays an important role in software engineering education. There are a variety of modeling techniques; some are intuitive and quite accessible to novices, while some are highly sophisticated and attract theory oriented students and researchers. Thus, educators have freedom in selecting appropriate models in accordance with the level and the disposition of students.

In this chapter, we show that teaching multiple software modeling techniques from a unified viewpoint is a good way of obtaining balance between the scientific aspect and the practical aspect of software engineering education. At the same time, it is pedagogical to let students notice the difference between different models. Some models, particularly when illustrated as diagrams, look quite similar but such similarity is often misleading. It is emphasized in this chapter that explicitly teaching differences between models is also very important.

1 Introduction

Software engineering education at universities faces a common problem, i.e. regular students do not usually have experience of developing software for practical use and thus are not motivated for software engineering aiming at high quality software production by a project team or a persistent organization. On the other hand, those students may have received training on abstract and formal way of thinking through other subjects of computer science.

There may be another type of students, who already have real experience in industry. In our case, there are currently five Ph. D. students under the author's supervision, who are working at companies as well as doing research in our lab. They are well motivated for studying and applying software engineering methods but, in some cases, not much prepared for abstraction-oriented technologies.

Software engineering by nature possesses the scientific aspect as well as the practical aspect. In education, a good balance between these two aspects should always be pursued. In our view, teaching various software modeling techniques is a good way to achieve balanced software engineering education. For the first-type students with little "real" experience, modeling may appeal to their intellectual curiosity. It is expected that they will become interested in real problems through learning and applying various modeling techniques. For the second-type students with industrial background, learning modeling will provide them good opportunities for re-thinking their problems in a systematic way.

P. Inverardi and M. Jazayeri (Eds.): ICSE 2005 Education Track, LNCS 4309, pp. 59–70, 2006.

It is needless to say that *model* is a key concept and *modeling* is an essential skill in software engineering. There are a variety of modeling techniques; some are intuitive and quite accessible to novices, while some are highly sophisticated and attract theory oriented students and researchers. Thus, educators have freedom in selecting appropriate models in accordance with the level and the disposition of students.

In this chapter, we would like to show that it is effective to teach multiple modeling techniques from a unified viewpoint. It is based on the author's experience of teaching software engineering courses at several universities in Japan. In 2004, the author published a textbook on software engineering, specifically focused on software modeling (unfortunately, it is written in Japanese)[13]. The book covers the whole area of software engineering, including design, testing and evolution but the modeling part has a role of attracting interests of intelligent students, who may not have much experience in developing real scale software systems. It also gives a consistent viewpoint penetrating through various techniques employed in different stages of software engineering. At the same time, it is also pedagogical to let students notice the difference between different models. Some models, particularly when illustrated as diagrams, look quite similar but such similarity is often misleading. It is emphasized in this chapter that explicitly teaching differences between models is also very important.

Of course, software modeling education had better be accompanied by software projects simulating real scale software development, particularly for the regular students. There have been reported some successful cases [3,6] and also similar activities will be covered by other chapters of this book.

2   Modeling Techniques

In software engineering, models are used for various purposes, e.g. life cycle model, process model, project model, product model, quality model, domain model, requirements model, design model, object model, and data model. In the following, we basically focus on requirements and design models but most of the discussions will hold for other kinds of models.

Teaching modeling is almost equal to teaching abstraction. Models are constructed through capturing the crucial properties and structure of the target, abstracting away irrelevant details. Thus, learning how to model is a good training for mastering abstraction.

2.1   Graph Representation of Models

Many software models are represented with diagrams. Wide acceptance of UML symbolizes the trend that diagrams are often preferred to textual languages. Among many types of diagrams, graph structured diagrams are by far the most widely used. The reasons are presumed as follows.

1. A most fundamental way for human mind to understand the world is by regarding it as a set of conceptual units and a set of relations between them. Conceptual units can be naturally illustrated with boxes or circles or whatever closed figures and relations can be illustrated with lines or arrows connecting such figures, corresponding to vertices and edges of graphs, respectively.

Table 1. Graph structures of typical models

model	vertex	edge
Data flow	process	data flow
ER	entity	relationship
State transition	state	transition
JSD	process	data stream connection
		state vector connection
Flowchart	process	control flow
	decision	
Petri net	place, transition	fire and token flow

2. It is easy to draw graph structured diagrams by hand or with drawing tools.
3. Concepts and algorithms of the graph theory are available and often useful in analyzing models represented by graphs. A typical example is reasoning on transitive relations by tracing along paths of graphs. Also, the concept of subgraph is highly useful in decomposing higher-level models or clustering lower-level models.

Accordingly, a number of models share the same structure of graphs. Table 1 shows graph structures of some typical models.

2.2   Ambiguity and Confusion in Graph Representation

Graph structures are simple and appeal to intuitive understanding, so much so that their use is not confined to software modeling. Graph like diagrams with boxes or circles connected by lines or arrows can be found daily in newspapers, magazines, reports, proposals and other documents. However, intuitive understanding often causes confusion. Semantics of vertices and/or edges are often not consistent within the same diagram. For example, the same shape of a box is used as a process in some part and as a data in another. An arrow represents a causality relation somewhere and a temporal relation somewhere else.

One way of avoiding such ambiguity is to divide vertices and/or edges to different groups, assigning a different symbol to each vertex/edge group. For example, data type vertices may be represented by boxes and process type vertices by ovals. But if you introduce too many vertex types or edge types, it will harm the simplicity of graph representation.

A diagram with too many symbol shapes often indicates serious flaws in the model. Fig. 1 shows an example taken from a Web page at the University of Tokyo (now it is replaced by a much neater diagram). The original figure illustrates sexual harassment complaint procedure at the campus but the texts labeling the vertices and edges are deliberately removed.

In this small diagram, there are six different vertex shapes and six different edge shapes. Moreover, there is even an edge bridging not a pair of vertices but a pair of edges!

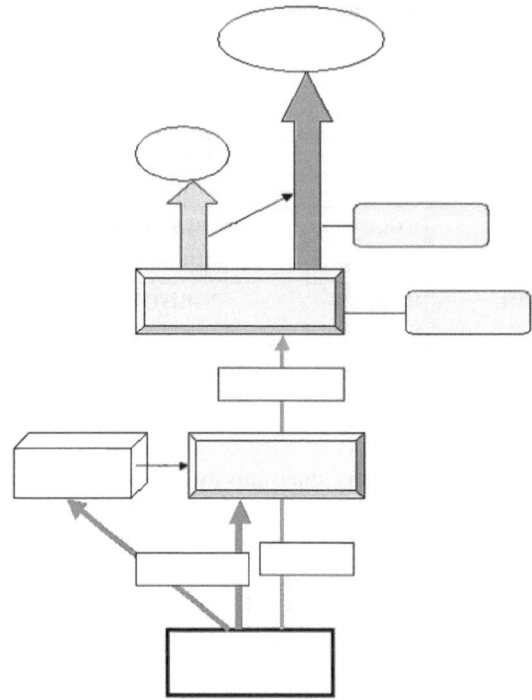

Fig. 1. Confusing Diagram

2.3   Commonality and Difference Between Models

We must be careful not to let students fall into such confusion. Although it is pedagogical to let students notice the common structure shared by a number of models, the
apparent resemblance often causes misunderstanding. Thus, it is important as well to
make students consciously aware the difference between different models. We often experience that when we let students draw data flow diagrams, the diagrams turn out to be
something like control flow graphs, although they appear to have understood the data
flow model perfectly.

To show the difference, it is instructive to categorize models represented by graphs.
Basically, there are two categories.

1. Static models:
   An edge connecting vertex A and vertex B represents a relation between A and B.
   When the edge is undirected, it means "A and B are in some relation" and when
   directed, it means "A has a relation with B". Typical examples include entity relationship model, class diagram and semantic network.
2. Dynamic models:
   An edge from vertex A to B denotes a move from A to B. The edge in this case is
   always directed. There are two sub-categories:

(a) The case where a view of control moves from A to B. Examples are control flow model and state transition model.

(b) The case where data or objects flow from A to B. Examples are data flow model, work flow model, and transportation flow model.

Static models and dynamic models may not be easily confused but confusion between different dynamic models are often observed, e.g. confusion between data flow and control flow or confusion between state transition and activity transition. Since graphs are intuitively understandable, their semantics are apt to be understood ambiguously or misunderstood. The author often emphasizes the following points at his class.

Difference between data flow and control flow diagrams. Although the data flow model can be classified as a dynamic model, it also possesses static nature. The point becomes clear when you ask a question "where am I?" While the question has a meaning for the control flow model or the state transition model, it does not make sense for the data flow model. Indeed, it is meaningful to ask on which activity the control lies *now* in the control flow graph or on which state the machine is in *now* in the state transition graph, but for the data flow model, there is no notion of the "current time".

Difference between state transition and activity transition diagrams. The activity diagram of UML essentially represents a control flow model. Students and even engineers with certain experience often confuse state transition(ST) with control flow(CF). It is effective to teach the differences explicitly.

1. Meaning of vertices: A vertex in ST represents a state, while a vertex in CF represents a processing unit.
2. Location where "execution" takes place: *Execution* takes place at an edge during transition in ST models, while *execution* takes place at a vertex in CF models.
3. Transition trigger: Transitions are triggered by events in ST models, while transitions are triggered by termination of processing at vertices in CF models.
4. Interaction with outside: Interaction with the outside environment is regularly conducted through event capturing and generation in ST, while there is no interaction with the outside environment except specific IO operations (read/write) in CF during processing.

2.4   Use of Graphical Analysis Techniques

In the preceding section, we emphasized differences between models but we should also note that the common graph structure brings benefit of applying various analysis methods well-studied in the graph theory. For example, algorithms for identifying connected components corresponding to different definitions of "connectivity" are useful in capturing a diverse or concentrated structure of the target model. Path analysis is a versatile technique that can be employed in many models. Especially, when the relation represented by directed edges of the graph has the transitive property, path enumeration is essential in identifying the scope of the property. It is also strongly related with search algorithms explored in AI and Operations Research.

Algorithms and data structures for graphs are typical subjects taught at computer science classes but when they are applied to concrete problems encountered in software engineering, students' understanding will be deepened, bringing benefit in both topics.

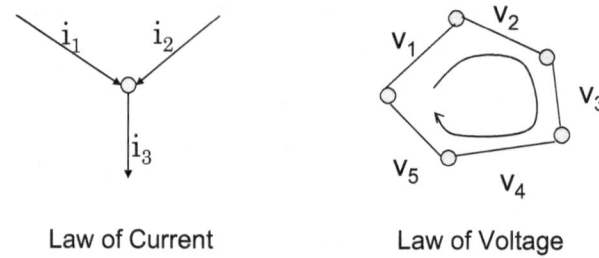

Law of Current   Law of Voltage

Fig. 2. Kirchhoff's Law

2.5 Physical Quantities on Graphs

Graphs give topology of models as incidence relations between vertices and edges. In many cases, vertices and edges in a model are associated with some sort of physical quantities. A typical example is an electric circuit modeled with a graph, where each vertex is associated with electric potential and each edge is associated with electric current. The well-known Kirchhoff's law determines the relation of these physical quantities and the topological structure.

Kirchhoff's Law of Current. Total amount of electric current around a vertex summed over edges incident to the vertex is zero, where incoming current is counted positive and outgoing current is counted negative.

Kirchhoff's Law of Voltage. Total amount of voltage summed along a closed path is zero.

Many of typical software models may not involve quantities like current and voltage but still it is often effective to analyze a model in terms of information around a vertex or information along a path. For example, we can check consistency of a data flow model by considering whether a set of incoming data and a set of outgoing data are appropriate as input and output to the process determined by the vertex. Also, we can trace a path in a data flow model to capture a sequence of processes that transform data as a probable behavior of the model.

As seen above, data flow clearly has a nature of current but it is not measured in quantity. However, data flow studied in the field of compiler optimization and static program analysis such as definition-use chains [7] has a rigorous definition and obeys a law of balance, i.e. total data flow-in plus data generation and minus data destruction balances with total data flow-out. This kind of problems can be found in other areas such as the shortest path problem, the finite state automaton, and the network reliability problem and can be uniformly formulated and solved using the concept of lattice [11].

An example of quantitative flow dealt with in software engineering is execution counts along execution paths, measured in program profiling. A conservation law just like Kirchihoff's law of current holds in this case. For example, if i_1 in Fig. 2 left is regarded as the execution count of the left path and i_2 as that of the right path, $i_3 = i_1 + i_2$ must be the execution count of the path downward from the vertex.

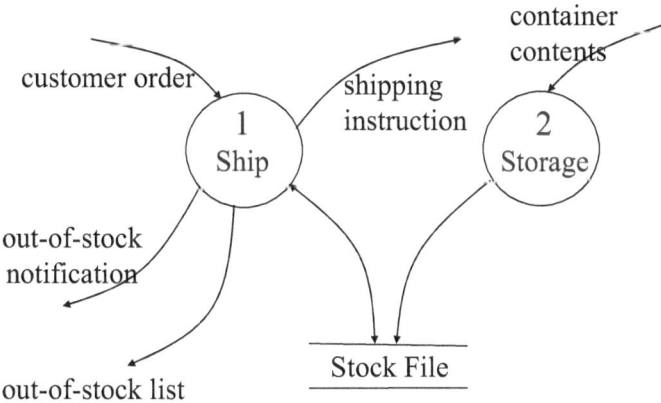

Fig. 3. Top level DFD of the Sakaya Warehouse Problem

So far, we have seen only current-like entities but what about voltage- or potential-like entities? When we divide execution counts by execution time, we get a measure of performance whose dimension is more like electric current (flow volume per time). Corresponding to this entity, processing power of the processor measured by something like MIPS(million instructions per second) can be regarded as an entity representing voltage. Such a relation is actually used in performance models represented by simulation networks.

2.6 Recursive Structure

A model with a graph structure may have a property such that when a vertex is decomposed to a sub-level model, the sub-model has the same graph structure as the upper level model. A typical example is the data flow model where a vertex denoting a process can be decomposed into another data flow model, so that a recursive hierarchical structure be naturally constructed.

For example, Fig. 3 shows a top-level data flow diagram for the *Sake Warehouse Problem* [12].

Process 1 of Fig. 3 is expanded to the second level of data flow diagram as shown in Fig. 4.

The recursive structure embodied in data flow diagrams corresponds to the concept of subgraphs in the graph theoretical terminology. A subgraph is defined by a subset of the edges of the original graph together with a set of vertices incident to those edges. When a subgraph is connected, a subgraph can be collapsed to a vertex to show a macroscopic structure. Conversely, a vertex can be expanded to a subgraph to show a microscopic view as shown in Fig. 5. This figure depicts the recursive relation as given by Fig. 3 and Fig. 4.

A control flow model like the activity model also has this recursive property, for a process in the model can be decomposed to a lower level control flow model. Statecharts by D. Harel [4] share the same property. On the other hand, a class diagram of object-oriented modeling does not have this hierarchical property, for in general a class cannot

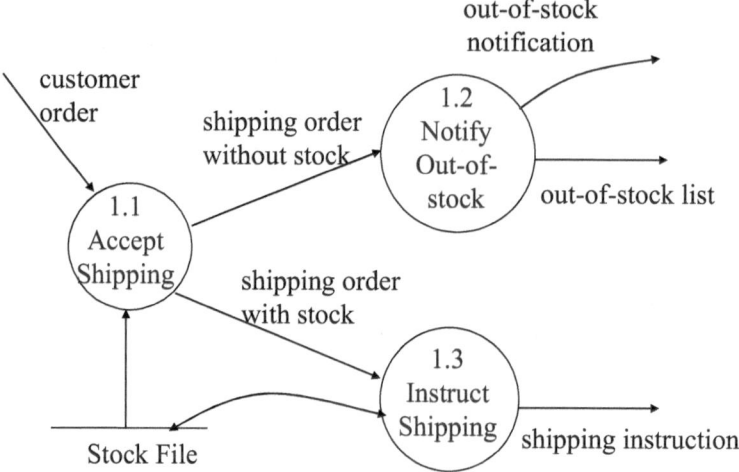

Fig. 4. Second level DFD of the Sakaya Warehouse Problem

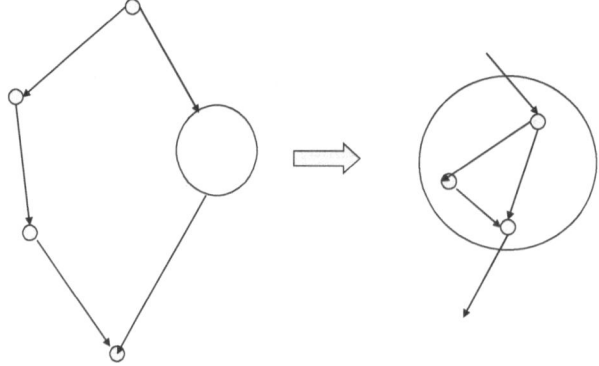

Fig. 5. Subgraph

be decomposed to another level of class diagram. This may be one of the reasons why the class model is harder to comprehend and handle than the data flow model or the activity model. The package in UML has a weak recursive structure. It may contain classes or packages, thus forming a tree-like structure, where a leaf is a class. However, interface of a package is not defined as interface of a class. Moreover, while a class is a primitive concept of object-orientation, a package is a secondary concept introduced to group classes.

Another popular diagram that does not possess a natural recursive structure is the sequence diagram. This may be a reason that although sequence diagrams appeal to intuitive understanding, its expressive power is rather limited.

3 UML Diagrams with Overly Rich Constructs

UML diagrams can be viewed in terms of graph structures. Table 2 shows graph structures of five UML diagrams.

Table 2. Graph structures of UML diagrams

diagram	vertex	edge
class diagram	class	generalization, composition, association
state machine	state	transition
activity diagram	activity	control flow
collaboration diagram	object	message flow
sequence diagram	message anchor point	message flow

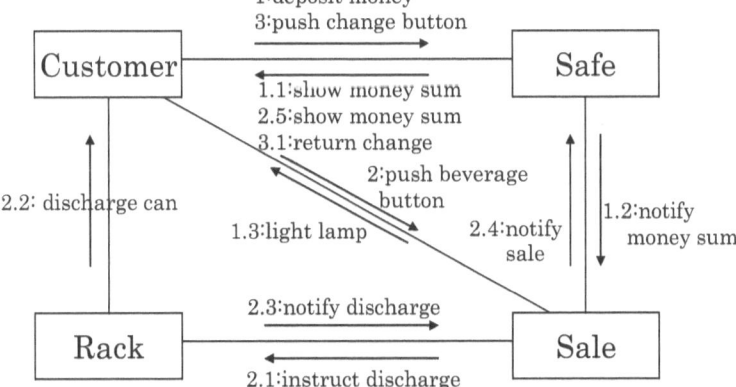

Fig. 6. Collaboration diagram of a beverage can vending machine

It is usually not desirable to teach UML per se. UML is a collection of miscellaneous diagrams and its specification is continuously changing. For the pedagogical purpose, UML had better be regarded as a catalogue of analysis and design know-how collected around diagrammatic representations. Diagrams should be selected according to the policy of how to teach modeling methods.

Each UML diagram contains overly rich constructs, which sometimes blur the essential property of the model. What M. Jackson wrote in his book [8] must be highly respected.

> "The diagrams used in many OO methods are horrendously complicated and ill-defined. But you don't have to use all the complications."

Thus, we had better not only select diagrams to teach but also purify them to capture their essence. We will see some examples of UML diagrams overloaded with multiple concepts and functions.

Activity diagram. The activity diagram is essentially a control flow diagram. But its definition in the current UML (UML 1.4 or 2.0) also includes a notation for data flow

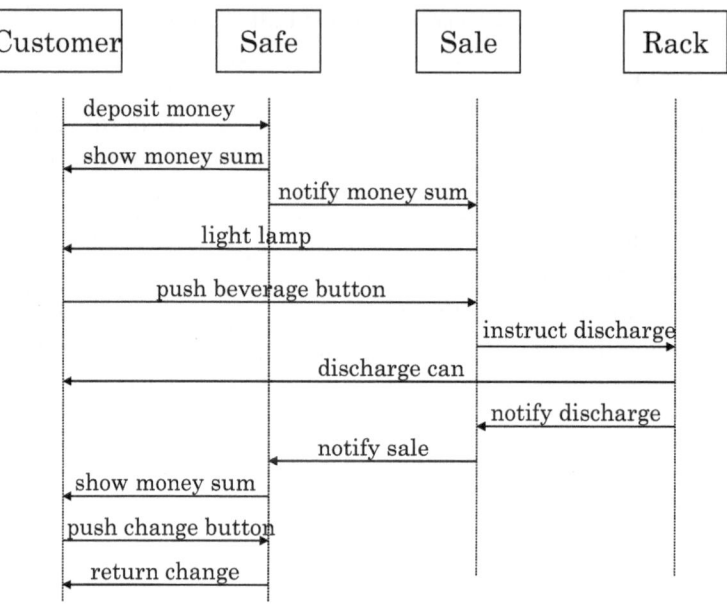

Fig. 7. Sequence diagram corresponding to the collaboration diagram of Fig. 6

description. From the stance of emphasizing differences between various models, it is not appropriate to include such ad hoc constructs.

It is interesting to note that the activity diagram inherits and still retains a shortcoming of the flowchart, even though it is overly enriched with miscellaneous constructs. In 1970's, the flowchart was criticized for "unstructuredness", reflecting code with "goto"s. Many structured versions of control flow diagrams were proposed, including Nassi-Schneiderman's chart [10], PAD [2] and others [1]. These efforts for introducing structured constructs of selection (if or case structure) and iteration (loop structure) are ignored in the activity diagram.

Collaboration diagram. The collaboration diagram in UML (renamed to *communication diagram* in UML 2.0) is explained to have the equivalent semantics as the sequence diagram. Figure 6 shows an example of a collaboration diagram modeling a beverage can vending machine.

In UML, this model is supposed to be equivalent to the one represented by the sequence diagram of Fig. 7. The equivalence is materialized by the sequence numbering that labels each message along an edge. The number determines the temporal order of the messages so that the message sequence of Fig. 7 is equivalently expressed.

The first question is why we need two different models if they are equivalent. As the appearance of collaboration diagrams is quite different from that of sequence diagrams, it is natural to expect that the collaboration diagram has its own role. The author prefers to regard it as showing collaboration relations between objects, integrating a set of different sequence diagrams. When we remove the numbers from the collaboration

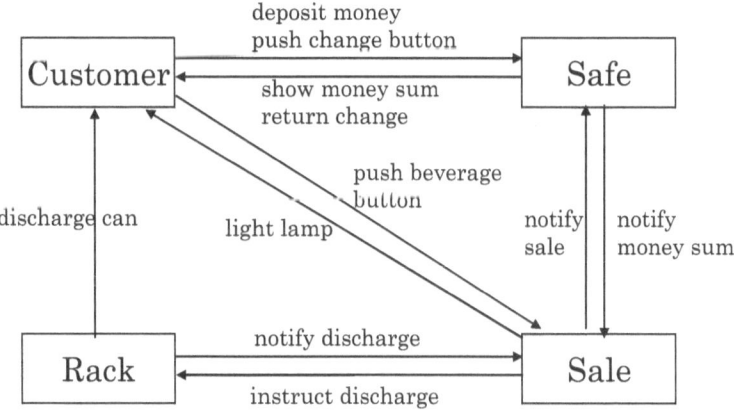

Fig. 8. Revised collaboration model

diagram of Fig. 6 and also remove redundant messages, we get a diagram as shown in Figure 8.

In fact, Harel & Politi [5] uses a similar diagram in their reactive system modeling method, calling it a *module chart*. Magee & Kramer [9] also uses a similar diagram in their concurrent system modeling method, calling it a *structure diagram*. All of these share the basically same graphical notation and semantics.

4   Conclusion

Software modeling is important by itself but teaching modeling in the software engineering course has at least two additional meanings. One is to give a bird's-eye view to the whole software engineering through the standpoint of modeling technology. The other is to attract interest of good students who may not have much experience in developing a real-scale software but possess intelligence and will to attack complexity of modern software construction.

References

1. M. Aoyama, K. Miyamoto, N. Murakami, H. Nagano, and Y. Oki. Design specification in japan: Tree-structured charts. *IEEE Software*, 6(2):31–37, Mar. 1983.
2. Y. Futamura, T. Kawai, H. Horikoshi, and M. Tsutsumi. Development of computer programs by problem analysis diagram(pad). In *Proceedings of the 5th International Conference on Software engineering*, pages 325–332, 1981.
3. W. G. Griswold. Teaching software engineering in a compiler project course. *Journal on Educational Resources in Computing (JERIC)*, 2(4), Dec. 2002.
4. D. Harel. Statecharts: A visual formalism for complex systems. *Science of Computer Programming*, 8:231–274, 1987.
5. D. Harel and M. Politi. *Modeling Reactive Systems with Statecharts*. McGraw-Hill, 1998.
6. J. H. Hayes. Energizing software engineering education through real-world projects as experimental studies. In *CSEE&T*, pages 192–206, Feb. 2002.

7. M. S. Hecht. *Flow Analysis of Computer Programs*. Elsevier, NorthHolland, 1977.
8. M. Jackson. *Software Requirements & Specifications: a lexicon of practice, principles and prejudice*. Addison-Wesley, 1995.
9. J. Magee and J. Kramer. *Concurrency – State Models & Java Programs*. John Wiley & Sons, 1999.
10. I. Nassi and B. Shneiderman. Flowchart techniques for structured programming. *ACM SIGPLAN Notices*, 8(8):12–26, 1973.
11. T. Tamai. A class of fixed-point problems on graphs and iterative solution algorithms. In A. Pnueli and H. Lin, editors, *Logic and Software Engineering*. World Scientific, 1996.
12. T. Tamai. How modeling methods affect the process of architectural design decisions: A comparative study. In *Proc. 8th International Workshop on Software Specification and Design (IWSSD'96)*, pages 125–134, Paderborn, Germany, Mar. 1996.
13. T. Tamai. *Foundations of Software Engineering*. Iwanami Shoten, Tokyo, Japan, 2004. in Japanese.

Do Students Recognize Ambiguity in Software Specifications?
A Multi-national, Multi-institutional Report

Tammy VanDeGrift[1], Beth Simon[2], Dean Sanders[3], and Ken Blaha[4]

[1] Electrical Engineering & Computer Science,
University of Portland, Portland, OR 97203
vandegri@up.edu
[2] Computer Science & Engineering,
University of California, San Diego, La Jolla, CA 92093-0404
esimon@cs.ucsd.edu
[3] Computer Science & Information Systems,
Northwest Missouri State University, Maryville, MO 64468
sanders@nwmissouri.edu
[4] Computer Science & Computer Engineering,
Pacific Lutheran University, Tacoma, WA 98447
blahakd@plu.edu

Abstract. Successful software engineering requires experience and acknowledgment of complexity, including that which leads designers to recognize ambiguity within the software design description itself. We report on a study of 21 post-secondary institutions from the USA, UK, Sweden, and New Zealand. First competency and graduating students as well as educators were asked to perform a software design task. We found that graduating seniors were more likely to recognize ambiguities in under-specified problems than first competency students. Additionally, participants who addressed all requirements in the design were more likely than others to recognize ambiguities in the design specification. The behavior of recognizing ambiguity and gathering information appear to be independent of past performance, as measured by course grades.

1   Introduction

Software engineering requires many skills, some of which include gathering information about the domain, designing, implementing, testing, debugging, and documenting [13,12]. Tension between prioritization of sub-tasks, evaluation of proposed solutions, and the constant management of process can lead to breakdowns in the design process, even among professionals [9]. Among the many skills involved in design is the ability to recognize ambiguity in a software engineering project. Recognizing ambiguity is an important part of the design process in that it enables designers to gather information and refine assumptions. The book *Are Your Lights On?* suggests that a designer should raise several questions when trying to understand a problem's specification [8]. Hilburn states

P. Inverardi and M. Jazayeri (Eds.): ICSE 2005 Education Track, LNCS 4309, pp. 71–88, 2006.

that students need more and better training for the inspection of formal specifications [10].

This work reports results from a multi-national, multi-institutional study of student-generated software designs [6]. We describe results pertaining to participants' recognition of ambiguity in the design specification used to prompt initial software designs. We say that a participant recognized ambiguity by asking questions, other than those of process, or by making assumptions during the design process.

Prior work in comparing the design processes of freshman and senior engineering students found that seniors made more requests for additional information and made more than three times as many assumptions [5]. Recognizing and addressing ambiguity is important because ambiguities in requirements can propagate to errors in the designed solution. It is cheaper to recognize and resolve ambiguities early in the design process [3]. Recognition of ambiguity in the software design specification reflects design maturity, and our work shows that, across a diverse and multi-national sample, recognition of ambiguity is associated with designs that address more requirements. This work should spur discussion on how to educate students with regard to recognizing ambiguity and its importance in the software design process. If explicitly addressing ambiguity is not commonly part of homework assignment specifications, students have little practice in developing this important skill.

Following the introduction, we provide information about the research study, including the subject population, research questions, and the data gathered for analysis. We describe the results from the data collected and offer conclusions based on our work.

2   Research Study

This study reports on 21 post-secondary institutions in the USA, UK, Sweden, and New Zealand participating in the Scaffolding Research in Computer Science Education, an NSF-sponsored workshop [1,6,7].

2.1   Tasks

Participants in the research study were asked to perform two tasks related to software engineering. The first task, called the *decomposition task*, asked participants to design a solution from a design brief (See Figure 1). Each participant was asked to provide a solution (a design) for a "super alarm clock".

Participants were explicitly invited to ask questions and to take as long as they wished. Upon completion of the design solution, participants were asked to talk about their designs and to describe each part and its function. Their verbal descriptions were recorded and transcribed for later analysis.

Following the decomposition task, participants were asked to perform a *design criteria prioritisation task*. Participants were given 16 cards, each describinga

Design Brief

Getting People to Sleep

In some circles sleep deprivation has become a status symbol. Statements like "I pulled another all-nighter" and "I've slept only three hours in the last two days" are shared with pride, as listeners nod in admiration. Although celebrating self-deprivation has historical roots and is not likely to go away soon, it's troubling when an educated culture rewards people for hurting themselves, and that includes missing sleep.

As Stanford sleep experts have stated, sleep deprivation is one of the leading health problems in the modern world. People with high levels of sleep debt get sick more often, have more difficulties in personal relationships, and are less productive and creative. The negative effects of sleep debt go on and on. In short, when you have too much sleep debt, you simply can't enjoy life fully.

Your brief is **to design a "super alarm clock" for University students** to help them to manage their own sleep patterns, and also to provide data to support a research project into the extent of the problem in this community. You may assume that, for the prototype, each student will have a Pocket PC (or similar device) which is permanently connected to a network.

Your system will need to:
- Allow a student to set an alarm to wake themselves up.
- Allow a student to set an alarm to remind themselves to go to sleep.
- Record when a student tells the system that they are about to go to sleep.
- Record when a student tells the system that they have woken up, and whether it is due to an alarm or not (within 2 minutes of an alarm going off).
- Make recommendations as to when a student needs to go to sleep. This should include "yellow alerts" when the student will need sleep soon, and "red alerts" when they need to sleep now.
- Store the collected data in a server or database for later analysis by researchers. The server/database system (which will also trigger the yellow/red alerts) will be designed and implemented by another team. You should, however, indicate in your design the behaviour you expect from the back-end system.
- Report students who are becoming dangerously sleep-deprived to someone who cares about them (their mother?). This is indicated by a student being given three "red alerts" in a row.
- Provide reports to a student showing their sleep patterns over time, allowing them to see how often they have ignored alarms, and to identify clusters of dangerous, or beneficial, sleep behaviour.

In doing this you should (1) produce an initial solution that someone (not necessarily you) could work from (2) divide your solution into not less than two and not more than ten parts, giving each a name and adding a short description of what it is and what it does – in short, why it is a part. If important to your design, you may indicate an order to the parts, or add some additional detail as to how the parts fit together.

Fig. 1. Design Brief for the Decomposition Task

single design criterion. For example, "Knowing how each part of the solution could be implemented" and "Making sure that un-related things are linked via a narrow (internal) interface" were two of the design criteria. For a complete description of the design criteria, see [6].

2.2   Participants

Three populations were asked to perform the tasks above. The first population, defined as *first competency students* (FC), are students who could program a simple calculator as defined by the problem in [12]. Not all FC participants were majors in Computer Science, but all had taken the required courses necessary to program a simple calculator.

The second population consisted of *graduating students* (GS), defined as Computer Science students within the last one-eighth of a Bachelors degree program. Many graduating seniors were completing the final term prior to graduation.

The final population included in the study were *educators* (E). Educators were defined by those holding faculty positions and teaching Computer Science in the undergraduate curriculum. Details pertaining to the participants may be found in [6].

In total, the study included 314 participants from 21 institutions (FC = 136, GS = 150, E = 28). The student participants were also assigned descriptors specifying their level of technical competence. The descriptors ranged from 1 being a Picasso to 5 being a failing student. The descriptors were accompanied by a protocol to determine the allocation of students to each category. Transcripts for each participant contributed to an average GPA calculation in Computer Science courses. On a four point (4.0) GPA scale (used in the USA), the divisions occur at: 4, 3.7, 2.7, 1.7 and 0 where these numbers represent the bottom of the category in question. A Picasso has a 4.0; a 3.7 or higher falls into the Top category. In terms of percentages, these would mean: 100%, 93%, 67%, 42% and 0. In terms of letter grades, this roughly maps to: A+, A, B-, C- and F. Here, a "D" was considered to be synonymous with failure (although this is considered a pass in some contexts). Note that the performance bucket classifications are in order from 1 to 5, with 1 being the most technically competent and a 5 being the least technically competent. All performance buckets contain at least one GS participant and one FC participant. Table 1 shows the number of participants in each performance category.

Table 1. Performance Bucket Percentages for FC and GS Populations

	1 (Picasso)	2 (Top)	3 (High)	4 (Low)	5 (Fail)	No Data
FC (N=136)	11% (15)	18% (24)	41% (56)	19% (26)	7% (9)	4% (6)
GS (N=150)	6% (9)	23% (34)	58% (87)	13% (19)	1% (1)	0% (0)

2.3   Data Analysis

To study participants' recognition of ambiguity and the level to which they addressed requirements in the design brief, the following questions were asked of the data corpus:

1. Did the participant ask at least one question about ambiguities/omissions in the specification (as distinct from procedural questions and questions about word meanings)? (Yes or No)
2. Did the participant make at least one explicit assumption in the oral description, written representation, or other recorded responses about ambiguities/omissions in the specification? (Yes or No)
3. Did the subject address the requirements of the specification? (Yes, Partially, Hardly, No)

Nine distinct requirements were used when determining the answer to question 3. See Appendix A for a list of the requirements. If all nine requirements were addressed, the participant was deemed as "yes" for satisfying the requirements. If five to eight were satisfied, the participant was classified as "partially". If one to four were satisfied, the participant was classified as "hardly" and if no requirements were addressed, the participant was classified as "no".

3 Recognition of Ambiguity

We define two subpopulations for the purpose of classifying participants in the study. The classification is based on observable participant behavior that indicates whether or not the participant recognized ambiguity in the design brief specifications. The observable events we considered for evidence as recognizing ambiguity are question-asking and oral/written assumptions. A participant who asked at least one question about the specifications had recognized that the specification was underconstrained, had omissions, or needed further clarification. A participant who wrote assumptions or explicitly stated assumptions during the interview recognized that the specification was underconstrained and made assumptions to progress to the design phase.

The *recognizers* are participants who either asked a non-procedural question or made an explicit assumption in the design process. Both spoken and written assumptions are classified as explicit assumptions. The *information gatherers*, a subset of the recognizers, asked questions and may or may not made observable assumptions. A participant who made an assumption but did not ask a question was classified as a recognizer, but not an information gatherer. Table 2 shows the classification of recognizers and information gatherers based on the observable events of making assumptions and asking questions.

Participants who gathered information asked questions such as:

- Who decides if a student should get more sleep?
- What does it mean by 3 red alerts in a row? Over a period of days? 3 nights in a row?
- What happens when the student does not wake up with the alarm?
- Does the mother own a Pocket PC?
- Is the two minutes before or after the alarm is going off?
- How will the report to someone who cares be transmitted? Should it be email, a letter, or what?

Table 2. Criteria Used to Determine Recognizers and Information Gatherers

Made Assumption	Asked Question	Category
Yes	Yes	Recognizer Info Gatherer
No	Yes	Recognizer Info Gatherer
Yes	No	Recognizer Non Info Gatherer
No	No	Non-Recognizer Non Info Gatherer

– Is the device an aid or an enforcer? Do we have to worry about people lying? Should it be belligerent, annoying when people need sleep?

The participants' procedural questions that did not indicate recognition of ambiguity include the following:

– So you are really not looking for actual code, but just how you would go about doing this?
– So you are looking for a description in English, not in code?
– What are you looking for? . . . do I need to write . . . just . . . an outline?
– So when you say design what do you want? I mean how much detail? You want a list of features? You want a basic design an overall system . . . maybe a block diagram?
– How much detail do you want? Do you want pseudo-code?
– Can I use a calculator?

Spoken or written assumptions about the alarm clock system indicated recognition of ambiguity. Participants' spoken assumptions during the design process include:

– Average number of hours [of sleep] for each student would be 8.
– Made assumption about user always entering when they wakeup and when they go to sleep.

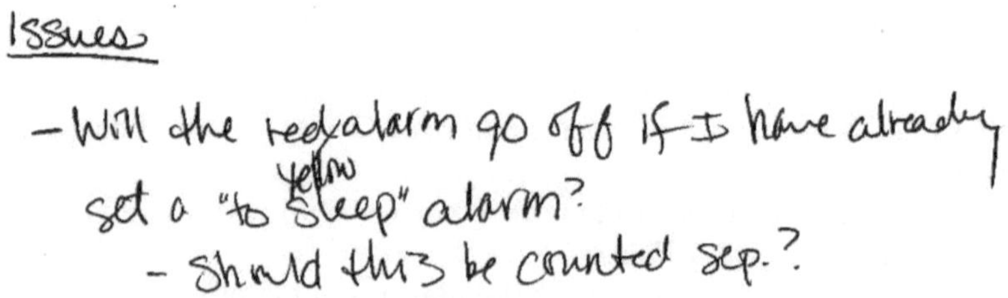

Issues

– Will the red alarm go off if I have already set a "to Sleep" alarm?
    – Should this be counted sep.?

Fig. 2. Example of recognition of ambiguity in design document

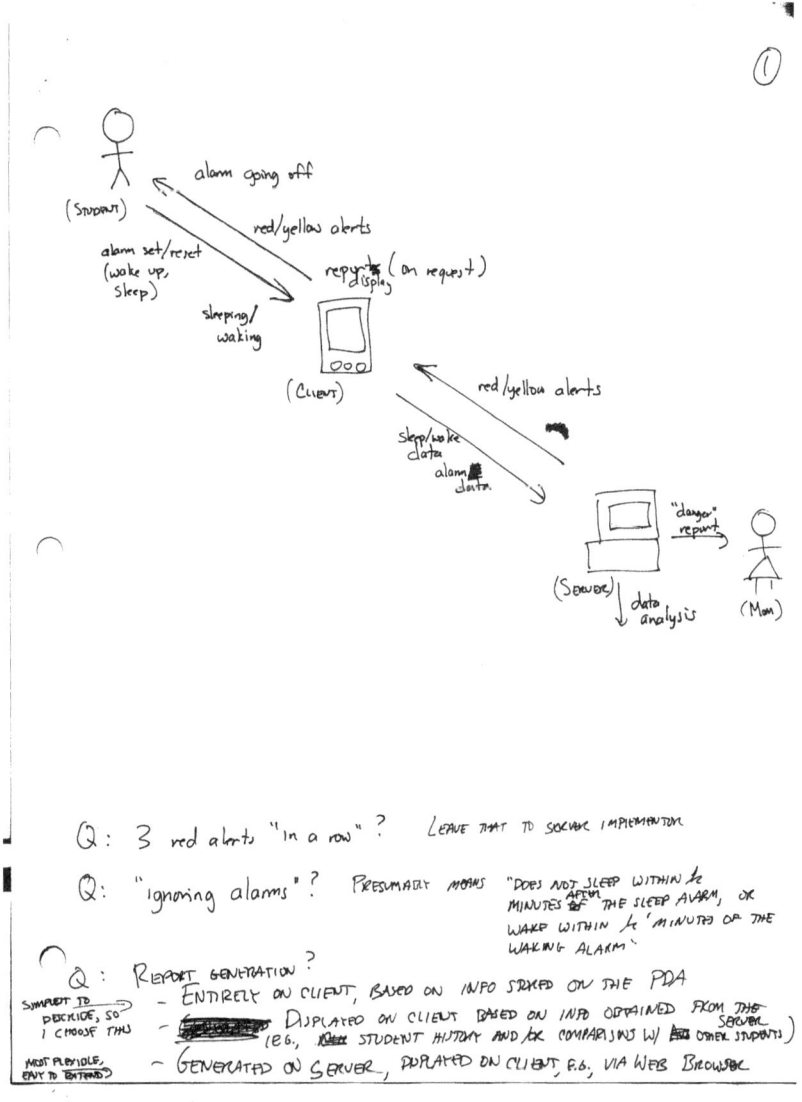

Fig. 3. Example of recognition of ambiguity in design document in the form of written questions. See bottom of figure.

- Red alerts are reset if there is a day without red alert.
- What I like is 7-8 hours of sleep - that is me personally. So I'm going to use that.
- yellow alert to beep user after fourteen hours of wake up time, red alert to beep user after sixteen hours of wake up time.
- I assume that the PDA has yellow lights.
- I'm assuming Java since it is the only programming language I know.

- It would be the "sleep time reminder". And, uh, that could be set for any time during the day, as long as it was set for at least seven hours before the wake time.
- umm, i was going to ask about the capabilities of a pocketPC, but I thought I could just assume that is had sort of the capabilities of a handheld computer.

Participants could also express their recognition of ambiguity in the documents they created. Figure 2 shows an example of one participant who explicitly wrote down the issues encountered while producing a design solution. Another participant wrote down questions, shown in the lower half of Figure 3.

We recognize a source of bias in that our definitions of subpopulations are based on observable behavior (asking questions and making explicit assumptions). Participants making assumptions without externalizing them are not defined as recognizers in this work and, consequently, the number of participants making assumptions may be larger than reported.

A second source of bias is introduced when determining if a participant's verbal or written declaration represents a non-procedural question or an assumption. In the few cases where the participant could not be classified, the participant is coded as "Don't Know". One reason why a participant could not be classified is due to illegible handwriting on design sheets, and a confident decision could not be made regarding the nature of the scribble as an assumption or not. Due to the nature of the study, participants' interviews were tape recorded. In some cases, the tapes are inaudible so determining whether a participant did or not not recognize ambiguity in spoken form was impossible. Each investigator classified the participants that he or she interviewed. In most cases, the investigator was an educator at the institution where participants were recruited. Concensus about what constituted a non-procedural question and written/spoken assumption among all 21 investigators took place prior to classification.

4   Performance Analysis

Our data analysis includes a breakdown of recognizers and information gatherers by participant population (FC, GS, and E), the number of requirements addressed in the design solution, and performance bucket. We also analyze the time taken to perform the task. Of the 314 participants, 11 could not be classified as recognizers or non-recognizers because of a "Don't Know" response from the researcher reporting the data, so 303 participants were used in the data analysis.

By Population. Table 3 shows that a greater percentage of graduating students recognized ambiguity than first competency students. The same can be said of information gatherers. Educators overwhelmingly recognize ambiguity. Note that 36% (78/216) of recognizers simply made assumptions without gathering information. Of FC recognizers, 48% simply made assumptions. This is consistent with the practices of beginning engineering students [5].

Results on the impact of experience (defined by population level) was statistically significant for both recognizers and information gatherers. A chi-squared test with a desired significance of 0.05 leads us to reject the following hypotheses:

H1: The distribution of recognizers is independent of experience (population) level. (p ≤ 0.025)
and
H2: The distribution of information gatherers is independent of experience (population) level. (p ≤ 0.01)

Table 3. Recognizers and Information Gatherers

	FC (N=131)	GS (N=145)	E (N=27)	All (N=303)
Percent Recognizers	63% (82)	76% (110)	89% (24)	71% (216)
Percent Information Gatherers	33% (43)	50% (73)	81% (22)	46% (138)

Addressing Requirements. Recognizers were also more successful at addressing the requirements outlined in the design task. Each participant's design was categorized by how well it addressed requirements: Yes (all 9 requirements addressed), Partially (5-8 addressed), Hardly (1-4 addressed), No (0 addressed), NA (no data about requirements). Table 4 shows the performance of each group in satisfying the requirements. Almost half of the recognizers addressed all the requirements, while only 26% of non-recognizers did. The results for information gatherers are similar.

Additionally, of those who addressed all requirements (N = 120), 81% were recognizers and 52.5% were information gatherers. Of those who partially addressed the requirements (N = 151), 67% were recognizers and 44% were information gatherers. A weighted average was used to estimate the number of requirements addressed by recognizers and non-recognizers. We assigned Yes the value 9, Partially the value 6.5, Hardly the value 2.5, and No the value 0. Using these values as an estimate of the number of requirements addressed by participants assigned to each category we found that recognizers addressed an average of 7.3 requirements and non-recognizers addressed an average of 6.5 requirements.

The differences in rate of addressing requirements is statistically significant when comparing recognizers versus non-recognizers and also when comparing information gatherers and non-gatherers. A chi-squared test with a desired significance of 0.05 leads us to reject the following two hypotheses:

H3: Recognizers and non-recognizers address requirements at the same rate. (p ≤ 0.01)
and
H4: Information gatherers and non-gatherers address requirements at the same rate. (p ≤ 0.025)

However, when comparing information gatherers versus the subset of recognizers who do not gather information (i.e. those that merely make assumptions), we cannot reject the following hypothesis:

Table 4. Addressing Requirements By Population

	Yes	Partially	Hardly	No	NA
Recognizers (N=216)	45% (97)	47% (101)	6% (14)	1% (2)	1% (2)
Non-Recognizers (N=87)	26% (23)	58% (50)	14% (12)	2% (2)	0% (0)
Info Gatherers (N = 138)	46% (63)	49% (67)	4% (5)	1% (1)	1% (2)
Non Info Gatherers (N = 165)	35% (57)	51% (84)	13% (21)	2% (3)	0% (0)

H5: Information gatherers and those who recognize but do not gather information address requirements at the same rate.

Performance Buckets. When looking at recognizers and information gatherers with respect to performance bucket (1 = Picasso . . . 5 = Fail), one might expect that participants in the higher buckets would tend to be the recognizers and the information gatherers. However, our data do not support this hypothesis. Figures 4 and 5 show the distributions of recognizers and information gatherers across the five performance buckets. A performance bucket could not be determined for six FC participants.

Figures 4 and 5 provide a visual representation of the percentage of recognizers and information gatherers, respectively, in each of the five performance buckets. From these graphs, it is evident that there is little difference between the performance buckets, but there is a consistent difference between first competency participants and graduating seniors. Across all buckets, as shown in Table 3, the percentage of recognizers increases from 63% for first competency participants to 76% for graduating seniors. Similarly, the percentage of information gatherers increases from 33% for first competency participants to 50% for graduating seniors. The largest deviations in percentages of recognizers and information gatherers appear in performance buckets 1 and 5, but these deviations in percentages are probably artifacts of the sizes of these buckets rather than general trends.

What is more interesting is that the difference between first competency participants and graduating seniors is greatest in performance bucket 1 (Picasso). This could be a result of the size of the bucket. The size of the Picasso bucket for FCs is 15, and the size of the Picasso bucket for GSs is 9. Because FC participants have taken few Computer Science courses, the GPA measurement of FC participants may not be a representative measurement of performance. It could also be that beginning participants with exceptional skills are over confident. As these students mature and gain experience they might recognize the importance of addressing ambiguities in a design specification. Of the 15 first competency participants in bucket 1 only 4 asked questions about ambiguities and/or omissions in the specification. Among graduating seniors classified as Picassos, 5 out

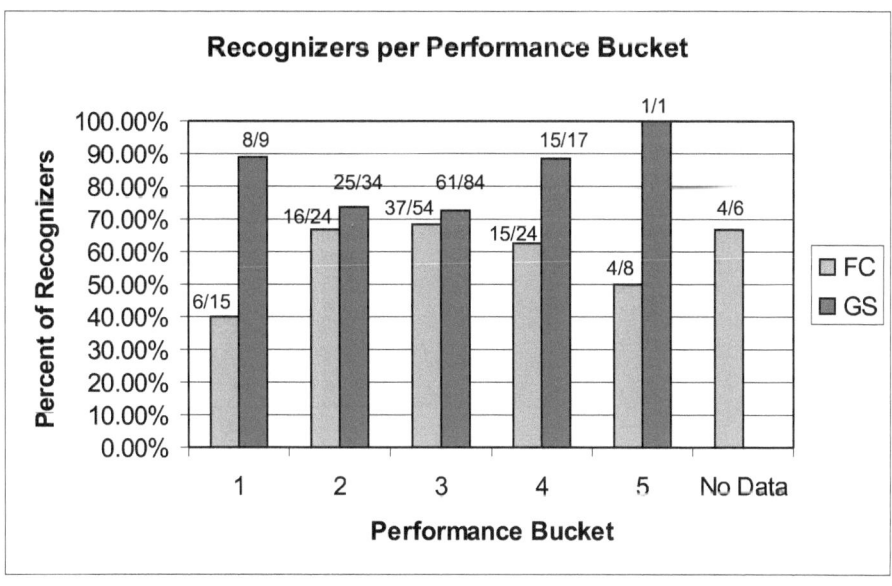

Fig. 4. The percentage of recognizers per performance bucket (1 = Picasso, 2 = Top, 3 = High, 4 = Low, 5 = Fail). The absolute numbers of participants falling into each performance bucket are listed above the bars.

of 9 asked a question clarifying the specification. If one looks at participants in bucket 1 that asked a non procedural question and made an assumption we find that 5 out of 9 graduating seniors fall into this category as compared to only 2 out of the 15 first competency participants.

Statistical tests on the distribution by performance bucket for either recognizers or information gatherers could not be found to be statistically significant. Specifically, chi-squared tests with a desired significance of 0.05 would not allow us to reject the following hypotheses:

H6: The distribution of recognizers is independent of performance bucket.

and

H7: The distribution of information gatherers is independent of performance bucket.

Time. The average amount of time taken to perform the design decomposition task (before talking about the design aloud) was 41.2 minutes for recognizers and 31.7 minutes for non-recognizers. Information gatherers took, on average, 44.0 minutes and non information gatherers spent 33.8 minutes on the design task. This result is not too surprising, since the act of recognizing ambiguity and asking questions takes time during the initial design phase. Figures 6 and 7 show the distributions of time taken by recognizers and information gatherers, respectively.

Per Institution. If we look at the percentage of recognizers and information gatherers, separated by institution we see that some institutions have a high number

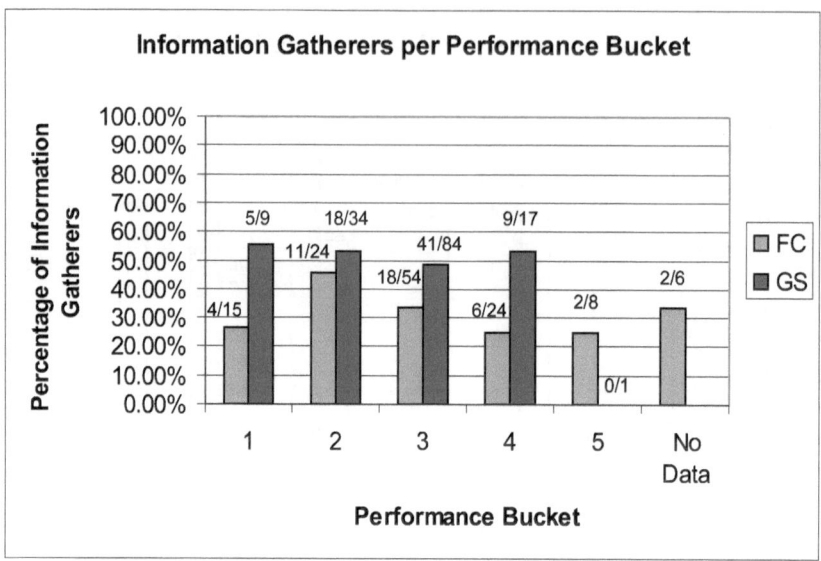

Fig. 5. The percentage of information gatherers per performance bucket (1 = Picasso, 2 = Top, 3 = High, 4 = Low, 5 = Fail). The absolute numbers of participants falling into each performance bucket are listed above the bars.

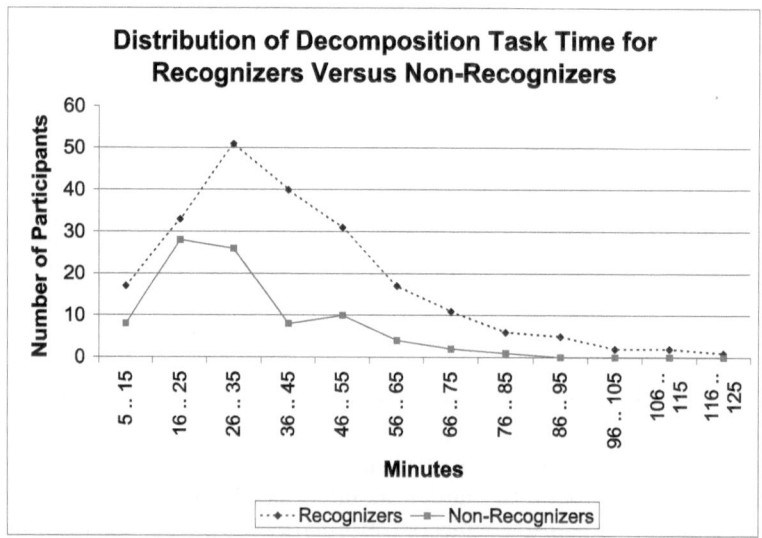

Fig. 6. Distribution of time taken to complete design decomposition task, separated into recognizers and non-recognizers

of recognizers. Five of the 21 institutions had all participants who recognized ambiguity. The data in Figure 8 indicate that all institutions had at least one recognizer and at least one information gatherer.

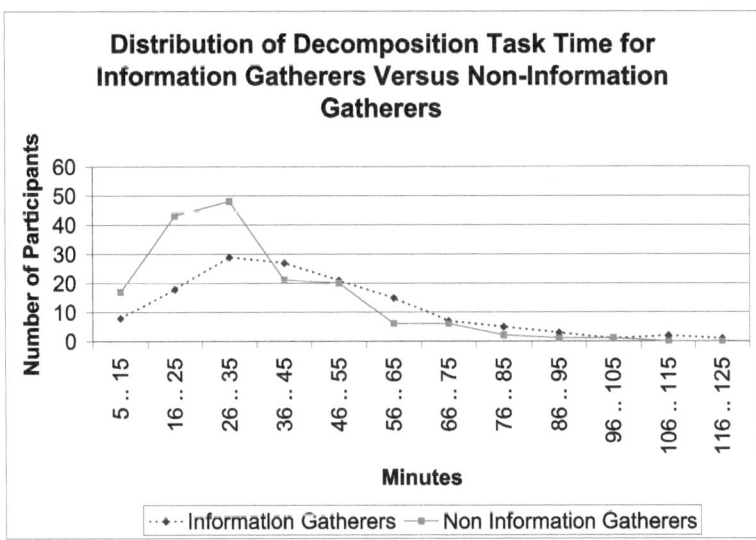

Fig. 7. Distribution of time taken to complete design decomposition task, separated into information gatherers and non information gatherers

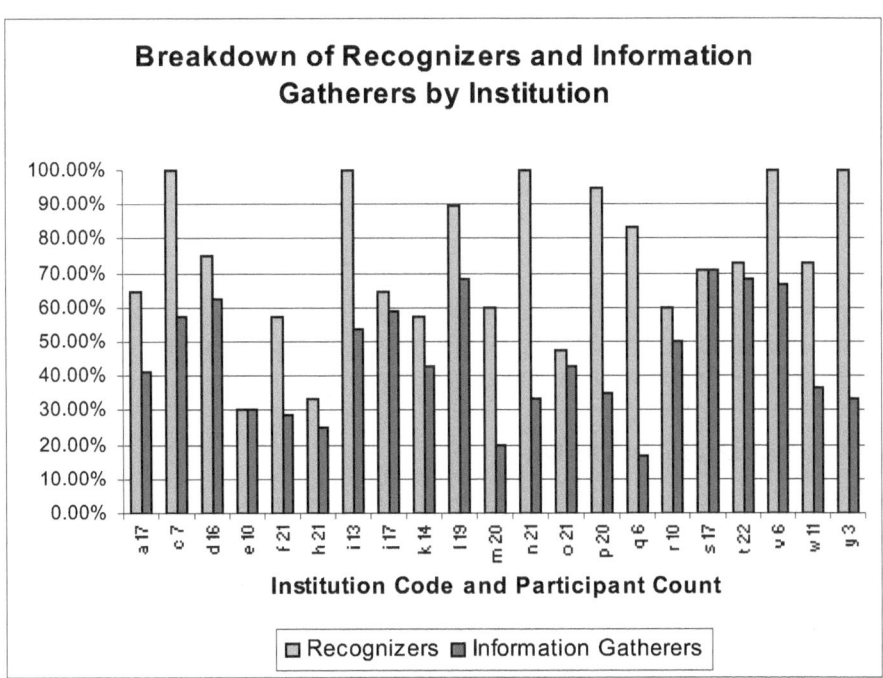

Fig. 8. Breakdown of information gatherers and recognizers by institution. Each institution is labeled by a letter and a number on the x-axis. The number indicates the total number of participants interviewed at the institution.

5 Discussion and Future Work

This work describes a multi-national, multi-institutional study of student designs which reveals that recognition of ambiguity is more common among graduating seniors than first competency students and that recognizers tend to address more requirements in the design. The majority of participants (81%) who addressed all requirements in the design also recognized ambiguity. Additionally, those participants who recognized ambiguity addressed an average of 7.3 requirements while non-recognizers addressed an average of 6.5 requirements. The result of more seniors recognizing ambiguity is consistent with the findings of Atman *et al.* [5]. In our study, 48% of the first competency students made assumptions without requesting additional information, while 34% of graduating seniors fell into this category. (These participants were recognizers but not information gatherers.) Making assumptions without gathering information appears to be a characteristic of less experienced designers.

The study presented here categorized participants as recognizers and information gatherers. Table 2 indicates the criteria for determining recognizers and information gatherers. We did not attempt to distinguish information gatherers who did not make assumptions versus information gatherers who did make assumptions for most of the analysis presented in this paper. Future analysis using all four categories in Table 2 may reveal additional trends among the FC, GS, and E subpopulations.

The study included three metrics for comparing participants and their designs. The first metric, performance buckets, affords a comparison of participants from different institutions and is independent of the software design produced by the participants. The other two metrics, number of requirements addressed and time needed to complete the task, are directly related to the design task but do not convey the quality of the design. At this point, no attempt has been made to assess the quality of participants' designs, but others have attempted to compare designs based on formal notation, grouping and interaction of parts, communication between parts, and hierarchical organization. More details can be found in [6] and [14]. These other metrics could prove useful for studying recognizers and information gatherers.

5.1 Research Study Design

The study investigation took place at 21 different institutions, requiring explicit instructions for recruiting participants, receiving human subjects approval, gathering data, and performing data analysis. The investigation was a collective research component of the Scaffolding Research in Computer Science Education, a NSF-supported project to train Computer Science faculty in educational research methods [1]. The overall investigation posed the questions: Can computer science students decompose a problem into parts? and What criteria do students use when evaluating and producing designs? Because the questions are broad, the authors narrowed the focus to students' recognition of ambiguity in the alarm clock description. In the data collection instructions, the researchers were asked to instruct students back to the alarm clock design brief if they had any questions about the specification and to make any necessary assumptions. Had the study investigation focused on the recognition of ambiguity from its inception, data specific to our research questions could have been collected.

The alarm clock design problem proved valuable, in that the problem statement is complex enough to produce a variety of designs. The design brief also includes statements open to interpretation, which is necessary to study recognizers and information gatherers. Each investigator recorded interviews with the participants, but making a full transcript of the sessions was not mandatory for the investigators. As a result, full transcripts are not available for every participant. If we conducted this study again, we would require full transcripts for every participant, so that complementary and more detailed research questions could be asked about participants' designs and interviews.

5.2   Implications for Educators

This work raises some important questions for educators. Recognition of ambiguity and information gathering appear to be independent of a student's academic achievement. It is our hope that these questions will be discussed and fleshed out by interested investigators and will lead to new studies and interventions to better understand the possibilities and benefits of addressing ambiguity in the undergraduate curriculum.

The recognition of ambiguity in underconstrained design environments is an important skill in the design process. Our research study shows that a higher percentage of graduating seniors recognize ambiguity than do first competency students. This could be a result due to the educational experience of the participants. Perhaps first competency students are provided with fully specified problems to solve, while upper-division students are more likely to solve underconstrained problems. In many Computer Science curricula, upper-division students have the opportunity to take capstone courses, independent studies, and industry-partnered courses where underconstrained design problems are likely to occur. A recommendation based on the results of this study is that educators provide and discuss strategies for handling underconstrained design problems at all levels in the curriculum. If the initial design phase of problem-solving is not explicity addressed in introductory computing courses, educators may want to include such a discussion in the course and provide activities for students to practice recognizing ambiguity.

Participants who recognize ambiguity tend to address more design requirements. We did not attempt to classify participants' designs with regard to quality, but making an attempt to address most or all requirements is a quantifiable measurement necessary for high-quality designs. A recommendation to educators is to include a specific mapping phase in the design process where students can clearly link each design element to a specific requirement in the specification.

The recognition of ambiguity does not appear to reflect past performance, as measured by grades. One interpretation is that grades themselves may not measure students' skills in recognizing ambiguity, as this part of the design process may not be included in the overall grade assigned to homework assignments. Additionally, first competency students usually had recorded grades for just one to three computing courses; therefore, FC grades may not accurately indicate design skill. A recommendation to educators is to formally assess design process elements, such as recognizing where more information is needed to carry out a design, in addition to the final product.

Stepping back from our role as researchers, we observed the utility of the design brief exercise and the design criteria task as useful activities in the classroom. It was quite illuminating for us to see and hear students describing their designs and their design process. Because we were in the "researcher" role and not the "educator" role, we could focus on students' processes rather than the products. As educators, much of what we can "see" of students' process is during office hours, when they usually have questions, and in documentation of the final product. Some students tried to write code for their designs while others simply described which component would satisfy each bullet point in the design brief. Once students completed the decomposition task for the alarm clock, they described "parts" of their design to us. Their definitions of what a part is in software design may be of interest to their instructors. Educators may want to use such a design exercise to learn about how students interpret a specification and produce an initial design.

5.3 Future Work

The results of the study raise new questions for future investigation, both informally as action research for Computer Science educators and more formally as multi-national research studies similar to the one described in this paper.

- What can we do to help students recognize ambiguities in specifications?
- How should students be taught to resolve ambiguity in specifications? How should we teach them to gather information and how does that impact our traditional evaluation mechanisms?
- At what point in an undergraduate curriculum should we intentionally introduce ambiguity into problem statements? Brown points out the benefits of having students in CS1 write formal program specifications [4]. Is teaching students how to recognize and respond to ambiguity in the first year feasible or advisable? Is it so important that we address it in the first class, or will that only add to confusion?
- Will addressing the issue of ambiguity more directly in instruction really improve students' design abilities? Put another way, is becoming a better designer a matter of maturity, an intrinsic ability, or something that can be taught and learned?
- Are there exemplary curricula that help students learn to recognize and resolve ambiguous specifications?

Acknowledgments

We thank the participants and leaders of the Scaffolding Workshop for CS Education Research for their help in data collection and analysis. We especially thank all the students and educators who participated in the study. This material is based upon work supported by the National Science Foundation under Grant No. DUE-0243242. Any opinions, findings, and conclusions or recommendations expressed in this material are those of the authors and do not necessarily reflect the views of the National Science Foundation.

References

1. http://depts.washington.edu/srcse/.
2. R. S. Adams, J. Turns, and C. J. Atman. What Could Design Learning Look Like? In *Expertise in Design: Design Thinking Research Symposium 6, Sydney, Australia*, 2003.
3. B. W. Boehm. *Software Engineering Economics*. Prentice Hall, Upper Saddle River, New Jersey, 1981.
4. D. A. Brown. Requiring CS1 student to write requirements specifications: A rationale, implementation suggestions, and a case study. In *Proceedings of the 19th SIGCSE Technical Symposium on Computer Science Education*, pages 13–16, 1988.
5. K. M. Bursic and C. J. Atman. Information Gathering: A Critical Step for Quality in the Design Process. *Quality Management Journal*, 4(4):60–75, 1997.
6. S. Fincher, M. Petre, J. Tenenberg, K. Blaha, D. Bouvier, and *et al.* Cause for alarm?: A multi-national, multi-institutional study of student-generated software designs. Technical Report 16-04, Computing Laboratory, University of Kent, Canterbury, September 2004. http://www.cs.kent.ac.uk/pubs/2004/1953.
7. S. Fincher, M. Petre, J. Tenenberg, and *et al.* A multi-national, multi-institutional study of student-generated software designs. In *Proceedings of the 4th Annual Finnish / Baltic Sea Conference on Computer Science Education*, 2004.
8. D. Gause and G. Weinberg. *Are Your Lights On?* Winthrop Publishers, Cambridge, MA, 1982.
9. R. Guindon, H. Krasner, and B. Curtis. Breakdowns and processes during early activities of software design by professionals. In *Empirical Studies of Programmers: Second Workshop*, 1987.
10. T. Hilburn. Inspections of formal specifications. In *Proceedings of the 27th SIGCSE Technical Symposium on Computer Science Education*, pages 150–154, 1996.
11. R. Jeffries, A. A. Turner, P. G. Polson, and M. E. Atwood. *The processes involved in designing software, Cognitive Skills and Their Acquisition*. Lawrence Erlbaum Associates, 1981.
12. W. M. McCracken and *et al.* A multi-national, multi-institutional study of assessment of programming skills of first-year CS students. *SIGCSE Bulletin*, 33(4):125–180, 2001.
13. E. Soloway and K. Ehrlich. Empirical studies of programming knowledge. *IEEE Transactions on Software Engineering*, 10(5):595–609, 1984.
14. J. Tenenberg and *et al.* A multi-national, multi-institutional study of student-generated software designs. *Informatics in Education*, 4(1):143–162, 2005.
15. S. Wiedenbeck. Novice/expert differences in programming skills. *International Journal of Man-Machine Studies*, 23:383–390, 1985.

Appendix A

Requirements Used for Determining Satisfaction of Requirements

1. Allow a student to set an alarm to wake them up.
2. Allow a student to set an alarm to remind them to go to sleep.
3. Record when a student tells the system that they are about to go to sleep.
4. Record when a student tells the system that they have woken up, and whether it is due to an alarm or not (within 2 minutes of an alarm going off).
5. Make recommendations as to when a student needs to go to sleep. This should include yellow alerts when the student will need to sleep soon, and red alerts when they need to sleep now.
6. Store the collected data in a server or database for later analysis by researchers. The server/database system (which will also trigger the yellow/red alerts) will be designed and implemented by another team. You should, however, indicate in your design the behaviour you expect from the back-end system.
7. Report students who are becoming dangerously sleep-deprived to someone who cares about them (their mother?). This is indicated by a student being given three red alerts in a row.
8. Provide reports to a student showing their sleep patterns over time, allowing them to see how often they have ignored alarms, and to identify clusters of dangerous, or beneficial, sleep behaviour.
9. Wake the student up.

The Groupthink Specification Exercise

Michael D. Ernst

MIT Computer Science & Artificial Intelligence Lab
Cambridge, MA, USA
mernst@csail.mit.edu
http://pag.csail.mit.edu/~mernst/

Abstract. Teaching students to read and write specifications is difficult.
It is even more difficult to motivate specifications — to convince students
of the value of specifications and make students eager to use them. The
Groupthink specification exercise aims to fulfill all these goals. Groupthink is a fun group activity, in the style of a game show, that teaches
students about teamwork, communication, and specifications. This exercise teaches students how difficult it is to write an effective specification
(determining what needs to be specified, making the choices, and capturing those choices), techniques for getting them right, and criteria for
evaluating them. It also gives students practice in doing so, in a fun environment that is conducive to learning. Specifications are used not as
an end in themselves, but as a means to solving realistic problems that
involve understanding system behavior.

Students enjoy the activity, and it improves their ability to read and
write specifications. The two-hour, low-prep activity is self-contained,
scales from classes of ten to hundreds of students, and can be split into
2 one-hour sessions or integrated into an existing curriculum. It is freely
available from the author (mernst@csail.mit.edu), complete with lecture slides, handouts, a scoring spreadsheet, and optional software. Instructors outside MIT have successfully used the materials.

1 Introduction

Specification (along with related verification activities such as testing) is critical to the success of any real software system. However, many students view
specification as a dry, tedious, and impractical topic.

One problem is that many undergraduate programming classes fail to integrate specification into the curriculum in a realistic way. Writing a specification
for the purpose of being graded takes specifications out of the context in which
they are used, so students gain little appreciation for their utility. Additionally, typical class assignments are simple, so techniques that are crucial for more
complex software may not be cost-effective. Students learn the (incorrect!) lesson
that specification is pointless.

This paper describes Groupthink, a two-hour group activity that teaches students about specification — conveying its utility, illustrating how to do it (and
how not to do it), and emphasizing the importance of teamwork and communication during the process — through hands-on experience with a realistic problem.

P. Inverardi and M. Jazayeri (Eds.): ICSE 2005 Education Track, LNCS 4309, pp. 89–107, 2006.
© Springer-Verlag Berlin Heidelberg 2006

In small teams, students are given a set of requirements and asked to specify the behavior of a simple desktop telephone with integrated answering machine. They then play a game to determine how successful their specification was. The game poses questions about the behavior of the telephone, and each team member must answer the questions individually. There are no right or wrong answers; rather, the goal is for all team members to give the same answer, indicating they have constructed a specification that they can all understand and that covers all possible behaviors. Finally (though they are not told this beforehand), they are given a second chance to improve their specification and to continue to play the game.

The author has run the activity 9 times since 2002, involving over 850 sophomores from the MIT School of Engineering. The activity has also been run outside MIT. At MIT, the activity is part of the January inter-session UPOP (Undergraduate Practice Opportunities Program) engineering "boot camp". This is an intensive week-long program intended to teach engineering sophomores a variety of engineering and management skills that are often not taught in regular classes but are important for industrial jobs [9].

The objective of the exercise is to teach students

- the importance of creating precise, complete specifications
- the difficulty of doing so
- specific methods for eliciting requirements and creating specifications
- strategies for information representation when expressing specifications
- effective teamwork and group communication
- the importance of ensuring understanding among all team members
- time management
- the value of iteration and how to learn from mistakes

No brief activity can teach all these skills, and different students bring different skill sets to the activity. Therefore, the exercise is intended to teach different lessons to different students. As explained in Section 4, the exercise meets its objectives. Students find the activity enjoyable, they report learning these lessons, and they demonstrate better success on a specification task afterward.

Our three major goals in designing the activity were as follows.

1. We wished to pose students a well-motivated, practical, concrete, realistic problem. Such a problem is not a dry academic exercise, but has a clear connection to real-word work. The problem needed to be small enough to be easily comprehensible and to look easy at first glance, but hard enough that undisciplined approaches were unlikely to be successful, so that the students appreciate the advantages of using a specification.
2. We wanted to run an interactive and lively event. Many people learn best by doing (e.g., active learning [1], which is promoted by a variety of teaching guides [3,10,11,2]), and hands-on activities are more likely to be fun and to inspire students. Iteration gives students an opportunity to learn from and to correct their mistakes, gaining a feeling of accomplishment and illustrating how and why undisciplined alternative approaches fail. Interaction with other

people exposes students to multiple technical and organizational approaches to a problem. An element of competition — both with other teams and with a team's own previous performance — made students more energetic and focused them on the task.

3. We aimed to appeal to students with many different backgrounds. The activity should equally engage computer science students and computer-phobes, and those with years of job experience or none at all. This implies that the activity must teach different skills and concepts to different people, and it should encourage participation by all students. For example, we wished to force "techies" to talk to "non-techies", which teaches better communication skills to both groups.

2   The Activity

The activity starts with a very brief lecture on specifications. The introductory lecture motivates why one would care about specifications, and who should care about specifications. Writing and understanding specifications is important to everyone:

- designers – to communicate their ideas to others
- implementers – to faithfully reproduce the ideas
- testers – to ensure compliance
- managers – to understand what the technical team is doing
- technical support – to understand what behaviors are desired
- salesmen/marketing – to communicate to customers
- users – they cannot use, and will not buy, what they cannot understand

Students then form small teams and are given a partial specification of a system, plus a set of requirements for its behavior. The specification is incomplete and inconsistent in somewhat subtle ways. Each team is asked to develop a better and complete specification that prescribes the system's behavior under all possible user interactions. There is no right or wrong specification as long as the requirements are met. The goal is for each team to agree upon the specification and to understand what they have agreed upon. The exercise is motivated in part by imagining that the students are working for different divisions of a company that wants to bring the system to market.

The Groupthink framework provides a way of running an activity that emphasizes teamwork and consensus. Instructors use Groupthink along with a content module that sets students a specific task. As of this writing, one content module, called "Answerphone", is distributed with the Groupthink Specification Exercise. Appendix A reproduces the requirements handout that is given to students.

Answerphone is a desktop telephone with integrated answering machine. Other systems would also work well. The system should be relatively familiar to students to minimize confusion and reduce time requirements, and should have a moderate level of feature interactions to make the specification rich but tractable.

Each team of students had 30 minutes to agree upon the system's behavior. After 20 minutes, facilitators such as instructors or TAs (teaching assistants) may gently guide teams that are struggling very badly: for instance, some students are not engaged, so they aren't participating, or some students don't understand the team's solution. TA intervention should be rare, because we found that students learn best when they struggle, make their own mistakes, and then correct them. Thus, TA involvement is primarily intended to let the team proceed to new experiences and mistakes that can teach new lessons. TAs should avoid making specific suggestions, but might point out that all team members must understand the solution, or note that the team is stuck on one relatively minor point, or ask whether the team has considered some important situation. The TAs should listen to all of the group's deliberations, in order to provide better feedback after the entire activity was over.

To evaluate their specifications, students play the Groupthink game that gives the activity its name. Teams are asked a series of questions about the system behavior, many of which focus on feature interactions. Each question is displayed on an overhead projector and is also read by the instructor. A sample question is:

> The user is connected to an outside party. The outside party hangs up.
> Can the user hear dial tone?
> A. The user hears dialtone (the phoneline is in the lineactive state)
> B. The user does not hear dialtone (the phoneline is in the lineidle state)

Each team member individually answers the questions. There is no right answer. Instead, the challenge is for all team members to give the same answer, without communicating with one another, based on the specification they have developed. It is important to emphasize that differences in answers are a failure of the team to develop a specification that everyone understands, not a failure of any individual.

Displaying a running tally of scores promotes excitement and involvement in the game. Each team receives as many points as the size of their plurality answer, plus a bonus of 10 points if all answers agree. For example, suppose that a team has 9 members. If 4 team members answer "A", 3 answer "B", and 2 answer "C", the team receives 4 points. If 1 team member answers "A", 1 answers "B", and 7 answer "C", the team receives 7 points. If all 9 team members answer "B", the team receives 19 points (9 points plus 10 bonus points). Students quickly realize that winning or losing the game depends primarily on the number of bonuses earned.

After a round of questions, the instructor moderates a class discussion that conveys the core of the material the students will learn. Students explain what strategies were and were not successful. We believe that students hearing from one another in their own words is more effective than a lecture: it is more convincing to hear from someone who has actually tried a particular technique. This approach also forces reflection (introspection), which is itself a successful learning strategy [6,2,12]. An instructor moderates the discussion, following up to emphasize or expand upon certain points, or to draw connections. Section 3 lists some common student observations.

After the discussion, though they are not told this beforehand, the students are given more time to improve their specification before a second round of the game (see Section 2.1). Students use their mistakes from the first round to help them improve. This iterative learning experience is key: students get to make mistakes, learn from them, and then do a better job, which solidifies the learning and leaves them with a positive feeling [16].

After the game, the activity concludes with a lecture that reinforces the points made by the introductory lecture, the class discussion, and the exercise.

2.1   Round 2 of the Game

The second round of the game — after students have played the first round, then improved their specifications based on their experiences — makes four scoring-related changes.

Two changes keep all teams involved in the game. These changes prevent any team from getting so far ahead in the first round as to discourage other teams.

- All point values are doubled (including bonus points; just double the overall score).
- There are two winning teams: the one with the highest overall score and the most improved team.

Two other changes require students to produce a quality specification. These changes make the second round more challenging, and they prevent participants from "gaming the system" by creating an unrealistic system that is easy to answer questions about.

- Some answers are marked as wrong, because the behavior violates requirements or the operation of the telephone network. When scoring, we disregarded wrong answers when determining the plurality answer.
- Some answers are marked as legal but questionable — for instance, they do not provide the functionality that users would desire. If such an answer is the plurality, the team's score is not doubled.

Before introducing new questions, the second round repeats all the questions that the first round asked. (Students are *not* appraised of this beforehand.) After the repeated questions, the instructor should ask whether any teams missed any of the questions, ask why, and emphasize the importance of learning from one's mistakes. Then, continue with the new questions.

3   Lessons for Students

During the class discussion, students commonly report having learned the following lessons. Instructors may wish to emphasize these points, or to raise issues that they observed but that no student voices.

Student remarks tend to fall into two categories: technical approaches and team organization. Some common technical approaches are:

- Draw state diagrams with transitions among states.
- Draw state diagrams showing the state of all components (switches, phone-line, etc.).
- Explore a set of "use cases" or scenarios, and decide what happens in each circumstance. This was effective when the participants predicted the questions, but less so when they did not.
- Draw a flow chart indicating the sequence of events.
- Focus the specification around the communication protocol among system components.
- Rank all actions: give some priority over others. An extension of this is to create a rule-based system with a set of (prioritized) rules.
- Decompose behaviors into normal and exceptional cases, and treat each separately.

Common approaches to team organization include:

- Choose a leader to direct and focus the group's activity.
- Don't argue. To avoid wasting time, poll everyone, make a decision, and then move on.
- Choose simple behavior that is easier for everyone to understand; avoid bells and whistles. There is no need to add complicated features that are not explicitly noted in the requirements, such as call waiting.
- Make a schedule indicating how much time it is worth spending on each task, based on the value of each discussion or decision, and stick to the schedule.
- Listen to everyone—don't shut out some participants. Often quiet team members had very good points to make, and those with more forceful personalities need to listen carefully.
- Ensure that everyone understands—the team is only as strong as its weakest member. Team members comfortable with the technical terms used in the requirements should help the others. Students come to realize that although the exercise is couched in telecommunications and computing terminology, it does not rely on skills specific to those disciplines.
- Use a master copy so everyone can focus on it. When this is on the whiteboard, more people tend to participate then when it is on paper, and it is more useful than each person writing up a separate copy. If there are separate copies, they must be kept in sync.
- Spend a few minutes in which everyone reads the handouts before diving into a solution, in order to guarantee understanding of the problem.
- Divide and conquer: delegate different parts of the specification to different sub-teams. Re-group in plenty of time to explain the separate sub-teams' progress to the full team.

The instructor should emphasize that the technical aspects and the team organization are complementary, and neither can be ignored. If either is mismanaged, the project will be a failure.

4 Assessment

The Groupthink specification exercise has been a success. Students eagerly and intently attack the problems during the activity; they loudly cheer and groan as their team's fortunes change during the game; and they confirm their enjoyment and learning in a post-activity survey. TAs for the UPOP engineering boot camp [9] report that the activity is their favorite among the more than a dozen presented by engineering and management faculty.

We attribute the success to the design of the activity, which paid careful attention to the goals noted in Section 1. The problem was realistic enough to motivate students, hard enough to require use of specifications, and easy enough to give students a sense of accomplishment. Students got a chance to fail in an initial attempt, then a chance to succeed after reflecting on their experience and learning about a wide variety of other approaches taken by other teams [16]. Achieving high scores required full participation from every team member; this motivated students to communicate and explain their ideas in a simple and clear manner. Students with different backgrounds learned different lessons, whether technical, communication, or organizational.

4.1 Student Learning

This section reports results from four sources: team scores in the activity (collected from the scoring spreadsheets), student surveys, a post-activity followup by a student, and instructor observations of team behavior.

Student performance improved during the game. We compared (normalized) scores during the first round of play (before students had observed their performance and participated in a class discussion about various technical and organizational approaches) and the second round. The improvement ranged from 4% to 131%, with an average of 66%. Student self-assessment indicated that, compared to a control group, the UPOP students had greater improvement in their teamwork abilities [9]. (Before UPOP, 18% of students reported never having worked as part of a team either in class or on a job; 36% reported one such experience; and 46% reported 2 or more such experiences.)

A post-activity survey in 2002 asked students what big ideas they had learned that they could use in practice. The most common themes were clarity (12%), teamwork (12%), communication (11%), simplicity (11%), the importance of a written document (9%), completeness (5%), focus on the end goal (5%), and organization (5%), though students also cited a dozen other general ideas. Many of these themes are related, but the diversity also demonstrates that the activity can teach different ideas to different students.

When asked what activities they had enjoyed best in a session of the MIT UPOP program, student responses included "Answerphone brought out the big idea of communication with every member of the group," and "The Answerphone activity caused us to really gel as a group and communicate very effectively between ALL group members." Other students remarked that they enjoyed the analysis portion, and the friendly competition (see Section 4.3).

The activity turned out to be surprisingly realistic and practical. One student wrote to the organizers of the UPOP program during the summer of 2004:

> I am on my second day of work at my Internship at Orange (division of France Telecom), and I am looking at design specs for a product I am researching—a voice activated answering system. As I opened the packet, I saw a flowchart very similar to what we did in the Answerphone exercise back in UPOP. Good job on picking the activities we did.

Not every student or team learned the lessons presented in Section 3. Based on direct observation of 102 teams, the largest problem was individuals who were not engaged: when it came time to give an answer, those people too often gave a divergent answer, preventing the team from achieving unanimity (and gaining the bonus points). Two common reasons for disengagement were bossy individuals who ignored and alienated other team members, and individuals who had less technical background than others but failed to speak up to ask for clarification. Other common problems were failure to understand the problem domain, losing the big picture (overfocus on small issues, resulting in an end product that was missing large and important components), and poor technical approaches that were not corrected in time. On a few occasions, a team that had excelled during the first round became overconfident and did not use the second specification period effectively, and thus fared worse on the second round of questions.

4.2   Student Reaction

As noted earlier, students and TAs enjoy the Groupthink specification exercise. Students had three general complaints. The first complaint concerns teams of different sizes; see Section 5.3.

The second complaint is that some students tried to game the system. The introductory lecture emphasized that it is not acceptable to communicate during the questions nor to use meta-information, such as answering with the first listed answer in cases of ambiguity; students respected these restrictions. The complaints were rather that some teams had made unrealistically operable specifications that happened to be easy to reason about and answer questions regarding. Since simplicity and understandability are key lessons of the exercise and are crucial in real-world projects, this was not an unreasonable approach. We also addressed this issue in the second round of the game (see Section 2.1) by awarding lower scores for illegal and for strange answers.

The final complaint is that students wanted more time: they felt that they could have done a far better job if given the opportunity to further improve their specifications. We answered this complaint by noting that in real engineering situations, there is never enough time (it is constrained cost and time-to-market concerns), and that time management is one of the crucial skills that the exercise teaches. And though the time is artificially compressed in the exercise, the problem has also been made artificially simple (another point emphasized in the materials), so the time-to-difficulty ratio is not unreasonable.

All of these complaints have become less common as we have fine-tuned the game over time. For example, time management has become a more important theme of the activity over time.

4.3   Experience Without Competition

An instructor at another institution ran the activity without the competitive aspect.

> Each class was incredibly small (about 5 students), which is unusual. Because of that, I grouped all the students in each class into 1 group. The more advanced class set about doing it in a serious manner, while the "Intro to programming" class basically blew it off (since I'd mentioned that there were no points attached). Something I thought was really interesting is that the Intro class (which went second) accidentally saw the scores for the other class only after their first round of specification (which I'd forgotten to delete from the .xls file); they commented that had they known it was going to be competitive, they would have actually tried harder. Also interesting is that all 5 of those people were male, and I'd estimate the ages to be 18–26 ish or so.
>
> I found the exercise to be incredibly well-thought out, and greatly appreciate the handouts / slides / outline — it was incredibly helpful!

5   Mechanics

5.1   Schedule

We ran the exercise as a two-hour self-contained activity (see Section 5.2 for alternatives), following this schedule:

5 min	Brief introductory lecture
10 min	Explanation of requirements
30 min	Specification (round 1)
10 min	Game (round 1)
20 min	Discussion
20 min	Specification (round 2)
15 min	Game (round 2)
5 min	Game wrapup
5 min	Concluding lecture
120 min	Total

We have found that the introductory lecture is most effective when it is shortest. The explanation of requirements walked the students through most aspects of the telephone system and answered their questions. During the class discussion, we started with the teams with the highest and lowest scores, and after that proceeded around the room systematically. We made a representative from each team speak. The game wrapup can include more discussion (we found time to debrief in the individual teams very valuable), awarding of prizes, etc.

5.2 Integration into Curriculum

Because the Groupthink specification exercise is self-contained, it can easily augment an existing curriculum, for instance to motivate specifications or to replace dry lectures. Alternately, by incorporating more instruction about specifications, the problems presented in the game could be made more challenging.

The exercise can be split into two one-hour class sessions. The first session introduces the activity and plays the first round of the game along with limited discussion, and the second session includes the second round of the game, preceded and followed by more discussion. The exercise can also be integrated with more lectures or other instruction, enabling it to fit into an existing curriculum or the problems to be made more challenging.

Variations on the activity as run so far would be interesting. One example is to give students far more time to perform the activity, eliminating any time pressure (or perhaps increasing the complexity of the task). Another example is to perform a similar activity using formal rather than informal specifications.

Instructors can develop additional modules (in addition to the provided "Answerphone" module) by creating new handouts for students and new questions. Section 5.5 describes the voting techniques for the Groupthink specification exercise. When using the manual voting technique, the questions should be in slideshow format (e.g., PowerPoint), and when using the electronic voting technique, the questions should be in an XML format that is documented with the provided software.

5.3 Team Size

We run the activity with up to 13 teams of 9 students. While the team size is in part dictated by the physical setup of our lecture room, this size has worked very well in practice. It presents nontrivial, but surmountable, problems in agreement, coordination, and communication.

Instructors should keep the team sizes consistent, because smaller teams enjoy an advantage (they find it easier to reach consensus and earn the bonus points). But students in any size team will complain that teams of other sizes have an advantage.

5.4 Logistical Requirements

The activity requires an overhead projector with computer hookup. It works best in a room where students can work together in small groups (moveable chairs are crucial), preferably with access to blackboards or whiteboards.

The activity requires the following materials.

- For the instructor: slides for the lecture and game; scoring spreadsheet or PRS software (described in Section 5.5). All of these are provided with the Groupthink distribution (available from mernst@csail.mit.edu).
- For the students:
  - One copy of the handout per student, single-sided to permit easier reference.

- 16 small pieces of paper per student, for writing answers. This is necessary only if using manual vote collection technique (see Section 5.5).
- Optionally, token prizes for the highest-scoring team and the most improved team.

You may override the default team names in the spreadsheet (manual voting method) or program (electronic voting method).

5.5 Collecting Votes

There are two ways to collect votes and keep track of each team's score: manual and electronic. In the *manual* technique, each student writes his or her answer on a piece of paper, these are tallied by hand, and the result is entered into a provided spreadsheet. The spreadsheet tracks cumulative scores and (for round 2) improvement over the previous round. In the *electronic* technique, students use a hand-held remote control or other hardware to cast a vote, and the tallying and spreadsheet entry occur automatically. We provide software for the Personal Response System (PRS) from GTCO CalComp/InterWrite [7], which is a system of infrared remote control "clickers", but it could be ported to other hardware, including networks of workstations, PDAs, or cell phones.

Manual Voting Technique. For each question, students write their answer on a small piece of paper, turn it face down, and either give it to group's TA (or a designated team member) or place it in a common location such as the center of their table.

When all team members have voted, the TA reveals the answers. This ensures anonymity and prevents teams from blaming individuals who gave different answers than the plurality. Anonymity is important to make the participants think like a team: differences in answers are a failure of the team to reach consensus and to ensure understanding, not a failure of the individual. Having each student turn over his or her own answer would not achieve this goal.

It is necessary to know when each team is finished. We had up to 13 teams of 9 students, so we used the following mechanism (other mechanisms might work for smaller groups). The team's TA raises his or her hand as soon as the question is asked, then lowers it when all team members have answered. This makes it easy for the instructor to look around the room and see when everyone was done (when no more hands are up). One problem was that occasionally the designated person forgot to raise their hand and keep it raised until all answers were in. (The TAs preferred the use of the electronic voting technique described below.)

The instructor collects scores by calling out the name of each team, having that team's TA respond with the score, and typing these into a spreadsheet (see Figure 1). Communicating all the scores to the centralized location was somewhat clumsy, especially for large classes, and this was a complaint from some other institutions as well. (We mitigated the problem by collecting scores every two or three questions.) Projecting the spreadsheet so that everyone can see the current standings was popular with the students and increased the sense of excitement in the game.

Electronic Voting Technique. In order to overcome the clumsiness associated with manual vote tallying, we wrote custom software to support the Groupthink specification exercise. This software is distributed with the exercise for use by other instructors.

We had access to a classroom equipped with the InterWrite PRS, or Personal Response System [7]. This commercial system consists of remote control transmitters ("clickers") capable of transmitting a digit to infrared receivers that are positioned throughout the room. Typical uses for PRS are taking attendance and polling students during class to gauge comprehension. The vendor software has very limited functionality, so we wrote our own program instead, using the manufacturer's low-level interface to the hardware.

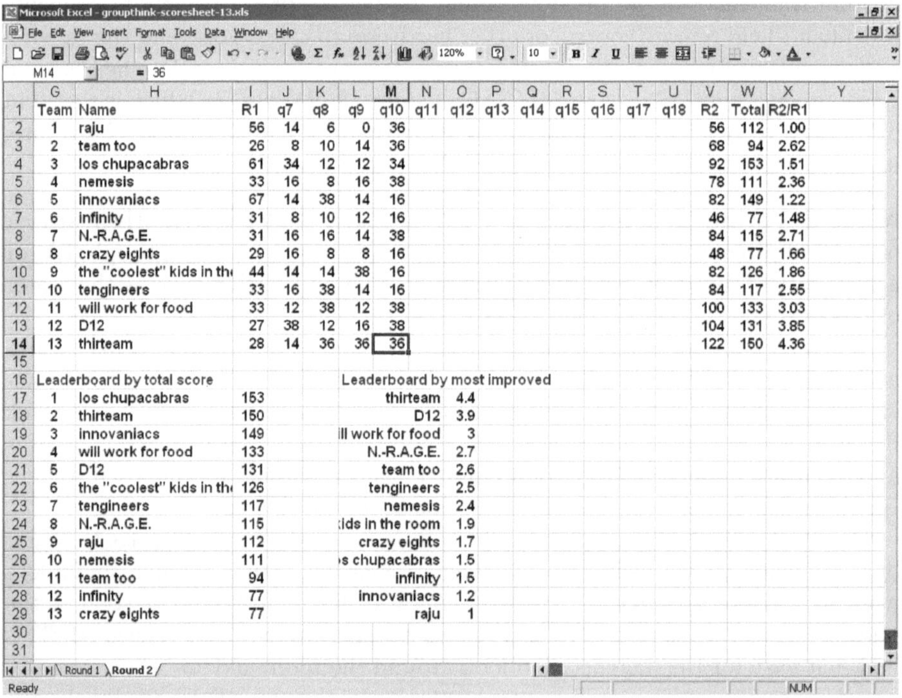

Microsoft Excel - groupthink-scoresheet-13.xls

M14 = 36

	G	H	I	J	K	L	M	N	O	P	Q	R	S	T	U	V	W	X
1	Team	Name	R1	q7	q8	q9	q10	q11	q12	q13	q14	q15	q16	q17	q18	R2	Total	R2/R1
2	1	raju	56	14	6	0	36									56	112	1.00
3	2	team too	26	8	10	14	36									68	94	2.62
4	3	los chupacabras	61	34	12	12	34									92	153	1.51
5	4	nemesis	33	16	8	16	38									78	111	2.36
6	5	innovaniacs	67	14	38	14	16									82	149	1.22
7	6	infinity	31	8	10	12	16									46	77	1.48
8	7	N.-R.A.G.E.	31	16	16	14	38									84	115	2.71
9	8	crazy eights	29	16	8	8	16									48	77	1.66
10	9	the "coolest" kids in th	44	14	14	38	16									82	126	1.86
11	10	tengineers	33	16	38	14	16									84	117	2.55
12	11	will work for food	33	12	38	12	38									100	133	3.03
13	12	D12	27	38	12	16	38									104	131	3.85
14	13	thirteam	28	14	36	36	36									122	150	4.36
15																		
16	Leaderboard by total score					Leaderboard by most improved												
17	1	los chupacabras	153				thirteam	4.4										
18	2	thirteam	150				D12	3.9										
19	3	innovaniacs	149				ill work for food	3										
20	4	will work for food	133				N.-R.A.G.E.	2.7										
21	5	D12	131				team too	2.6										
22	6	the "coolest" kids in th	126				tengineers	2.5										
23	7	tengineers	117				nemesis	2.4										
24	8	N.-R.A.G.E.	115				ids in the room	1.9										
25	9	raju	112				crazy eights	1.7										
26	10	nemesis	111				s chupacabras	1.5										
27	11	team too	94				infinity	1.5										
28	12	infinity	77				innovaniacs	1.2										
29	13	crazy eights	77				raju	1										

Round 1 Round 2

Ready NUM

Fig. 1. The scoring spreadsheet for the manual scoring technique, during the second round of the game. The instructor types team scores into the top part of the spreadsheet. The two leaderboards (just one, during the first round) are updated automatically.

The software could be adapted to other systems that support in-class multiple choice questions [20]; academic systems include ClassInHand [19], the Digital Lecture Hall [17,13], and ActiveClass [14] (and its followons Classroom Presenter and Ubiquitous Presenter), and commercial systems include CPS [4], PRS [7], H-ITT [8], and TurningPoint [18].

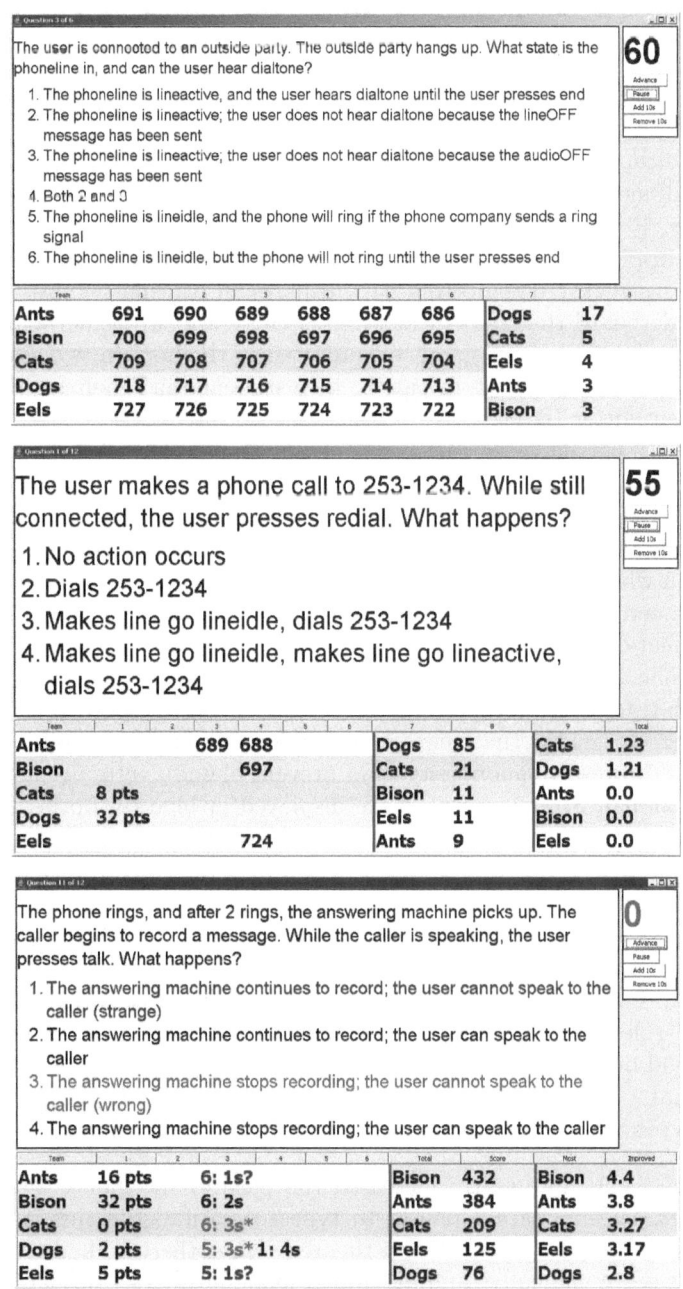

Fig. 2. User interface for the software for the electronic voting technique. The three screenshots were taken immediately after displaying a question, during voting on a question, and after voting was complete. The first screenshot was taking during the first round of the game, and the last two screenshots were taken during the second round of the game.

The program guides the class through the following phases:

Registration. Each student presses arbitrary buttons on his or her remote control and gets visible feedback. This makes students comfortable with use of the transmitter and gives them confidence that it is working properly. This also indicates which students are present, which is important for knowing when all members of a team have voted.

Questions. Figure 2 shows the user interface during voting. The top part of the UI displays a question, along with a countdown timer and a few controls for the instructor. The bottom part displays all transmitter IDs, along with the leaderboard that ranks the teams. (There are two leaderboards during the second round of the game, as indicated in the bottom two screenshots.) Color is used in the bottom part to help students find their team and their own transmitter ID.

  As each person votes, the corresponding transmitter ID is erased in order to indicate that the vote has been received. The middle screenshot of Figure 2 shows the user interface after some of the participants have voted.

  As soon as all members of a team have voted, the team's score is displayed (but not what the team members voted, as that could give guidance to other teams), and the leaderboard that ranks the teams is updated; see the middle screenshot of Figure 2.

  As soon as all teams have voted, or time runs out, a summary of all votes for each team is displayed, as shown at the bottom of Figure 2. The notation "3: 1s 2: 3s" means that there were 3 votes that were "1" and 2 votes that were 3. To preserve anonymity (and prevent blame), votes are not reported by individual. Strange answers are displayed in blue (in both the top and bottom part of the user interface), and wrong answers are displayed in red.

Display winner. After the end of the first round, the winner of the first round is displayed. This heightens the subterfuge that the game is over.

Show changed rules The changed rules for round 2 are displayed (see Section 2.1).

Questions. The second round of questions is like the first, but with modified scoring rules (see Section 2.1) and with two leaderboards: one for overall score and one for most improved, as shown in the bottom two screenshots of Figure 2.

Display winners. The game ends with a display of two winners.

Use of the software greatly increased the pace of the game, especially for large classes, by eliminating pauses to type scores into the spreadsheet. The software was also quite popular with the TAs, who otherwise had to determine each team's score manually (and inevitably made mistakes). In fact, use of the software enabled us to give lower scores to the "strange" answers, which we feel is an improvement. We did have to change two of the questions to conform to the software. One question had had three parts and a total of 18 possible answers; we split it up into two separate questions with 6 and 3 possible answers, respectively. Another question had several multiple choice answers but also a write-in possibility; we eliminated the (rarely-used) write-in option. Use of solely free response questions would have been more challenging and might have had greater pedagogical value [15], but in our view the logistical problems, including subjective judgment of agreement, outweighed the benefits. Furthermore, Wolfman [20, p. 190] notes many other drawbacks of non-computer-based systems.

Acknowledgments

John Chapin of Vanu, Inc. co-conceived the Groupthink Specification Exercise and assisted in running it. Michael Gebauer wrote the PRS software for displaying questions and scores and collecting votes. Steve Wolfman, Rachel Pottinger, and Catherine Howell provided helpful feedback on this paper. The development of the Groupthink Specification Exercise was supported in part by the NSF and by Microsoft. This paper is an extended version of one that appeared in ICSE 2005 [5]. Finally, we thank the instructors who have used the activity and provided feedback. We welcome feedback from other instructors; send mail to mernst@csail.mit.edu to receive a copy of the Groupthink materials or to provide feedback or suggestions.

References

1. C. C. Bonwell and J. A. Eison. Active Learning: Creating excitement in the classroom. ASHE ERIC Higher Education Report 1, The George Washington University School of Education & Human Development, Washington, D.C., USA, 1991.
2. J. D. Bransford, A. L. Brown, and R. R. Cocking, editors. *How People Learn: Brain, Mind, Experience, and School.* National Academy Press, Washington, D.C., USA, expanded edition, 2000.
3. A. W. Chickering and Z. F. Gamson. Seven principles for good practice in undergraduate education. *AAHE Bulletin*, 39(7):3–7, Mar. 1987.
4. eInstruction. eInstruction — the global leader in interactive response systems. http://www.einstruction.com/.
5. M. D. Ernst and J. Chapin. The Groupthink specification exercise. In *ICSE'05, Proceedings of the 27th International Conference on Software Engineering*, pages 617–618, St. Louis, MO, USA, May 18–20, 2005.
6. R. M. Felder and L. K. Silverman. Learning and teaching styles in engineering education. *Engineering Education*, 78(7):674–681, 1988.
7. GTCO CalComp. InterWrite products. http://www.gtcocalcomp.com/interwriteprs.htm.
8. HyperInteractive Teaching Technology. Hitt (classroom remote system). http://www.hitt.com/.
9. C. Leiserson, B. Masi, C. Resto, and D. K. P. Yue. Development of engineering professional abilities in a co-curricular program for engineering sophomores. In *ASEE Annual Conference*, Salt Lake City, Utah, June 20–23, 2004.
10. J. J. McConnell. Active learning and its use in computer science. In *ITiCSE'96: the 1st Conference on Integrating Technology into Computer Science Education*, pages 52–54, Barcelona, Spain, June 1996.

11. W. J. McKeachie. *Teaching Tips: Strategies, Research, and Theory for College and University Teachers*. Houghton Mifflin, Boston, MA, USA, 10th edition, 1999.

12. J. A. Moon. Reflection in learning — some fundamentals of learning, part 1. In *Reflection in Learning and Professional Development, Theory and Practice*, chapter 9, pages 103–119. Kogan Page, Sterling, VA, USA, Jan. 2001.

13. M. Mühlhäuser and C. Trompler. Digital lecture halls keep teachers in the mood and learners in the loop. In *ELearn*, pages 714–721, Montreal, QC, Canada, Oct. 2002.

14. M. Ratto, R. B. Shapiro, T. M. Truong, and W. G. Griswold. The ActiveClass project: Experiments in encouraging classroom participation. In *CSCL'03: the International Conference on Computer Support for Collaborative Learning*, pages 477–486, Bergen, Norway, June 2003.

15. J. A. Siegel, K. J. Schmidt, and J. Cone. INTICE — Interactive Technology to Improve the Classroom Experience. In *2004 American Society for Engineering Education Annual Conference & Exposition*, Washington, D.C., USA, June 2004.

16. L. Springer, M. E. Stanne, and S. S. Donovan. Effects of small-group learning on undergraduates in science, mathematics, engineering, and technology: A meta-analysis. *Review of Educational Research*, 69(1):21–51, Spring 1999.

17. C. Trompler, M. Mühlhäuser, and W. Wegner. Open client lecture interaction: An approach to wireless learners-in-the-loop. In *ICNEE'02: the 4th International Conference on New Educational Environments*, pages 24–46, Lugano, Switzerland, May 2002.

18. Turning Technologies, LLC. Audience response system, group response system. http://www.turningtechnologies.com/.

19. Wake Forest University Information Systems Research and Development Team. Classinhand. http://classinhand.wfu.edu/.

20. S. A. Wolfman. *Understanding and Promoting Interaction in the Classroom through ComputerMediated Communication in the Classroom Presenter System*. PhD thesis, University of Washington Department of Computer Science and Engineering, Seattle, Washington, 2004.

A   Answerphone Module

The next three pages reproduce the student handout for the Answerphone module.

Groupthink Specification Exercise

In this exercise, you will design the control for a simple telephone with integrated answering machine. You will specify the telephone's behavior when the user interacts with it.

PART 1: Specifying Behavior

As a group, read this document and decide upon the behavior of the telephone under all possible user behaviors. Your design may be written down or agreed upon orally. We do not care how you record it.

PART 2: The Groupthink Game

After deciding on the behavior of the telephone, you will be given a variety of scenarios in which a user interacts with the telephone. Each member of your group will *individually* answer questions about the telephone's behavior. Your group is scored not on what your answers are, but whether all of the members' answers are consistent. However, your answers must satisfy the requirements and must be plausible behaviors that a user would find reasonable.

In a real project, consistent answers would lead to components that interoperate correctly, behavior that is consistent with the documentation, etc. Problems due to diverging interpretations are common in software (and other!) development teams where the specification is ambiguous or underconstrained. We encourage you to think hard in part 1!

Here is an example question:

> The user is connected to an outside party. The outside party hangs up. What state is the phoneline in?
>
> A. Lineactive (the user hears dialtone)
>
> B. Lineidle (the user does not hear dialtone)

The group that wins the Groupthink Game will receive a prize. Your group may not give answers based on the form of the game; for instance, you may not agree to answer "A" if you aren't sure what else to do.

Definitions

lineidle	The phone is hung up or "on hook." In a traditional phone, this means the handset is lying in the cradle, but your phone uses the **end** key instead.
lineactive	The phone is picked up or "off hook." In a traditional phone, this means the handset is not in the cradle (it is "off hook"), but your phone uses the **talk** key instead.
ring signal	A +/- 24 volt AC signal sent over the phone line, which causes a traditional phone to ring. The phone company only sends a ring signal if it detects the lineidle state.

System Specification

TELEPHONE COMPONENTS

- Handset (includes both speaker and microphone)
- 24-character display
- Answering machine
- Keypad with keys labeled **talk, redial, ansmachine**, and **end**.

    *Simplification: The keypad also has 0 through 9, but in this exercise, you can ignore how those keypresses are handled. When the **talk** key is pressed, the digits previously entered by the user are delivered to the control software (much like a cellular phone). The **redial** key does not deliver any numbers. There is no hook or cradle as with a traditional phone, just the keys.*

FUNCTIONS

- The user places a call by pressing **talk** or **redial**. The user answers a call by pressing **talk**.

    Simplification: Your phone is not required to handle call waiting.

- The user begins using the answering machine by pressing **ansmachine** on the handset.

    Simplification: In this exercise, you will not be asked to specify the answering machine's behavior during message review.

- The user presses **end** to end a call or to stop using the answering machine.

REQUIREMENTS

- The display must show the appropriate information at all times.
  - If idle   show "READY"
  - If a ring signal is being sent
    by the phone company   show the caller ID information of the caller
  - If connected to an incoming call   show the caller ID information of the caller
  - If connected to an outgoing call   show the number being called
  - If using the answering machine   show "ANSWERING MACHINE"
- If a ring signal is delivered, the telephone must ring and show the caller ID of the caller. If the user doesn't answer the call within 2 rings, the answering machine must pick it up.

CHALLENGE

This specification may be incomplete or inconsistent. This is normal in any development effort! Your group should figure out the details needed to handle all possible scenarios that you might be asked about in the Groupthink Game.

System Architecture

The telephone has the following components. The messages that may be exchanged between the handset controller and the other components are labeled in the diagram. Analog audio links are shown with dashed lines. Switches (represented by ⊗) either make or break audio connections.

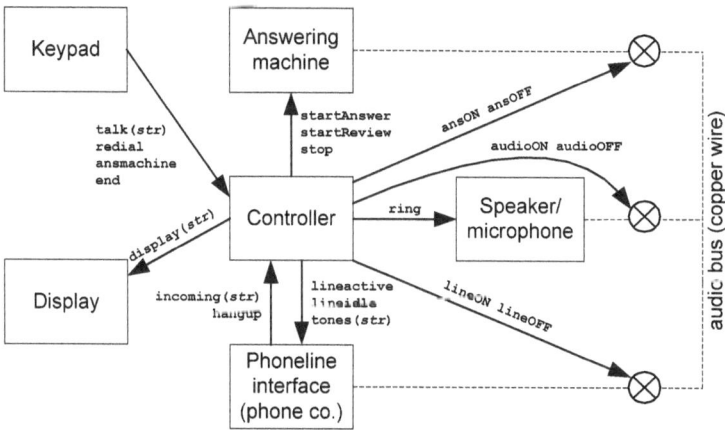

talk(_string_)	The user typed the digits in the argument string and then pressed **talk**
redial	The user pressed **redial**
ansmachine	The user pressed **ansmachine**
end	The user pressed **end**
display(_string_)	Makes the LCD display show the characters in _**string**_, a 24-character string
startAnswer	Play outgoing message and record the caller's message
startReview	Play back recorded messages and perform other user interactions
stop	Stop answering machine functions, return to idle state
incoming(_string_)	The phone company sent a ring signal with _**string**_ as caller ID information. This message is repeatedly sent (every 6 seconds) until the call is answered or the caller hangs up.
hangup	The phone company indicates that the remote party has hung up
lineactive	Put the resistance across the phone line that indicates the phone is active
lineidle	Put the resistance across the phone line that indicates the phone is idle
tones(_string_)	Send the digits in _**string**_ out over the phoneline as touch-tones
ring	Causes the speaker to play one ring tone
ansON ansOFF	Connect/disconnect the answering machine to the audio bus
audioON audioOFF	Connect/disconnect the speaker and microphone to the audio bus
lineON lineOFF	Connect/disconnect the phoneline to the audio bus

Simplification: Messages among telephone components are never lost or corrupted.

The Making of a Software Engineer
Challenges for the Educator

Clemens Szyperski

Microsoft, Redmond, WA 98052, USA
http://research.microsoft.com/~cszypers/

Abstract. Software engineering is foremost an engineering discipline. Engineering in general and software engineering specifically has to balance many factors to achieve viable tradeoffs–an understanding of the factors as well as the viability criteria is at the heart of the educational challenge. All engineering has one ultimate goal: the delivery of artifacts (products, commercial or not) that meet the needs of those using such artifacts. All engineering lives in the intersection of people, technology, domain, and opportunity aspects. Software engineering, however, is laden with its own specific difficulties. Software as an engineering medium fills a space between the fluidity of digital content, with which software shares the representation, and the nature of machines, with which software shares the flexible and repeatable application. This brief article covers some of the author's personal observations and suggestions with a hope to inspire (and provoke) those striving to improve software-engineering education.

1   Introduction

When aiming to educate people to join some profession, few standard recipes apply. That is no different in the field of software engineering. There are fundamental issues that need to be considered and this brief article is a survey of those the author finds most compelling. Then there is the need to synthesize the whole, a curriculum, and make it greater than its parts: pointwise factoids, glimmers of wisdom, and deliberate omissions. This article does not cover such larger curricular issues, despite their clear importance.

Software engineering is foremost an engineering discipline and as such has one ultimate goal: the delivery of artifacts that meet the needs of those using them. For the sake of brevity, the term product is used throughout this Article when referring to the spectrum of artifacts, but without implying any necessity of commercial form. Products can be artifacts anywhere from: the one-off work of an individual meeting an ad-hoc need, to the work of the many over long periods of time; from meeting the needs of the few at specific times to the needs of the many over long periods; from the commercial to the societal and to the charitable framing.

Engineering as a discipline of delivering the right products has to consider a wide array of tradeoff functions, including many that are only weakly defined.

P. Inverardi and M. Jazayeri (Eds.): ICSE 2005 Education Track, LNCS 4309, pp. 108–114, 2006.

Tradeoffs include technical requirements that are in mutual conflict (perfect security versus third-party extensibility), competitive drivers (time to market or process agility), opportunity drivers (windows of technological alignment in a changing world), and many more. A deep appreciation of this fundamental situation is at the core of all engineering and needs to be conveyed to the budding software engineer as well.

All engineering lives in the intersection of people, technology, domain, and opportunity aspects. Software engineering, however, is laden with its own specific difficulties. Software as an engineering substance fills a space between the fluidity of digital content, with which software shares the representation, and the nature of machines, with which software shares the flexible and repeatable application. Software-engineering education is thus challenged to draw on broader traditional engineering disciplines while clearly extracting how it is that software is different from other engineering substances.

2   Why Is Software Different?

One approach to understanding software as the substance of software engineering is to look at it from the perspective of crosscutting disciplines. For instance, how is software different from other engineering substances when considering the distribution of manufactured goods? Or the industrial supply chains? The opportunities of specialization in work force, industry, and society? In a recent book, David Messerschmitt and the author have analyzed these questions for a wide range of such disciplinary crosscuts [1].

In short, software is about engineering the equivalent of flexible manufacturing plants that are represented as streams of bits. That is, while traditional engineering is about the repeatable delivery of instances (a bridge), roughly following design templates that are well understood (classes of bridges), software engineering is about delivering systems (software) that then automatically deliver instances (configured, running) as needed.

It is noteworthy that traditional engineering turns to software engineering for insights when crossing the boundary into delivering automated delivery systems (such as flexible manufacturing plants [1]). The widely held myth that traditional engineering disciplines know so much better how to control their processes and the quality of their products does not generally hold. Engineering a bridge that falls outside of all known and proven templates is a costly undertaking, largely drawing on the prototyping and simulation of the specific instance to be built. Traditional engineering disciplines do tend to be more mature when it comes to established and certifiable processes that make it much more likely that defects are detected early. However, almost all such processes assume the working within an established framework and aid in the reproducable delivery of "more of the same".

As soon as the established envelope needs to be stretched or surpassed entirely, no engineering discipline is beyond the concepts of prototyping, exploration, and scientific experimentation. Software is, ideally, always about something new–or else it should have been automated already. It is true that there is still something to be learned from other engineering disciplines, such as the scientific recording of experimental settings and experimental results. However, it is also true that non-repeatability is, in some way, the essence of software engineering. Any such argument is guaranteed to raise concern–that it could be understood as an excuse for poor software quality. This is not the intention: avoidable mistakes need to be avoided and discipline and process that help in such a cause are therefore essential. Yet, accepting those mistakes that could not have been avoided in any systematic way (and using mitigation strategies to limit damage) is an equally important aspect of software engineering–and engineering in general. There is always a remaining risk of failure.

3   The Requirements Myth

The definition of engineering entails the concept of synthesizing products that meet their users' needs. A conceptualization of this simple observation extracts the users' needs as their up-front requirements that are then to be met. In textbook examples, this seems to work out well. After all, picking any successful product after the fact, we find it compelling to extract the requirements met by that product. However, faced with the truly new, requirements capture is often doomed to under-deliver. Yet, a disproportional number of system failures can be blamed on flawed requirements capture.

There are several reasons. First, most people think incrementally and are best at phrasing their requirements as desirable improvements over an existing situation. If incremental steps are small enough or if new projects are sufficiently close to previously successful ones, then requirements can be captured with a reasonable level of completeness and precision. This is probably the single most compelling reason to use agile processes with tight feedback loops in many software projects.

At the other extreme, disruptive technology can hold the greatest promise, but almost no one succeeds at eliciting requirements in areas of disruption. Since creating disruptive technology in small increments is almost a contradiction in terms, it is useful to consider research and advanced development processes in addition to agile development processes.

Second, only products aimed at the few in specific situations–and often at precise moments in time–are likely to target coherent requirements. Products aimed at the many have to unite individual needs and perspectives. Products aimed to generalize over many situations or to bridge over longer periods have to unite domains and embrace change. Techniques like focus groups can help gather requirements and feedback even then, but only in a less conclusive fashion.

Third, software could be cast to deliver a huge number of special-case solutions that meet pointwise requirements exactly, at least in theory. However, users of such solutions themselves move through time and space, facing varying situations. What started out as a highly specialized and perhaps optimal solution can quickly degenerate into something entirely inadequate. Aspects of training, economics, and predictability all push for solutions that are more malleable.

The reality is that engineers need to understand how to capture those requirements that can be elicited, while living with inevitable uncertainties. Agile engineering methods aim to shorten the feedback loop, but fall short on creating disruptive technology and paradigm shifts. Longer-cycle methods are better at addressing the latter, but need to be kept iterative and incremental nevertheless. The one process for all, the one tool kit for all, or the one education for all software engineers in all situations is unlikely to deliver the best overall results.

It is unfortunate that requirements and thus project goals are inextricably linked to project execution. After all, capturing requirements is known to be hard and project management and team skills are among the hardest to teach.

4   Daily Essentials in the Life of a Software Engineer

Engineering is the skillful conception and realization of tradeoffs. Almost as a law of nature, if there is the perfect solution, then it is not engineering. To be successful, engineers need to eliminate the impossible first. This is where theory contributes most forcefully–and where a lack of theoretical foundation can be most catastrophic.

Both a reasonably deep understanding and an intuitive command of the key results of central theories help. For software engineers, these include the following: computability, complexity, communication, measurement, type, and proof theory. A grasp of underlying laws of physics, such as the consequences of the inescapable speed-of-light limit or the law of the conversation of energy, help to keep the software engineer's mind grounded. Since so many tasks of the engineer are non-technical in nature, it is important to have a working understanding of social, economic, and societal mechanisms.

Having eliminated the impossible, an engineer then needs to focus on the practical. Here, it is important to open up the mind for the many different fields of influence that matter. Briefly, it is all about people, technology, domains, and opportunities (markets, society).

4.1   People, Roles, Processes

In a good approximation, software engineers never create ground-up new systems, so architecture, systems theory, services and components need to take a front seat. In addition, software engineers never deal with systems or situations small enough for individualists to cope. A good understanding of team and role models that have worked in practice needs to be paired with actual team experiences. Perhaps surprisingly, rigor and semiformal to formal methods may have their main strengths in enabling precise team communications, not in the formal securing of certain properties of the deliverables (unless largely automated).

Software development itself is obviously at the center of software engineering. However, it is critically important to understand and appreciate (rather than merely tolerate) the critical roles played by Quality Assurance (the subject formerly and improperly known as Testing), Architecture, Program and Project Management, Accessibility and Usability Engineering, User Education,

Sustaining Engineering, Escalation Management, Operations, and Systems Management. Some of these roles only show prominently in large or complex projects, but–more likely than not–any software engineer will encounter them at some point.

Processes, their understanding, appropriate formalization, and desirable agility, are at the center of team effectiveness and team efficiency. Itself a rapidly evolving field, it is important that the new software engineer has a good initial understanding of what can (and cannot) be obtained by applying processes. For instance, test-driven development–an approach that effectively encourages the writing of specifications in the form of tests to pass–is an example of a technique that combines team communications with some level of automation (regression testing). Embedded as one of several key ingredients, it forms a pillar of most agile development processes.

4.2   Technology

Technology is easily the focus in software-engineering education, so there is less need to discuss this aspect here. Given the ever-changing nature of technology, educators need to take care to cover a broad range of technology. Presenting a comprehensive historic perspective is important if only to help engineers avoid the known mistakes of the past. (However, some mistakes were just inappropriate tradeoffs at the time and need to be reevaluated!) Futuristic outlooks, studies of Moore's, Amdahl's, and other laws, and cautionary tales of phenomena such as the memory wall–and the general trend towards latency dominance-help to keep everyone on their toes. Nothing that has been done in the past is ever good enough; nothing that is being done can ever be more than good enough.

Given the plethora of technical terms and categories that the software field produces on an ongoing basis, it is particularly important to have educators that are well-versed to project an image of currency and validity in the context of the rapidly moving blogosphere, trade press, research field, and industry developments. At the same time, the educator and indeed the entire curriculum are challenged to establish cohesion and effectiveness of mental models and tools. An example close to the author's heart [2] would be concepts such as objects, components, component frameworks, composition models, services, contracts, types, protocols, and the like. Finding plausible handles on such terms in a way that casts established technology into a framework while also helping to predict and cast coming developments is a challenge–and not one that has a single definitive answer.

4.3   Domain

Finally, yet perhaps most important of all, no engineer can function without appropriate domain knowledge. There is a huge and growing number of deeply specialized domains, so picking one or a few of them for good is a recipe for likely unemployment. Yet, educators and practicing engineers alike have to select and embrace a few characteristic domains deeply to avoid the biggest dilemma that befalls software engineering more than any other engineering discipline:

the theoretic potential to do the arbitrary paired with the practical inability to realize the specific.

No curriculum as such can be of much help here–the ancient master-and-apprentice model may well be the one approach that works. Designing educational programs to embrace deep and repeated contact with practice is therefore essential. A few longer encounters, such as year-long internships paired with reduced part-time continued studies, are likely more effective than several brief episodes. Models that encourage people to return to universities repeatedly over the course of their lifelong journey would help to balance education in a world of rapid change.

4.4   Opportunity

Anyone who has worked in a startup context (or in a risky long-pole incubation effort within a larger organization) knows that the one factor that cannot be ignored is the "window of opportunity". Itself a strangely elusive concept, such a window has to be predicted and yet, by definition, if it were perfectly predictable, it would not be an opportunity. Studying the principles of success that cause startups in some parts of the world to execute almost like clockwork (including the calculated folding of an acceptable percentage) yields many insights.

Regions like California's Silicon Valley have established a startup ecosystem that provides anything from early-phase consulting to venture capital, from companies that focus on building companies to companies that focus on devouring the leftovers of imploded efforts. For software engineers to participate in the innovation cycles that are so fundamental to the nature of software, it helps to understand the principles that govern markets. Besides economic and fiscal mechanisms, some attention should be paid to psychological ones as well.

Attempts to develop the perfect solution outside of a framework of a perceived and carefully monitored opportunity is generally a recipe for disaster. Given the constant flux of technology, domains, and even people-level processes and expectations, it is essential to strive for a balance between the technically "perfect" in a presumed-to-be-frozen universe and the pragmatically usable in an accepted-to-be-fluid world.

5   Conclusion

Personally, I like to challenge educational programs by asking three questions:

- If I had to design the perfect questions for a day of interviews when hiring a junior engineer "out of college", what would I hope to cover and what would I hope to find?
- If we assume radical changes in technology and our use of it, on an ongoing basis, what balance can I seek between the long-term valid and the short-term complete?
- How can we absorb today's realities to a functional and productive level, while remaining open and imaginative about what could be?

In the end, there is an area of even greater compromise and tradeoff than engineering: education of engineers.

References

1. David G. Messerschmitt and Clemens Szyperski. Software Ecosystem–Understanding an Indispensable Technology and Industry. MIT Press, Cambridge, Mass., 2003.
2. Clemens Szyperski, Dominik Gruntz, and Stephan Murer. Component Software–Beyond Object-Oriented Programming (2nd ed). Addison-Wesley, New York, NY, 2002.

The Challenges of Software Engineering Education

Carlo Ghezzi and Dino Mandrioli

Dipartimento di Elettronica e Informazione, Politecnico di Milano
Piazza L. da Vinci, 32, Milano, I-20133, Italy
{carlo.ghezzi, dino.mandrioli}@polimi.it

Abstract. We discuss the technical skills that a software engineer should possess. We take the viewpoint of a school of engineering and put the software engineer's education in the wider context of engineering education. We stress both the common aspects that crosscut all engineering fields and the specific issues that pertain to software engineering. We believe that even in a continuously evolving field like software, education should provide strong and stable foundations based on mathematics and science, emphasize the engineering principles, and recognize the stable and long-lasting design concepts. Even though the more mundane technological solutions cannot be ignored, the students should be equipped with skills that allow them to understand and master the evolution of technology.

Categories and Subject Descriptors
K.3.2 [**Computer and Information Science Education**]

Keywords: Engineering, software engineering, education, models.

1 Introduction

We discuss the technical skills that a software engineer should possess. Rather than focusing on the organization of a course (or set of courses) titled "software engineering", we take the global viewpoint of a school of engineering and put the software engineer's education in the wider context of engineering education. We believe that software engineering (SE) should be viewed as an *engineering discipline*, and that a software engineer should be viewed as primarily an *engineer*. On these grounds, we analyze the principles and practices that pertain to the engineering culture and also what is special in the case of software engineering.

We emphasize that in general no engineering artifact involves the knowledge of a single discipline; thus, engineering disciplines cannot be taught in isolation but their essentials must be mastered by any engineer, independently of his/her particular field.

Another main issue that we face in engineering is learning by studying (at school) vs. learning by doing (at work) [1]. Our strong belief is that the two ways of learning are necessarily different and complementary. It would be a mistake to try to fake learning by doing at school, and it is almost impossible to resume the typical "learning in class and through textbooks" during everyday's work. However, it would be a fatal mistake to adopt the idea that the two worlds should ignore—or even disparage—each other. Learning at school should equip the students with all the fundamental skills that will enable them to proceed to lifelong learning at work.

P. Inverardi and M. Jazayeri (Eds.): ICSE 2005 Education Track, LNCS 4309, pp. 115 – 127, 2006.
© Springer-Verlag Berlin Heidelberg 2006

In a continuously and rapidly evolving field like software, education should emphasize principles and recognize what are the stable and long-lasting concepts of the discipline. Even though the more mundane aspects of the state-of-practice (technology, tools, methods) cannot be ignored, the students should be equipped with skills that allow them to understand and manage the various technological waves without being overwhelmed by them and thus avoid the danger of rapid obsolescence.

In the following sections of this paper we explain in some detail why we believe in this approach and how it should be exploited in the organization of an engineering curriculum. The focus is obviously on teaching software engineering, but always keeping in mind that the software engineer's education is part of a wider process aimed at "forging an engineer".

Section 2 examines the fundamental skills of a software engineer, showing that they are shared by any engineer, but also pointing out important differences, which might generate challenges peculiar to the teaching of software engineering. Section 3 discusses how software engineering should be taught within university curricula. Section 4 focuses on "putting software engineering in context". Finally Section 5 draws some conclusions.

2   Knowledge and Skills of a (Software) Engineer

Like any other engineer, the software engineer must master

- the theoretical foundations of the discipline;
- the design methods of the discipline;
- the technology and tools of the discipline.

In addition, he/she has to be able to

- keep his/her knowledge current with respect to the new approaches and technologies;
- interact with other people (often not from the same culture);
- understand, model, formalize, analyze a *new* problem;
- recognize a recurring problem, and reuse or adapt known solutions;
- manage a process and coordinate the work of different people;
- ...

The above list, far from being exhaustive, is however sufficient to enlighten both the differences between learning by studying and learning by doing and the differences between learning these skills in software engineering and in other fields of engineering.

At the two extremes, certainly learning the theoretical foundations of a discipline is a typical school activity whereas much of managing a process and the psychology of interacting with people—whether one's manager, peer, employee, or customer—can be learned mostly through experience in the field and exhibits often sharply different requirements depending on the peculiar environment.

On the other hand, none of these skills—not even the above two extremes—should be learned exclusively in one way. Consider, for instance, the typical case of learning programming languages: some languages must be learnt in depth at school, but new ones will certainly appear and will have to be mastered at work. Therefore, teaching at school should focus on two related fundamental issues: how to apply good programming methods in any language, and how to understand the principles of programming languages. Such principles as program design via abstractions, modularization, decoupling, documentation apply to any programming language. Furthermore, a student who understands type systems, binding mechanisms, scope rules, runtime memory management, and other similar concepts, can more easily learn any new language and its specific subtle semantic features. It would be wrong to expose students to a plethora of different languages, "because they have to know all the possible tools they will encounter in practice". The other extreme, is exemplified by Dijkstra [2], who claims that initially students should learn only mathematical languages without running their programs on real computers. This, however, is equally counterproductive, and can mark a chasm between university and "the real world".

As another example, teamwork should be experimented in school project works. It is important that students, before they move to work, appreciate the need for scheduling their work with others in a team, negotiate requirements and specifications for the parts they are responsible of, etc.

In summary, learning at school should lay the foundations for all the skills we listed at the beginning of this section. The students should be mentored to learning most of what they will need to continue to learn after leave school, as part of their lifelong learning activity.

It is important to acknowledge that software engineering differs from the other more traditional fields of engineering in several specific points. These differences affect how is should be taught. Let us examine some typical cases.

- *Theoretical foundations are less mature, often "far" from being directly applicable, and hence less immediately useful.*

This is at least a common feeling among practitioners, perhaps shared even by several academics. A deeper insight, however, may help discover more commonalities, better understand differences, and derive suggestions to gain more acceptance of theoretical models in computing science.

As a first example, let us compare the difference between a Turing machine and a real computer with the difference between the notion of material particle (a body with a mass but no volume) and a real physical object, such as a car, an aircraft, a fly, etc. or the difference between the notion of a "perfect gas" and the air of our atmosphere. In both cases, such very abstract and oversimplified models would never be used to build real products, but in both cases they perfectly serve the purpose of teaching the foundations of their discipline. The notion of material particle is used to introduce the principles of dynamics and Turing machines, which capture the essence of algorithms in a much more elementary way than –say– Pentium, can help explain the notion of (un)computability. The study of these abstract notions, however, is viewed and well accepted in traditional engineering as a foundational starting point that should be part of the engineer's education, whereas theoretical computer science is often neglected in the software engineer's education and not well accepted by average students.

As a second comparative example, let us consider, instead, a few formalisms that are conceived to directly support application development. In traditional engineering such formalisms are often directly applicable; think, e.g., of the use of Fourier transforms in signal processing and in other fields of electronics. Hence they are widely used by practitioners more or less as "black boxes". Even when they abstract away from many details –thus introducing approximation errors- well-established methods are often available to the designer to manage and minimize the effects of such errors: for instance, piecewise linearization is widely adopted to enjoy most of the benefits of linearity for some nonlinear systems.

In computing science, instead, quite seldom a formal model is ready to be applied as it is explained in the textbooks: for instance, although it is certainly true that the core of a compiler is a pushdown automaton, the real structure of a compiler only maintains a vague similarity with the original abstract machine. Similarly, Petri nets have been widely appreciated as a simple and natural model for concurrent systems; however, to be applied to the modeling and analysis of real systems they most often had to be modified in such a way (e.g., by adding timing, by adding values to tokens and conditions to transitions) that one could question whether their very nature had been affected.

- *Well-established models and notations are still lacking.*
This point can be seen as the counterpart of the previous. Here too a striking example is provided by programming languages: it is somewhat astonishing that this field, which should be one of the most mature of computer science, still produces major novelties almost every year. Although one might argue that changes affect programming language technology rather than the underlying principles, it is certainly true that changes affect the teaching material used in even lower-level (undergraduate or earlier) education. Conversely, introductory courses on physics still teach classical mechanics as it was taught decades ago. They would never try to incorporate new parts to teach quantum mechanics and relativity theory to freshmen.

The situation is even more striking if we move to such aspects as requirements analysis, specification and architectural design, where the state of practice is still largely ad hoc, and methods, notations and tools are still largely ignored in the industrial world.

The states of the art and practice, however, are evolving. The standardization and the increasingly wider adoption of UML have had a positive impact on bridging several gaps. Not only has UML been a vehicle—certainly not perfect, but useful— to transfer some research results into the industrial world. But also it is an example of a notation that originated in the field of computer science that is now recognized and adopted even in other fields of engineering. For example, it has been applied in logistics and in industrial manufacturing. This is not the only example of a technology that originated in our field and later was imported by other engineering fields. For example, control engineers now use automata-based discrete events models (e.g. Petri nets) along with their original continuous process models. We will come back to this issue in the following.

- *The distinction between the essential and the accidental complexity of software [3] is crucial.*
This is the essence of engineering. When solving a problem, the engineer must neglect irrelevant details to focus on the essentials, otherwise he or she would be lost in an unmanageable complexity. The ability to separate concerns and focus on the relevant ones at each time is crucial for the engineer. This is quite different from the way mathematicians work. A mathematician works in a formalized world and

mostly cares about precision of solutions. The hard question, of course, is what, how and when something can be considered to be a detail that can be neglected and what, how and when should one instead add more detail to achieve better modeling and analysis. The answer is difficult and context-dependent in most cases: one aspect could be irrelevant from some viewpoint and at some phase of the development, whereas it could be crucial in other phases.

For example, in programming it is often useful to concentrate first on writing a correct program, ignoring such issues as performance and usability. These can be taken into account at a later point via correctness-preserving code transformations and by improving user interfaces.

Other fields of engineering have some well-established guidelines to apply such difficult choices. In most cases they are rooted in the metrics of the adopted mathematical models: "neglect quantity X—say a current in an electric circuit—with respect to quantity Y if they differ of orders of magnitude". Metrics, and consequently any notion of continuity are lacking or highly controversial in most computer science models. Thus, the software engineer must often resort to more generic principles such as the separation of concerns to decide about what to focus on.

- *Mastering different approaches to manage project complexity.*

The complexity of different software engineering projects, the diversity of application areas, and the lack of established common foundations makes it likely that the software engineer should master different methods and approaches and should be capable of choosing the best method and approach that fits the problem at hand. For example, the development process can follow a highly structured, top-down scheme (like in a waterfall lifecycle) or a flexible and iterative scheme (like in extreme programming). The process to choose depends on the size of the project, its criticality, the relationship with the customer, the stability of requirements, and so on. As another example, when a system is to be specified, different notations can be used according to the stakeholder's viewpoint. There is no universal process model and there is no universal notation. The engineer has to learn which to use, when, and why, depending on the problem at hand.

Any engineer should own such a skill. However, the principles and, mainly, the techniques to confront with the various problems are much more established and less subject to fashion and "buzzwording" in traditional engineering than in software engineering. Examples can be easily found in the evolution from structured analysis/design, to object-orientation, to extreme and agile programming, etc. In parallel, and often in contrast, academia has been advertising for a long time formal methods, but those too have been subject to a rather uncontrolled and unpredictable evolution (thousands of abstract machines; logic, algebraic, and attempts to apply category-theory based approaches)[1]. It is certainly hard not to get lost in such a mess of more or less "revolutionary solutions". And it is hard to discern substance from pure cosmetics.

- *More emphasis is needed on interdisciplinary culture and communication skills.*

As for any engineering field, software engineering aims at designing and building *products*, which have some intended use in the real world. Useful products cannot

---

[1] This is another example of the big gap between learning (and teaching) at school and learning (and teaching) at work.

be conceived based on purely technical grounds. They require engineers to understand the real world and to interact with domain experts to capture the real-world requirements. These needs justify why engineers should have a broad technical education, and why they need to be exposed to other sub-disciplines of engineering. These reasons are even stronger in the case of software products. Most software can be viewed as the "intelligent glue" that integrates a complex heterogeneous system: examples go from embedded systems to industrial automation systems, to office automation, to virtual reality, etc. The real world with which software interacts may be physical, as in the case of embedded control systems, or social, as in the case of information systems, educational systems, or entertainment systems. The software engineer, therefore, even more than other engineers, must be able to understand problems and models not coming from his or her field and to interact with their specialists (of course, he will not replace the application domain specialist, nor will she have to gain the same depth and breadth of knowledge in their field).

The above remarks, therefore, can suggest that, and explain why, the gap between learning by studying vs. learning by doing is deeper in software engineering than in other cases. Perhaps a consequence of this situation is that textbooks and courseware that aim at teaching practice are often wordy, purely descriptive, and overly informal. At the same time, textbooks and courseware that teach mostly theory are often unrealistic, only deal with toy examples, are not well understood and not well accepted by students (and instructors).

In summary, the widely practiced attitude of comparing software engineering with more traditional fields is still valid and thought provoking. It still shows important differences besides common needs and approaches. It also shows that often the younger discipline should strive to get closer to the better-established ones, but sometimes even the converse can produce important progress. Fortunately, much has been achieved since the birth of software engineering. But there is still a long way to go.

On the basis of the above analysis in the next sections we elaborate some recommendations that could and should be addressed not only in organizing the teaching of software engineering but could also be taken into consideration, more generally, in engineering education.

3 Consequences on (Software) Engineering Education

In this section we articulate some general guidelines, derived from the analysis of previous section, on teaching software engineering *as an engineering discipline* [5].

• *Focus on lasting principles rather than last-minute fashionable technologies and buzzwords*[6], [7].
  This can be harder for software engineering than for other engineering fields because, as we discussed in Section 2, principles and theory may not be directly applicable, i.e., they do not yield normative practical techniques. Yet students should be motivated to learning principles because principles shape their mentality and make their approach to solving practical problems more mature and systematic. Because the recognition of the value of principles may come only later, even after

years of experience, some "faith and trust" is needed from the students[2]. Furthermore, technology is evolving faster and often it is hard to distinguish between hypes and real new good approaches.

• *Integrate class teaching with projects.*

This is a very critical issue in software engineering education. On the one hand, just studying principles on textbooks and even doing clever and insightful exercises is not real "learning" without a practical experience. On the other hand, mimicking the complexity of real-life projects in an educational environment can be impossible. Thus we need to find innovative ways of integrating project work in curricula (see, for example, [1] and [4]). We argue that projects should be realistic, but students should be aware of the differences with the real life, in terms of team size, duration and man power needed to carry over the project, requirements for compatibility with legacy systems, unavailability of "real" stakeholders, etc. At the same time, project work should exploit the opportunities (research methods, prototyping, ...) that often are unavailable in the industrial world. Students may turn out to be carriers of innovation when they enter the business world.

• *Try to make things easy and understandable.*

Stated in this way, such a recommendation may even sound obvious. How to achieve this goal, however, is far from trivial and involves conflicts. Indeed, many details should be abstracted away to make problems manageable within the typical terms of a university course and to help focus attention on the core of the problem, possibly one issue at a time. This may lead to class examples and exercises that deal with "toy problems", a term that is often used in a derogatory sense, to mean unrealistic and ultimately useless or even misleading. We claim instead that toy problems may be quite insightful *if well chosen*; the literature is now rich of successful examples often carved from real-life problems but "cleaned up" from irrelevant and distracting details.

As a side remark, one might wonder why, in general, toy problems adopted in other fields such as mechanics are better accepted by students than in software engineering. For instance, why an exercise that asks students to compute the trajectory of a missile, where the missile is considered a material particle, is appreciated and well accepted, whereas the classical dining philosophers problem is often disparaged as a "toy problem" —not only by students? Perhaps the answer to such a question is more of a psychological than of a technical nature.

• *Teach how to select and evaluate different methods and approaches rather than follow them like recipes.*

Often methods force a normative behavior, but their application must be preceded by a careful and scholarly analysis of competitive approaches, a rigorous evaluation of the trade-offs and costs and benefits. As opposed to more traditional fields of engineering, software engineering has only a limited availability of ready-made normative methods that are scientifically supported. The ability to perform

---

[2] It is not uncommon experience for us teachers to receive "post factum" recognition from former students with sentences such as "When I attended your course I hated topic xx. Also, as soon as I have been hired in my first company I was shocked by doing things that seemingly had nothing to do with what I learned at school. But now, after several years of practical work I understand and appreciate the value and usefulness of that teaching."

cost/benefit analysis, however, is a general skill that is typical and common to all areas of engineering.

Here again we see how learning by studying and learning by doing should complement each other, the latter building on the foundations laid by the former. The teacher and the student should insist on a critical and comparative attitude; the teacher should encourage the student to experiment, to question claims taken for granted in the literature, in order to come to her own opinions and decisions. The junior software engineer probably will not have so much freedom in making choices and will have to accept and comply with company-wide decisions made by someone else, maybe even a long time before he or she has been hired. Nevertheless the engineer will certainly be better able to exploit the company's methods if previously trained to apply a critical—yet constructive—attitude. The senior software engineer or the manager, instead, will have to choose a project's or even the company's new standards, and in this case he or she will *have to* be critical, comparative, and open to evaluating novelties by distinguishing the real advances from rubbish.

4   Software Engineering in Context: Requirements on Curricula

Engineering is seldom highly specialized and narrowly focused. In most cases it deals with *systems*, often involving heterogeneous and interdisciplinary aspects; this is even more true in the case of software engineering. The ultimate purpose of software, in fact, is to allow computer-based systems to interact with their external environment, to control it, automate functionality, or provide service. The external environment may be the physical world of a controlled chemical plant or an intensive-care unit in a hospital. Or it may be the organizational world of a business unit to be supported in their sale operations; or a set of players who are competing in some Internet-based game.

Although a software engineer cannot be an expert in every physical domain, he or she must be able to interact with experts from those domains. Thus, *software engineering cannot be taught in isolation. It must be put in context*—how broad is an open issue.

We can categorize the context of software engineering as follows:

4.1 Mathematical Background

This is a controversial issue although there is a general consensus that mathematics provides the fundamental background for every engineer. It is also true, however, that the gap between mathematical foundations and engineering applications is wider and less understood in software engineering.

It is often claimed that traditional engineering needs continuous mathematics whereas software engineering needs discrete mathematics. We think that such a view is fairly narrow-focused and misses the real relationship between engineering and mathematics. We claim, on the contrary, that *any* engineer, not only a software engineer, must have a solid background in all fundamental areas of mathematics:

- traditional continuous mathematics (differential and integral analysis and calculus[3]);
- discrete mathematics (logic, combinatorics, algebra; more generally, "non-continuous mathematics");
- statistics and probability theory.

There are many strong reasons to support our view.

First of all mathematics fosters rigorous reasoning. Each branch of mathematics, however, exhibits some specific forms of "building its own truths" which, *all together*, provide a formidable background for solid reasoning. Continuous mathematics stresses the unavoidableness of errors but provides the ways to make them small enough so that they become tolerable. Combinatorics teaches how to "count" the members of a class of various elements and how to "arrange them according to some rule". Mathematical logic teaches how to build new truths from elementary ones and how to check whether a claim is true or false. Algebra teaches how to abstract and generalize particular cases into wider categories; Statistics and probability theory teach among other technical skills—how to build reliable information on the basis of uncertain or variable data. All these skills should be part of the foundational tools of any engineer!

We should also be careful and flexible when we judge the "usefulness" of mathematics in terms of direct practical application. It is certainly true that many software engineers will never have to solve a differential equation. Continuous mathematics, however, is often used to model the real world, and is also the basis for modeling and controlling embedded feedback systems. However, teaching only the mathematics that can be directly applied *now*, would be the same mistake as—say—teaching only the last minute middleware technology instead of the lasting principles of software construction. We simply cannot foresee what will be directly applied of what we are learning now; on the contrary we should be ready to learn, master, and apply some new technical and mathematical machinery whenever needed. The need for introducing some metrics in a new "domain of knowledge" and, consequently, the need to "make a distance as small as possible", which leads to the abstraction of a "continuous domain" and the concept of limit, may arise for the software engineer in several, often unpredictable, circumstances. For instance recent techniques in the security domain (e.g., SPAM filtering, misuse and anomaly detection) are based on some metrics defined on the message flows and identifying some threshold to separate the "good ones from the bad ones". Applications of continuous mathematics can also be found in other areas, such as learning algorithms or performance modeling and analysis.

Examples that show the need for software engineers to have a solid background in statistics and probability theory include software reliability modeling [8] and experimental methods applied to evaluating software quality, testing, and other empirical approaches.

---

[3] Notice that we used both terms *analysis and calculus*: the former emphasizes reasoning and understanding mathematical definitions and properties; the latter focuses on building algorithms to solve practical problems once they have been formalized through suitable equations and a conceptual solution has been proved by some theorem.

We do not claim that any engineer must have the same strong background in all types of mathematics—it would be enormous and unmanageable. The relative balance between the various branches of mathematics can vary among the various fields of engineering. Also, advanced studies in some fields of engineering can require going in depth into fairly sophisticated mathematical technicalities. However, the fundamental background should be based on a wide range of mathematical fields.

Last, but certainly not least, the already emphasized need for the software engineer to interact with people with a different cultural background requires the ability to "find a common language" with them. This certainly applies to the mathematical part of the language, although it has even more important implications that will be discussed later.

4.2 The Core of Computing Science

This is certainly the least controversial part, at least in its essentials. There is no doubt that topics such as programming and programming languages, computer architecture, operating systems, databases, networking, computation and complexity theory, etc. are an essential part of the culture of any software engineer.

Rather, there could be some discussion on the borderline between what is considered to be the core of computing science and what instead more properly belongs to software engineering [9]. As an example, does object-oriented programming belong to the basics or is it part of software engineering? What about testing? Certainly, one should learn some basics of testing even in introductory courses, but most testing methodologies belong to the more specialized world of software engineering. Software processes and their management also share many organizational aspects with other disciplines: this is in fact another example of strong intersections, but also of striking differences, between software and other engineering disciplines. On the one hand, it is clear that in both cases we deal with the problem of organizing, managing, coordinating, and monitoring the work of several people; on the other side the human intensive distinguishing features of software production makes it much less predictable than, say, organizing the construction of a dam.

However, stating a precise borderline between the core of software engineering and its computing and organizational context is not such a big issue, once the important topics are well taught in a well planned and well coordinated curriculum.

4.3 The Essentials of the "Physical World"

Software intensive systems do not exist in isolation. They are built to be part of a wider and more general environment. As we mentioned, the environment can be physical, as in the case of embedded control systems, or human-centered, as in the case of information systems, educational systems, or entertainment systems, or both, as in the case of complex human interfaces for avionics control systems. Therefore, any (software) engineer should possess the necessary background to understand such a global environment. This includes:

- Mechanics, thermodynamics, electricity, etc.
- The technology on which computing science and engineering is built: electronics, telecommunications, ...

- The "social physical world": economics, business organizations, communication, management, etc.

To some extent most of these disciplines are part of many computing curricula. However, their role, impact, and relative weight within curricula are highly controversial. Without going into a questionable quantitative evaluation, we claim that most often the teaching of the above topics is too superficial and descriptive. An even precise and accurate description of the physical phenomena is not enough to make their concepts and principles real *engineering tools*. Instead the typical engineering attitude that consists of

- observing a—not necessarily physical!—phenomenon,
- building a model of it,
- reasoning on it, both qualitatively and quantitatively, with the help of the model

should be emphasized and exemplified in some depth within the context of all these disciplines. We see several good reasons to do so, even sacrificing overspecialization in elective fields.

First, note that basic engineering principles—such as modularization, abstraction, modeling, verification, etc.—are quite general, and crosscut all engineering fields. They should be used systematically not only in teaching computing science topics, but also teaching "the essentials of the physical world". For example, one could stress the analogy between considering a component of an electric circuit as a *black-box*, of which only the external behavior is known, and the principle of information hiding, through a clear separation between module interface and its implementation.

Also, a broad culture helps reasoning by analogy and therefore fosters reuse. The ability of reusing any type of knowledge has been listed above as a major skill for the software engineer.

Once again, the need for the software engineer to interact with people with a different culture imposes the ability to understand and to master at a basic level their own models.

Let us also point out that here we are referring to the activity of formally reasoning on models of the real world. Such a real world is not exclusively the world of physical objects (plants, cars, aircrafts, etc.) but also the world of human organizations (banks, agencies, offices, hospitals, even courts of justice, etc.). These entities too have to be abstracted into a suitable formal model in order to be managed with the aid of software, which is formal by its very nature. This is not to say, however, that the activity of an engineer must be based exclusively on formal and mathematical reasoning on abstract models. Experience, common sense, intuition, … are fundamental tools of the engineer as well as of most other professionals. These skills, however, are acquired as a result of experience in the real world, rather than being learned by studying at school.

We would like to conclude this section by insisting that it is not only true that software engineering has to "learn" from traditional engineering, but also the converse is true. Software engineers cannot ignore continuous mathematics, but civil engineers, industrial engineers etc. cannot ignore discrete mathematics and logic. The software engineer cannot be an expert in mechanics or thermodynamics, but rather should possess the basic knowledge that would allow him or her to interact with the specialists in these fields, should the need arise in acquiring requirements for a new application. Similarly, the mechanical engineer should be able to communicate with the software engineer who is designing the software embedded in the cruise control of a new vehicle, understanding the feasibility of certain real-time functionality. No engineer can ignore the basics of computer science, nor how software, which permeates practically all projects, is organized, documented and built: poor quality software can hamper a global system no matter how fine and sophisticated are other components. Notice that by "the basics of computer science" we do not mean how to use the Internet, productivity tools or, in general, computer tools, but the *principles* of computing science.

Cross-fertilization with other engineering fields is needed, in both directions; no matter how focused the curricula in the various fields are.

5 Conclusions

In this paper we presented our viewpoint on the challenges of teaching software engineering. We restricted our discussion to teaching within a university setting, ignoring the important areas of continuous education, special purpose intensive courses, and material mostly devoted to professionals. Rather than addressing *what* to teach in a software engineering class, we focused our attention on *how to organize* a curriculum for a software *engineer* and how to *put it in the proper context*.

We based our analysis on the unavoidable and complementary differences between learning by studying and learning by doing [1] and on the comparison between software engineering and other fields of engineering. On the latter point, our viewpoint is somewhat complementary to what has been argued by Parnas [10].

We concluded that a major challenge for the software engineering education comes from a deeper gap that exists between the two forms of learning than it happens in other, better established engineering fields. We analyzed the technical and "social" reasons of such a circumstance and suggested a few remedies (no "silver bullets", of course!). We also pointed out that the state of the affairs is evolving in a positive direction.

We strongly believe that, by its very nature, software engineering cannot be taught in isolation but must be put in the proper context. This is true for practically all branches of engineering, since most of the engineering tasks have to do with designing, building, and managing of *systems* that are quite heterogeneous in nature.

This remark broadens the scope of the challenge, because it leads to the question of what should be the foundations and the basic principles of engineering education, not just software engineering. At the beginning of engineering as a systematic discipline, it was fairly natural to define the core knowledge of any engineer. The continuous advances in science and technology inevitably led to a high level of specialization. For instance, presently our Technical University offers an order of 500 different courses for approximately 20 curricula that provide a degree in engineering. The mere proliferation of courses without caring about cohesion of the underlying foundations may lead to disasters.

We claim that the more the specialized culture and technology advance, the more education should strive to build a solid common mentality and culture that must serve as a foundation on top of which the special knowledge of a peculiar branch should be rooted and integrated with its context. The definition of such a common basis, however, should not be equated with keeping the same subjects that were taught for decades, before computing entered the engineering scene. Moreover, the common basis is not so much defined by identifying a common core set of disciplines, but rather a common approach that is based on building abstractions (models), reasoning about them and using the results to interpret the phenomena under study.

As we argued, the basics of continuous mathematics and classical physics should be still viewed as fundamentals in any engineering field. Moreover, since software permeates practically any engineering artifact and process, every engineering student should be exposed to the principles and the mathematical foundations of computing.

The challenges of education in a rapidly and continuously changing world should call universities, and in particular engineering schools, to rethink their educational mission. Success (and even mere survival) in such a world requires identifying the long-lasting principles and strengthening the foundations. This is true for software engineering as for any other engineering field.

References

1. Jazayeri, M., Education of a Software Engineer, Keynote presentation at Automated Software Engineering, Linz, Austria, 2004.
2. Dijkstra, E.W., "On the Cruelty of Really Teaching Computer Science", *Communications of the ACM*, *32*, *12*, 1989, 1398-1404.
3. Brooks, F.P., "No Silver Bullet: Essence and Accidents of Software Engineering," *Computer*, *20*, *4* (April 1987).
4. Baker, A., Navarro, E.O., van der Hoek, A. "An Experimental Card Game for Teaching Software Engineering Processes", *Journal of Systems and Software*, to appear.
5. Ghezzi C., Jazayeri M., Mandrioli D., *Fundamentals of Software Engineering, II edition,* Prentice-Hall, Englewood Cliffs, 2002.
6. Abran, A., Seguin, N., Bourque, P. Dupuis, R., "The Search for Software Engineering Principles: An Overview of Results", Proceedings of the 1st Int.l Conference on the Principles of Software Engineering, Buenos Aires, Argentina, November 2004.
7. Kramer, J. "Abstraction is Teachable?", Keynote at IEEE ACM SigSoft 16th International Conference on Software Engineering Education and Training; submitted for publication.
8. Musa, J.D., Iannino, A., Okumoto, K., *Software Reliability: Measurement, Prediction, Application*, McGraw-Hill, New York, 1987.
9. Parnas, D.L., "Software Engineering Programs Are Not Computer Science Programs", *IEEE Software*, *16*, *9*, 1999, pp. 19-30.
10. Parnas, D.L., "Software Engineering: An Unconsummated Marriage," *Communications of the ACM* 40(9), p.128, September 1997.

A Strategy for Content Reusability with Product Lines Derived from Experience in Online Education

Victor Pankratius and Wolffried Stucky

AIFB Institute
University of Karlsruhe
76128 Karlsruhe, Germany
pankratius@aifb.uni-karlsruhe.de,
stucky@aifb.uni-karlsruhe.de

Abstract. We present our experience made in the course "Information Systems Development" which is entirely taught online at the Virtual Global University (VGU). We identify current technical, economic, and pedagogical problems as well as challenges in online education, which are of interest to educators teaching software engineering online. We argue that despite the existing standards in the area of online learning, the reuse concepts of educational content are still immature, especially with respect to a reuse strategy. Building upon our own experience, we therefore present a proactive strategy to develop and reuse educational content, which is based on concepts that come from the area of software product lines.

1   Introduction

Online education and e-learning are becoming more and more popular, as the Internet simplifies the delivery of content and enables new forms of learning. In addition, e-learning is frequently offered nowadays in a combination with classroom learning, termed "blended learning". Therefore, these developments are not only important for distance education, but for the improvement of education in general. E-learning and blended learning offer also for software engineering education numerous new opportunities to help students delve into details of various subareas.

Our institute has actively participated for more than 3 years in a course related to software engineering, which is still held entirely online at the Virtual Global University [VGU06]. Our experience can be of interest to other educators who plan to use online learning technologies for software engineering courses. Within our course, we have noted that the existing concepts for the reuse of educational material are still immature, and that there are hardly any general reuse strategies around that are used for educational content. Based on our experience, we have developed a more general reuse approach which uses concepts from software product lines.

P. Inverardi and M. Jazayeri (Eds.): ICSE 2005 Education Track, LNCS 4309, pp. 128–146, 2006.

We present the details (which extend [PS05]) organized as follows. We give more details on the Virtual Global University in section 2. Thereafter, we describe our experience in section 3 with respect to technical, economic, and pedagogical issues. Derived from our experience, we present in section 4 a reuse approach for content that uses concepts from software product lines. Finally, we summarize the main issues and present opportunities for future work in the last section.

2   The Virtual Global University

The *Virtual Global University (VGU)* consists of a network of professors from more than 15 European universities [VGU06]. The courses at the VGU focus on Business Informatics, combining methodologies from computer science, information systems, and business administration. Furthermore, the courses and the corresponding exercises and labs are entirely taught online, using the Internet as a medium for the delivery of educational material, communication, and collaboration. The VGU is targeted at students who already have a Bachelor's degree, and who are already on the job. They are "physically" enrolled at the university in Frankfurt/Oder, Germany, from which they finally get a "real" Master's degree in Business Informatics. The VGU is successfully accredited by the German government and by the Foundation for International Business Administration Accreditation (FIBAA). In addition, the VGU has cooperation partners spread all over the world, for example in Germany, Slovenia, Russia, India, Pakistan, Malaysia, and Taiwan.

Within the VGU, there are several courses that cover different areas in software engineering. For more than 3 years, our institute has offered the course "Information Systems Development" that mainly covers requirements engineering, cost estimation, modeling and design (e.g., UML, ER-Diagrams, Petri-Nets), and, as a transition to other courses, a short part on implementation and testing.

3   Experience with Online Education

In the following, we describe our experience with online education which we consider to be of general interest, and the main problems we encountered in the technical, economic, and pedagogical areas.

3.1   Technical Issues

In online education, *Learning Management Systems (LMSs)* are currently used to ease administrative tasks such as the management of students, progress tracking, event scheduling, putting material online, or, using appropriate extensions, to manage content [ACP02]. In addition, it is current practice to package reusable pieces of content into so-called "Learning Objects" (LOs) which may consist simply of files (in formats such as HTML, Powerpoint, or PDF) and additional metadata (such as keywords, course outline, file paths, version numbers, etc.) that is often stored using XML [OPS05]. The metadata is intended to help to ease the migration of learning objects between different LMSs.

In the VGU, many different courses are provided by different parties, which have different technical requirements. This makes the choice of an LMS difficult, imposing a "one LMS fits all" solution. A learning object in our course basically consists of a Powerpoint file with slides on a specific subject (e.g., requirements engineering) and an online exercise. One initial requirement in our course was that the online lecture should support the presentation of slides annotated with video and audio. WebCT [Web06], the chosen LMS, however did not support the authoring of content in which lecture slides are synchronized with a video stream, which lead us to use Powerpoint Producer [Pow06], an external tool which automatically produces Web pages showing the video stream, the synchronized slides, and a navigation bar. However, we experienced severe reusability problems with such video-based courses when slides had to be added or changed, because the old video did not fit any more. The maintenance of such videos is always problematic since for example for a newly added slide, a new video sequence may have to be recorded, and the environment in the new video will not be exactly the same as in the existing slides (e.g., a lecturer may have different clothes on, the daylight may be different, etc.). Since many students said that they did not need the video anyway, we decided to abandon the synchronized video in future courses. Instead, we have used a feature of Powerpoint to add audio comments to every single slide[1], and distribute the resulting PPT-file as an executable file with an integrated viewer. The viewer allows every student to see the slides with audio comments, search for keywords, or print out slides. This approach improved the maintainability of material since local modifications or deletions affected only the audio comment of the respective slide. Concerning the LMS architecture problem, we think that further research is needed. A reconfigurable architecture for LMSs based on Web services [PV03, PSS04] may help to configure a LMS on-the-fly with functionality needed by particular customer groups.

A specific problem related to software engineering education was encountered in online-testing. At the moment, XML-based e-learning standards for online tests (e.g., QTI [QTI06] which is also used in WebCT) offer descriptions only for a limited number of test types, such as multiple choice or text. For more complex test types that are not supported by the standards (such as the submission of diagrams), one often has to resort to a submission of additional files by email. This requires additional external tools and the files submitted by email complicate the management for a larger number of students. There is also no support in the standards to help online educators correct diagrams, such as for example adding graphical annotations, marking an association or cardinality wrong, or adding missing model elements in a way that students see their old model and the correction in an appropriate way (e.g., in different colors). Such types of exercises are used frequently in our course and are likely needed in other online courses on software engineering. Thus, e-learning standards need to be extended, and future LMSs need to be equipped with better (i.e., integrated) management functionality for diagram submissions and corrections.

---

[1] All slides and audio comments are stored within the same PPT-file.

3.2   Economic Issues

The cost to produce and deliver content suitable for e-learning is often underestimated. Based on our experience, these are some of the most important costs:

1. Costs of the initial setup
2. Costs of creating material
3. Costs of maintaining material
4. Costs of communicating with students
5. Costs of various organizational tasks

Firstly, there are the costs of setting up the overall infrastructure. These include also the license fees for an LMS, travel costs, or costs to attract students.

Secondly, there are the costs of creating educational material, which must contain more detailed explanations than in traditional lectures because of a reduced degree of interactivity in distance education. For the context described above, one learning object for our course with audio comments and exercises took one person about four weeks (full-time) of preparation.

Thirdly, the cost of maintenance is very important, since educational content has to be updated and maintained (e.g., correct mistakes, include new standards and notations such as UML 2, etc.). Our experience so far shows that "old" e-learning content can be difficult to maintain without proper planning at the beginning [PV05]. This is also one of the main problems in e-learning at the moment, since the maintenance phase in the life-cycle of educational content is often "forgotten", assuming that the content will not be changed after its initial creation. If the original sources of material delivered in maintenance-unfriendly formats such as Flash, PDF, or JPG are lost, this inevitably leads to redevelopment from scratch[2]. Creators of software engineering courses sometimes have no choice but to store diagrams as pixel-based images, in order to embed them for example into HTML. Therefore, a clear strategy needs to be developed for the content in the maintenance phase which defines the location of sources and tracing links from them to their corresponding files. It is obvious that well-known concepts of configuration management, tracing, or versioning can and should be borrowed from traditional software development.

Fourthly, communication costs directly affect the choice of pedagogical methods and the way software engineering is taught online, especially with respect to the degree of individual learner support. Qualified teaching assistants have to be available to support the students and correct the exercises. In our course, it turned out that the students had slightly different problems when modeling diagrams using UML, which, despite the available news group, lead to individual emails that required extensive but similar answers to be written by the teaching assistant. Furthermore, it seemed that learners who are willing to pay for e-learning also expect a certain degree of individual support. However, such communication costs increase with the number of students.

---

[2] It is possible to use reverse engineering tools or decompilers (e.g., for Flash) to extract pieces of content to some degree. However, additional effort is needed and the results may be unsatisfactory.

Finally, there are costs produced by organizational tasks, such as the organization of supervised final exams, which can be taken every year at different locations, depending on the geographical region where the most students come from.

3.3 Pedagogical Issues

We have a direct comparison between the course taught online and a course taught in class that partly covers the same modeling techniques. The students in class seem to be better prepared to understand abstract concepts, but sometimes have difficulties with their application in practice. At the VGU, there are two ways to gain experience and apply software engineering theory: on the job *and* doing internships in enterprises that follow the VGU guidelines. The students at the VGU seem to have well-developed practical skills (most of them are on the job), but some of them seemed to have difficulties working with abstract concepts. In our opinion, teaching more complex issues and modeling techniques requires a lot of interaction with the students. Our teaching philosophy encourages exploratory learning. For example, we use vague descriptions in the tasks to "simulate" realistic situations in which users do not specify exactly what they want. The resulting (guided) interaction should uncover the way students find relevant information and the level of needed detail. Unfortunately, this approach was very difficult and impractical for online learning, because it often results in very long individual emails. LMSs need to provide better support for awareness and "mass interactivity" between teachers and students in real-time, such as for example a collaborative development or modification of diagrams.

In the online course, all lecture material was accessible from day one, so that each student could set his/her own pace of learning (no additional books were needed). Exercises are only available for one week. Figure 1 shows the student behavior reconstructed from the WebCT activity logs. In the logs, activities such as "quiz started", "quiz redisplay", "save question X", or "submit quiz" were continuously recorded. As can be observed, activity bursts occurred on the one hand in the evening hours, and on the other hand shortly before the submission deadline. All students were within the same time zone which they did not change during the period of the course. This pattern can be explained by the fact that the students were already on the job (also asked in a questionnaire). However, in a global scenario, many different students might be active in various time zones, which can lead to other activity patterns. From a business perspective, learners (as paying customers) will possibly demand to have teaching assistants available at times when they need them most. Thus, it is conceivable that in the worst case, teaching assistants will have to be available 24-hours a day – a situation resulting from the time lags and the aggregated availability demand patterns in a global scenario.

One final problem we address is that of unsupervised, distributed online testing. To our knowledge, there is no satisfactory solution to this problem, especially on how to prevent cheating effectively. One solution can be to work with partners like the European Computer Driving Licence (ECDL) Foundation [ECD06]

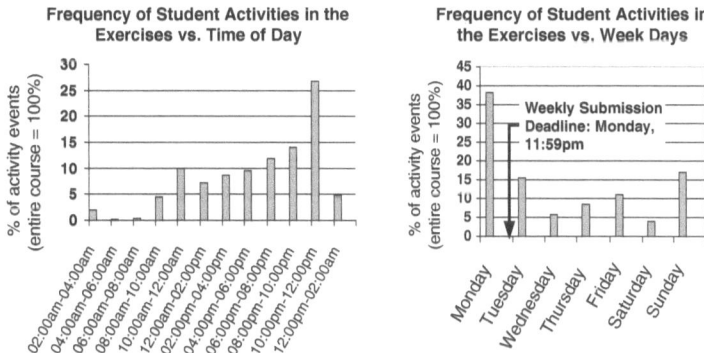

Fig. 1. Student behavior in the course of 2004

which already has a worldwide network of test centers. Another problem in online testing is the usage of multiple choice tests which can be problematic, especially in the context of modeling techniques. The most important step in modeling tasks is the ability to abstract from the real world (which is mostly a textual description in the exercises) and to produce appropriate models. The problem with multiple choice is that the correct model and some additional wrong solutions have to be shown to a student in order to allow him to make a choice. However, since the correct model has to be presented right away, the abstraction step (i.e., how to get from the informal descriptions in the real world to the more precise model) is not solved by the student, but by the educator. Therefore, online tests of this kind may not prepare the students with sufficient problem-solving capabilities. From this point of view, the extension of LMSs and standards to support types of tests that go beyond multiple choice seems necessary.

4   Improving Reuse of Content with Product Lines

We focus below on the technical part of online learning, and in particular, on a more efficient reuse strategy for educational content. Our experience has been that such content is not developed in isolation and that some important parts are also used in other courses (e.g., in class). Furthermore, a successful and sustainable reuse strategy needs planning in advance and should not rely on an opportunistic reuse of components or a "copy-and-paste" approach which, by the way, has already proven unsuccessful for code in software engineering [Bos00]. Empirical studies [NTD03, War03, Fri04] have shown that the current metadata standards used for learning objects do not necessarily improve reuse, since the completion of many parts is optional, and only a few of the many descriptive elements are ever used, sometimes in inconsistent ways. These are again more arguments in favor of a strategy for content reuse.

We briefly describe next the main concepts of software product lines which represent a proactive reuse approach for software. Using these concepts as a foundation, we present thereafter our own approach.

4.1   Software Product Lines

We briefly introduce some ideas and notions from software product lines, which will be used later in our own approach. Software product lines focus on the development of a similar set of programs and follow a proactive reuse approach. They borrow concepts from traditional product lines, such as for example from car manufacturing, where manufacturers use common platforms to create different variants of cars. This requires a longer-term strategy with an explicit definition of the commonality and variability found in product variants. Parnas in the mid-70s [Par01] proposed the idea of program families as a means of organizing reusable components. Since then additional techniques have been suggested to support reuse such as objects, patterns, frameworks, components and architectural styles. However, it has been meanwhile realized that ad-hoc reuse – with no strategic planning in advance – does not really work for software [Bos00].

Although in the beginning some authors distinguished between software product families and software product lines, this distinction is not emphasized any longer, and a consensus of what a software product line is has been reached recently in the following definition [CN02]: "A software product line is a set of software-intensive systems sharing a common, managed set of features that satisfy the specific needs of a particular market segment or mission and that are developed from a common set of core assets in a prescribed way". The definition touches a number of important points for reuse. Firstly, it is realized from the beginning that more than one system is developed, and all systems must have some features in common[3]. Secondly, there are predefined core assets which are used for the creation of a system (i.e., a software product). The same common set of (possibly parameterizable) core assets, which can be artifacts such as code components, architecture descriptions, or test cases, is used for the creation of any system in the product line, and thus the focus of the final creation is often shifted from programming to assembly. Thirdly, there is a "prescribed way", i.e., a predefined strategy and a description (often called a production plan) on how to proceed.

The development process of software product lines is typically divided into domain engineering and application engineering [PBvdL05]. Domain engineering covers aspects related to all products in a product line (these products are actually product variants). Feature diagrams are frequently used to model common and distinct parts of product variants in the product line. Design decisions with respect to concrete configurations are delayed until application engineering [CE00, KLD02]. For example, such a diagram specifies which feature must occur in every program variant, which feature is optional, or which other constraints are there (e.g., if certain choices of features mutually exclude each other). Thereafter, core assets have to be developed (or extracted from existing products) which help to implement the features. In application engineering, the focus is on a single

---

[3] In the marketing literature, product lines are understood to be formed possibly also by other than technical commonalities; they might be related to each other because they are sold to the same customer groups, use the same distribution channels, or fall within certain price ranges. See [KA05] for details.

software product that is configured according to its specific requirements, using an instantiation of the feature model developed in domain engineering. Based on the selected features it is determined which core assets are required to implement them, and if additional assets need to be developed. It is an important goal that the product line is designed in such a way that individual, product-specific extensions (which must also satisfy the overall product line requirements) are rarely needed or realizable with little effort. Furthermore, the possible parameters of the required core assets are bound to concrete values, and the assets are assembled to a final product. At this point, we omit further details on software product lines that would exceed the scope of this article, and refer the interested reader to [CE00, Bos00, JRL00, CN02, PBvdL05].

4.2   The PLANT Approach

The **P**roduct **L**ines for Digit**a**l I**n**formation Produc**t**s (**PLANT**) approach has been developed in our institute to tackle the reuse problem for content in a more general way. We have realized that the problems presented in the previous sections for e-learning also occur in the context of digital information products in general. We understand a *digital information product* to be a product in purely digital form whose core benefit is the delivery of information or education. For information, we adopt the definition given in [LL03], where it is generally understood as data that has been "shaped into a form that is meaningful and useful for human beings". For example, an online newspaper can be regarded as a digital information product whose core benefit is the delivery of news content; as an extended benefit, it may allow full-text search, e-mail alerts, or personalization. In the context of e-learning, we regard learning objects (see Sect. 3) as digital information products. One important aspect is that digital information products may consist of a mix of content and software. For example, current content of educational material may consist of more than just text, since in many cases it incorporates animations (e.g., written in Flash), or programs (e.g., Java applets).

During our preparations of educational material for our lectures and for online learning, we have observed that

1. most content development builds upon existing content;
2. the newly developed versions are often different variants of existing content which have numerous identical parts and few distinctive (i.e., variable) parts; and,
3. the variability of distinct parts is in many cases small or predictable. This experience is similar to that of software systems in the context of software product lines.

The PLANT approach uses these insights to improve reuse for digital information products. The main activity areas of PLANT are depicted in Fig. 2 and are exemplified in the remainder of the article for the education context. The PLANT approach has three perspectives which influence each other: domain engineering, application engineering, and family engineering[4]. *Domain engineering*

---

[4] These are actually sub-processes of the overall development process. However, the word "process" is often omitted in the literature.

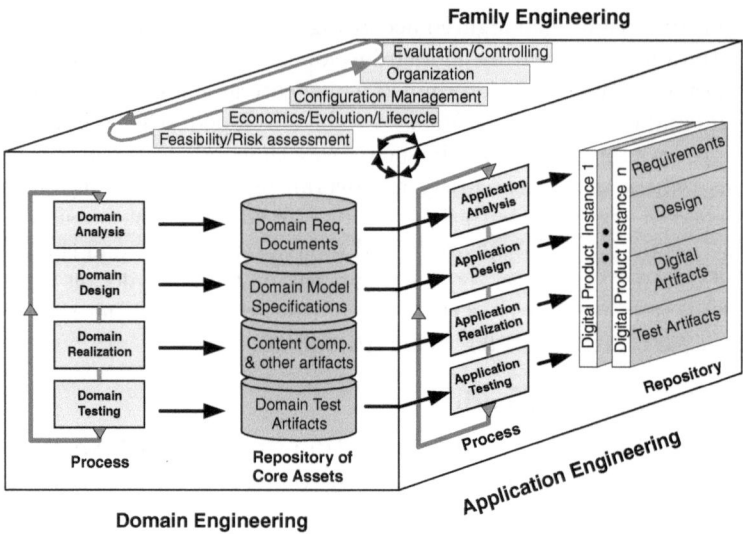

Fig. 2. An overview of the activity areas in the PLANT approach

has a perspective on all products of an entire domain. The biggest part of the overall effort has to be invested here. An important output is the feature model which describes all available features with the commonalities and variabilities of product variants, and which constrains valid feature combinations for a product. The term "feature" is used in this context to denote a related set of material. In addition, all reusable core assets (e.g., content components) which are used to implement the predefined features are defined in domain engineering. A uniform component model is defined for the core assets that represent content components, which specifies how each content component should look like, the level of granularity, uniform layout or metadata guidelines, or other constraints. In practice, content component models could be defined to be for example: an HTML page containing only text; an HTML page with text, videos and Java applets; a PPT file; an XML file with a predefined structure. The key idea is that later, in *application engineering*, most parts of a particular digital information product will be generated and assembled using the predefined core assets. Of course, minor adaptations or extensions are allowed for individual products, but only if they satisfy the product line constraints (i.e., if they do not change the globally defined component model, granularity, layout, or metadata format). In well-designed product line, however, such adaptations will not be done frequently. Using the results from domain engineering, there should be less effort than in a traditional development – the payback of the investment in domain engineering. In PLANT, we stick to the term "application", since as already explained, digital information products may in general consist of a mix of content and software. To manage the data produced throughout the approach, a relational database is used. Furthermore, there are two repositories for domain engineering and application engineering which store the created artifacts; in principle, all artifacts created during domain engineering are core assets. The *family engineering* perspective addresses issues related to the family as a whole and contains activities crosscutting domain engineering and application engineering. The details of each perspective are presented next.

4.2.1   Domain Engineering

The domain engineering process is subdivided into further sub-processes: domain analysis, domain design, domain realization, and domain testing. Their sequence is not intended to be strictly waterfall-like, and if needed, steps backwards are allowed. Throughout the overall development, it is even possible that there are several iterations between two of the sub-processes, before one moves on to the next sub-process.

Domain analysis is a process which scopes the domain and the focus of attention to the relevant parts of the domain of digital information products (e.g., "Information Systems"). In addition, it captures the relevant requirements for all products in the product line, and relates them to the three categories of common, optional, and alternative requirements. *Common requirements* have to be implemented in all information products (e.g., a particular layout that must be used, or content that should be included in all products); *optional requirements* can be implemented in some products (e.g., some specific content); *alternative requirements* define a set of alternatives from which a specified minimum and maximum have to be implemented in a product. Furthermore, a component model for the core assets which represent reusable content is defined, along with the level of granularity that will be uniform for all of these core assets. For example, in our courses a content component is a Powerpoint file which covers a certain topic, and all other content components are kept uniformly on the same abstraction level. We omit in this presentation the related online exercises, which can also be defined to be part of the same content component (the content model is then defined to contain a Powerpoint file and an additional XML file for online exercises). The final product will be a complete course, which will be packaged and delivered in several separate lectures.

Next, *domain design* uses the previously defined requirements to create a feature model of the domain for which educational material should be produced. The feature model defines the possible configuration space for a course in the domain. Although several notations for feature models exist in the area of software product lines (e.g., [KCHP90, CE00]), we have developed an own notation for a feature model (similar to UML) that is better suited for digital information products. We briefly explain the model elements and the semantics of the feature model using Fig. 3 as an example. The model depicted there is a simplified version of our own feature model. The feature model in the PLANT approach is a tree with three types of nodes: domains, atomic features, and crosscutting features, which have unique labels. All leaves are either atomic features or crosscutting features, and domains are inner nodes. *Domains* denote a sub-area of interest (e.g., "DB Modeling") and contain atomic and/or crosscutting features. A domain is used to bundle related features. *Atomic features* represent a content granule that is not subdivided further, and such a feature (e.g., "ER Model" and "Relational Model") is realized later using a predefined content component from the repository of core assets. *Crosscutting features* are modularized pieces of material that will be merged (in a precisely defined manner during application engineering) with all atomic features in their same domain and all sub-domains (e.g., a Powerpoint master file for layout, or a cascading stylesheet for HTML). Crosscutting features cannot occur "alone" – that is, there must be at least one other atomic feature in the same domain or in one sub-domain. Crosscutting features are similar to aspects in aspect-oriented programming [FECA04]. The overall feature model is used to create model "instances" with individual choices for a particular product (in this case, a particular course on information systems). For the creation of an instance, one can imagine that every node has a tag that captures whether it has been selected for that instance. Additional constraints for the selection are imposed by the types *common, optional,* and *alternative,* which belong to domains and atomic features. A *common domain* must be implemented in every product if its parent in the tree is selected to be implemented, and a common domain must contain at least one common feature or one other common domain; the root of the tree represents the domain as a whole and is, by definition, selected for every product instance. An *optional domain* can be selected, if and only if its parent node was selected. It is implied that if an optional domain is selected, then all its directly attached common domains and common features must also be selected. For example, if an educator chooses to cover the domain "Data-Oriented View", then he/she must also select the common feature "Introduction to DB" and the common sub-domain "DB Modeling". An *alternative domain* contains only features of type alternative, and features of this type are only used in alternative domains. If the parent of an alternative domain is selected, then a specified minimum and maximum of alternative features from the alternative domain must be selected; the exact cardinalities are noted in a (min, max) notation after the $<<$ *alternative* $>>$ stereotype. For example, if "Process-Oriented View" is selected, then from "WF Modeling" at least "Petri Nets" or "Event-oriented Process Chains" or both of them have to be selected. More details for the creation of an instance are presented in the part on application engineering.

As an addition to the feature model, all atomic and crosscutting features are linked to a corresponding core asset version graph (Fig. 4). We use this directed, non-cyclic graph at the realization level for artifacts that are used to implement a feature. The graph defines which versions of an artifact are there (nodes), and which other versions evolved from a particular version (using arcs). Versions that are not there yet will be implemented in the ·phases to follow. A node contains for a version additional metadata such as file path, file type, comments, etc. An arc can also have metadata, for example, with comments of what was changed. Every feature in the feature model is linked to exactly one graph, meaning that a particular feature can be implemented by choosing one version from the corresponding core asset version graph. In our case, each atomic feature is linked to a core asset version graph whose nodes reference Powerpoint

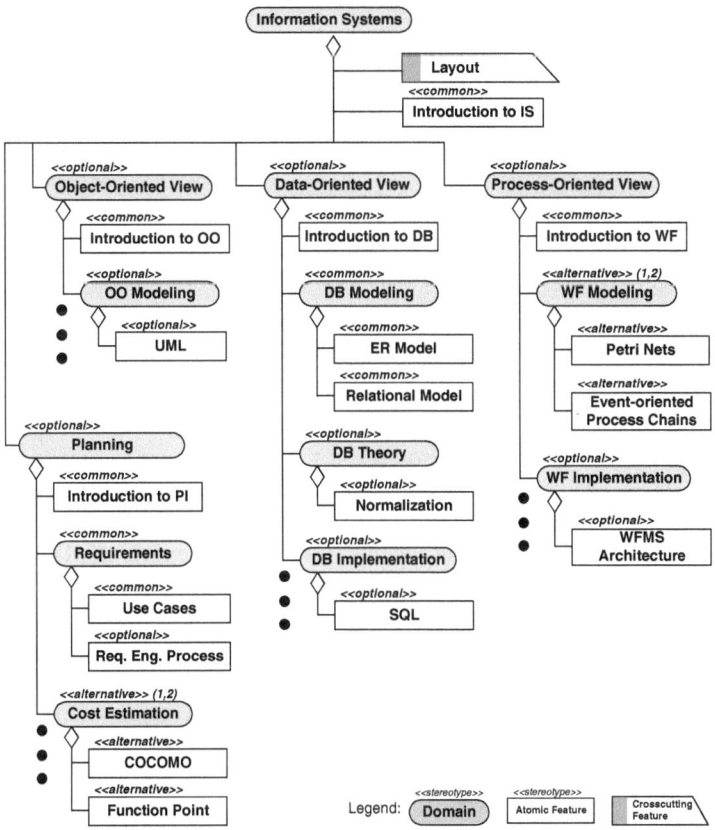

Fig. 3. An example for a feature model for courses in the domain "Information Systems"

files; each crosscutting feature is linked to a core asset version graph whose nodes reference Powerpoint master files (with predetermined layouts). A core asset version graph can be implemented within the aforementioned relational database.

Each product variant can have a different focus on the general area of information systems. As can be observed, the feature model does not specify the order in which features will be built into products, how crosscutting features are merged with atomic features, or how they are digital information products are finally packaged for delivery. For this, we use a separate production plan that is modeled as a workflow based on Petri nets (see [Pet77, Mur89] for an introduction). This workflow is designed in domain modeling for the whole product line and defines how features will be included into courses by calling which programs with which parameters. In addition, the workflow models all possible choices (derived from the feature model) for the configuration of a course. The actual workflow execution is performed later in application engineering. We have extended classical Petri nets to better suit our context: during the workflow

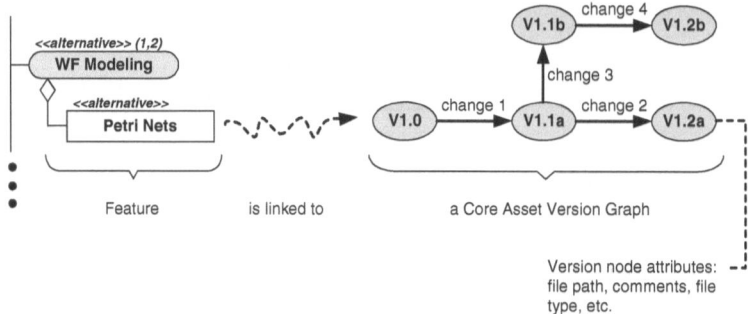

Fig. 4. A core asset version graph for the atomic feature "Petri Nets"

execution, external programs can be called (to construct features), and SQL queries can be executed on a relational database that belongs to the workflow net, for example to automatically update configuration data, insert paths of the created files, or extract data that is handed over to the called programs [OPS05]. As an example for such a workflow specification which consists of places (circles) and transitions (squares), we show a small excerpt in Fig. 5. Transitions represent tasks that can be executed to create a feature of a product. In our context, different Powerpoint files can be appended after each other to create a Powerpoint file for a lecture (e.g, from Fig. 3, "Relational Model" can be inserted after the last slide of "ER Model" to create the lecture for "DB Modeling"). During the execution of a task (i.e., occurrence of a transition), three steps can be executed: 1) updates or inserts can be made on the relational database, for example to mark that a feature was chosen in a course; 2) an external program can be called with some parameters (e.g., a program created in our group that can append a given Powerpoint file to another Powerpoint file, or another program that applies a Powerpoint template on an existing file); 3) other updates/inserts can be made in the relational database, for example to insert a new version number and the path of the created file. The control flow will move on if and only if all three steps have been executed successfully.

In the *domain realization* phase, all core assets used in the product line are created. This can be either from scratch or by reengineering existing material [PV05]. In particular, all content components and all layout files are developed. The content (here: a Powerpoint file) has to satisfy the specifications from the domain analysis phase. If content components or layout files are derived from existing ones, then the corresponding core asset version graphs have to be updated.

In *domain testing*, various methods can be applied to check if the created core assets have the desired properties. For example, content components can be checked whether they are displayed correctly (this is especially important for HTML files displayed on different browsers on different systems). Furthermore, content components should be validated to contain the correct content, and especially make sure that the allowed combinations according to the feature model make sense and do not have "semantic gaps" (e.g., when inside the content something is mentioned that was not introduced before). Another area which

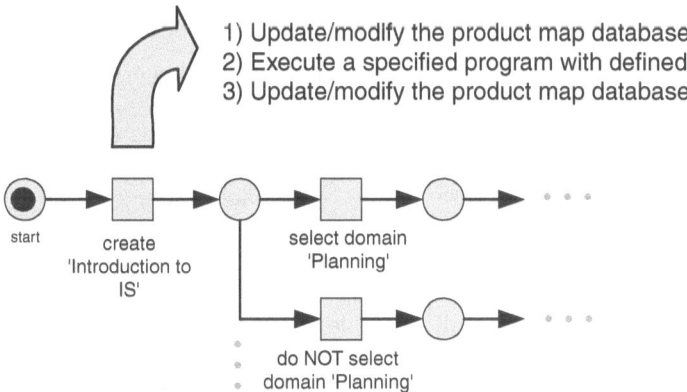

Steps that may occur during execution of a task
(either all successfully or none of them executed)

1) Update/modlfy the product map database
2) Execute a specified program with defined parameters
3) Update/modify the product map database

start   create
'Introduction to
IS'

select domain
'Planning'

do NOT select
domain 'Planning'

Fig. 5. A workflow model for the creation of digital information products

requires testing is for example that of online tests, where various test cases may
be needed.

4.2.2   Application Engineering

The application engineering sub-process has phases similar to domain engineering: application analysis, application design, application realization, and application testing. The difference, however, is that the focus is now on the creation of
a single digital information product, using the artifacts prepared in domain engineering. Furthermore, most of the work consists of configuring and assembling
existing artifacts.

Application analysis captures the requirements relevant for a particular
course, for example the one given in the VGU. Ideally, the requirements of a
particular course should match a subset of the requirements defined in domain
engineering (otherwise, this feedback should be forwarded to domain engineering for corrections). For example, the specific requirement "there should be a
lecture on UML" matches in domain engineering the optional requirement "a
course may provide lectures on UML". According to the collected requirements,
the domain feature model is customized for the application, which is done in
application design.

In *application design* a valid instance of the feature model is created, i.e., valid
sets of features are selected. As an example, we use the model in Fig. 3 and list
some sets of features which occur in valid instances; we omit the root and write
the features contained in domains in parentheses.

$CourseVariant_1$:= {Layout, Introduction to IS, Planing (Introduction to Planning, Requirements(Use Cases)), Object-Oriented View (Introduction to OO, OO
Modeling(UML)), Data-Oriented View (Introduction to DB, DB Modeling (ER
Model, Relational Model)), Process-Oriented View (Introduction to WF, WF Modeling (Petri Nets))}

$CourseVariant_2$:= {Layout, Introduction to IS, Data-Oriented View (Introduction to DB, DB Modeling (ER Model, Relational Model), DB Theory (Normalization), DB Implementation (SQL)) }

An instance of the feature model contains only the features that will be available in one final course. As can be seen in the example, the feature model has enough flexibility to allow the creation of courses with a different focus (more general vs. more specialized), with the advantage that the management of the material sources can be planned and reuse can be coordinated more systematically. Before the construction workflow can be executed, a more detailed specification is needed to define which core asset will be used to realize which feature. The PLANT approach uses for this a *product map* as shown in Fig. 6. In principle, the product map is a matrix where all available features are listed in rows (with headings on the left), and all products (or courses) to be developed are listed in columns (with headings at the top). Furthermore, the domains to which the features belong to are also shown (based on the feature model), although the domains are not an essential part of the product map. In a "cell" at an intersection of a row and a column, a version number of a core asset can be inserted to denote that a particular feature is implemented in a particular product using a specific version from the core asset version graph of that feature. The feature model imposes for a product the constraints in which cells version numbers can be inserted, depending on already inserted version numbers.

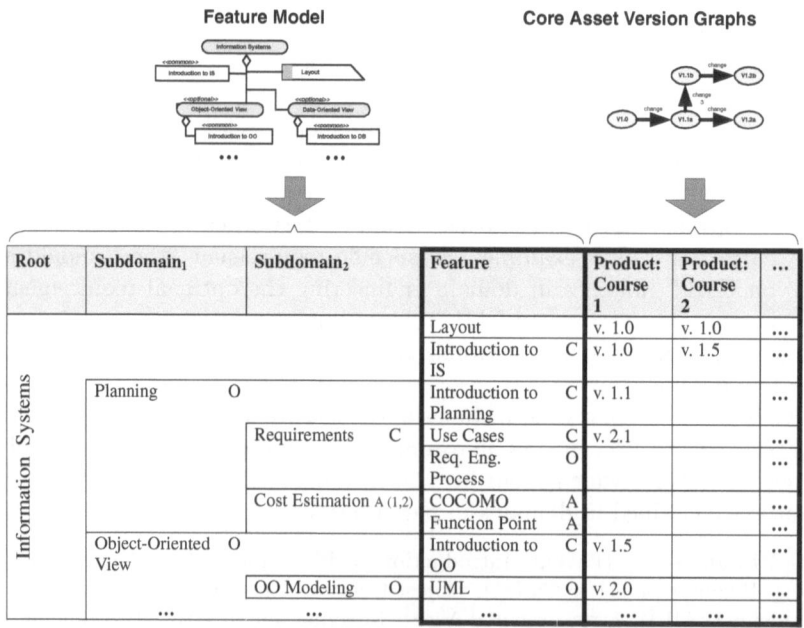

Fig. 6. A product map

In *application realization* the concrete course is created using the production plan defined in domain engineering. In principle, the existing workflow specification is only adapted to use the particular core asset versions from the product map, and to produce the packages of material as desired (e.g., the whole course in one file, several files for every lecture, or create ZIP packages out of several created files). Then, the workflow is executed.

Finally, in *application testing* the resulting courses have to be checked if they were generated correctly.

4.2.3   Family Engineering

In PLANT, family engineering focuses on tasks that concern the product line as a whole. It is assumed that after the initiation of the product line, the sequence of sub-processes is executed at specified time intervals, realizing a monitoring function for the product line.

Initially, the *feasibility and risk assessment* evaluates if a product line makes sense for digital products in a domain, and if the domain is stable enough (otherwise, frequent and tedious changes may be necessary).

Thereafter, an *economic analysis* should clarify whether it is more profitable to have a product line or several independent products. This can be analyzed for example using the net present values of the estimated profits (see [BMM03]) with and without the product line. The *evolution* has to be anticipated and planned, i.e., which extensions will likely be needed in the future, and how this will affect domain and application engineering. *Lifecycle* planning may define life spans for particular digital information products or the product line as a whole.

Next, *configuration management* can be considered from two perspectives: market-based and product-based. The market-based view summarizes which product configurations are demanded by customers – in our case, which courses should be given within the faculty and the department. This has to be transferred to the product-based view (realized in domain and application engineering) which defines the technical details. In principle, the aforementioned product map is the technical implementation needed for the product-based view of configuration management. The management has to make sure that the market-based and product-based view match sufficiently.

Another important issue is the management and the set-up of a running *organization* that supports product lines, i.e., who is responsible for domain and application engineering, how and when certain activities are performed, etc. Depending on the growth of the product line, it has to be continuously regularly whether the current form and the number of staff is still efficient. Furthermore, quantitative metrics have to be defined, for example how to measure progress, efficiency, profitability – these may depend on the specific application context.

The *evaluation and controlling* phase monitors the development and checks whether all assumptions made in the beginning are still valid.

4.2.4   Initiating PLANT

We briefly sketch how to proceed when the PLANT approach is initiated (c.f. Fig. 7). The process is initiated in family engineering. Here, the sub-processes

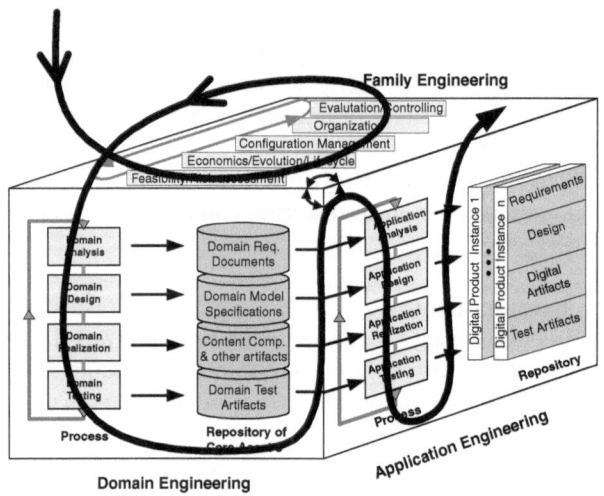

Fig. 7. Initiation of the PLANT approach

feasibility/risk assessment, economics/evolution/lifecycle, configuration management (market-based view), organization, and evaluation/controlling are executed. Then, if there is a decision in favor of the product line approach, the work of domain engineering can begin with domain analysis, domain design, domain realization, and domain testing. After the first pass of domain engineering, there is a base of artifacts for future use. After this, individual products can be created in application engineering, in which application analysis, application design, application realization, and application testing are executed for every product. After the creation of a product, the control is handed over to family engineering. The consecutive phases in family engineering are executed at specified time intervals, or triggered by predefined events, e.g., finishing a pass of domain or application engineering.

5 Conclusion

We addresses problems and challenges that are currently encountered in online education, and in particular we present our experience from our own course on information systems development which is taught entirely online at the Virtual Global University (VGU). In this context, we address several issues of general interest from a technical, economic, and pedagogical point of view. On the technical side we have identified a strong need for a reuse strategy for content in education. The strategy we propose here – Product Lines for Digital Information Products (PLANT) – tackles the reuse problem for content and borrows ideas from the area of software product lines with a planned and proactively coordinated reuse.

With the focus on the technical side, we aimed to illustrate that during the development of educational material, systematic approaches from software engineering can indeed be applied. A systematic development and a reuse approach becomes in the future even more important, as the complexity of educational content and the effort needed to produce content continues to grow. Although we have presented the PLANT approach in the context of online learning, we mention that it is general enough to manage content reuse and to be applied also in other contexts of digital information products, such as for example for digital newspapers or audio books. In our institute, there is ongoing research on the PLANT approach, especially with respect to tool support for the efficient management and execution of workflow models, as well as process reuse during the construction of digital information products.

References

[ACP02]   H.H. Adelsberger, B. Collis, and J.M. Pawlowski, editors. *Handbook on Information Technologies for Education and Training.* Springer-Verlag, Berlin, 2002.

[BMM03]   Richard A. Brealey, Stewart C. Myers, and Alan J. Marcus. *Fundamentals of Corporate Finance.* McGraw-Hill/Irwin, 2003.

[Bos00]   Jan Bosch. *Design and Use of Software Architectures.* Addison-Wesley Professional, 2000.

[CE00]   Krzysztof Czarnecki and Ulrich Eisenecker. *Generative Programming: Methods, Tools, and Applications.* Addison-Wesley Professional, 2000.

[CN02]   Paul Clements and Linda M. Northrop. *Software Product Lines: Practices and Patterns.* The SEI Series in Software Engineering. Addison Wesley Professional, August 20 2002.

[ECD06]   European Computer Driving Licence (ECDL) Foundation. http://www.ecdl.com, February 2006.

[FECA04]   Robert Filman, Tzilla Elrad, Siobhan Clarke, and Mehmet Aksit. *Aspect-Oriented Software Development.* Addison Wesley Professional, 2004.

[Fri04]   Norm Friesen. Final report on the "International LOM Survey". Technical report, ISO/IEC JTC1 SC36 N0871, September 8 2004.

[JRL00]   Mehdi Jazayeri, Alexander Ran, and Frank Van Der Linden. *Software Architecture for Product Families: Principles and Practice.* Addison-Wesley, 2000.

[KA05]   Philip Kotler and Gary Armstrong. *Principles of Marketing.* Prentice Hall, 11th edition, 2005.

[KCHP90]   Kyo C. Kang, Sholom G. Cohen, James A. Hess, and William E. Novakand A. Spencer Peterson. Feature-Oriented Domain Analysis (FODA) Feasibility Study. Technical Report CMU/SEI-90-TR-21, ESD-90-TR-222, Software Engineering Institute, Carnegie Mellon University, Pittsburgh, Pennsylvania, November 1990.

[KLD02]   K.C. Kang, J. Lee, and P. Donohoe. Feature-oriented product line engineering. *IEEE Software*, 19(4):58–65, 2002.

[LL03]   Jane Laudon and Kenneth Laudon. *Management Information Systems (International Edition).* Prentice Hall, 8th edition, 2003.

[Mur89]   T. Murata. Petri nets: Properties, analysis and applications. In *Proc. IEEE*, volume 77, pages 541–580, 1989.

[NTD03]   Jehad Najjar, Stefaan Ternier, and Erik Duval. The actual use of metadata in ARIADNE: an empirical analysis. In *Proceedings of the 3rd Annual ARIADNE Conference*, pages 1–6. ARIADNE Foundation, 2003.

[OPS05]   Andreas Oberweis, Victor Pankratius, and Wolffried Stucky. Product lines in e-learning. Technical Report 501, Institute for Applied Informatics and Formal Description Methods, University of Karlsruhe, Germany, August 2005. ISBN 398104410X.

[Par01]   David L. Parnas. On the design and development of program families. In Daniel M. Hoffmann and David M. Weiss, editors, *Software Fundamentals. Collected Papers by David L. Parnas*, pages 193–213. Addison-Wesley, 2001.

[PBvdL05] Klaus Pohl, Günter Böckle, and Frank J. van der Linden. *Software Product Line Engineering: Foundations, Principles and Techniques*. Springer, 2005.

[Pet77]   James L. Peterson. Petri nets. *ACM Computing Surveys*, 9(3):223–252, 1977.

[Pow06]   Powerpoint Producer. http://www.microsoft.com/office/powerpoint/producer, February 2006.

[PS05]   Victor Pankratius and Wolffried Stucky. Information systems development at the virtual global university: an experience report. In *ICSE '05: Proceedings of the 27th international conference on Software engineering*, New York, NY, USA, 2005. ACM Press.

[PSS04]   Victor Pankratius, Olivier Sandel, and Wolffried Stucky. Retrieving content with agents in web service e-learning systems. In *The Symposium on Professional Practice in AI, IFIP WG12.6*, Toulouse, France, August 2004.

[PV03]   Victor Pankratius and Gottfried Vossen. Towards e-learning grids: Using grid computing in electronic learning. In *IEEE Workshop on Knowledge Grid and Grid Intelligence, IEEE/WIC International Conference on Web Intelligence*, pages 4–15, Halifax, Nova Scotia, Canada, October 2003. Saint Mary's University.

[PV05]   Victor Pankratius and Gottfried Vossen. Reengineering of educational material: A systematic approach. *International Journal of Knowledge and Learning (IJKL)*, 1(3):229–248, 2005.

[QTI06]   IMS Question & Test Interoperability Specification. http://www.imsglobal.org/question/, February 2006.

[VGU06]   Virtual Global University (VGU). School of Business Informatics. http://www.vg-u.de, February 2006.

[War03]   J. Ward. A quantitative analysis of unqualified Dublin Core metadata element set usage within data providers registered with the Open Archive Initiative. In *Proceedings of the 2003 Joint Conference on Digital Libraries*, pages 315–317, Houston, May 27–31 2003. IEEE Computer Society.

[Web06]   WebCT. http://www.webct.com/, February 2006.

Informatics: A Novel, Contextualized Approach to Software Engineering Education

André van der Hoek, David G. Kay, and Debra J. Richardson

Department of Informatics, Donald Bren School of Information and Computer Sciences
University of California, Irvine
Irvine, CA 92697-3440 USA
{andre, kay, djr}@ics.uci.edu

Abstract. Over the past decade, it has been established that a good education in software engineering requires a specialized program of study different from traditional computer science programs. What should constitute such a specialized program of study, however, is still a matter of debate. Here we bring to this debate a new perspective that describes how we believe software engineering education should be framed, namely through the *context* in which software eventually is placed. That is, we must study software *and* information, development *and* design, technical *and* social issues, synthesis *and* analysis. At UC Irvine, we have designed and now offer a program of study that provides this focus – a four-year B.S. degree in Informatics. In this paper, we present our view of software engineering education, the principles underlying our Informatics curriculum, an overview of the curriculum itself and its pedagogy, some reflections on our experiences to date, and a concluding list of challenges that our approach addresses and that are critical for any approach to software engineering education.

1 Introduction

While software engineering has been a discipline for several decades, software engineering education is only now coming into its own. It is no longer considered adequate for software engineering to be relegated to one or two courses that are part of a traditional computer science education. Rather, it has been established, both philosophically and through experience, that an effective software engineering education requires a specialized program of study [1]. Such specialized programs are now appearing at universities around the world.

But deciding on exactly what to teach and how to teach it is difficult. Such decisions must be guided by an overall philosophy of how to frame the material for students. The McMaster University undergraduate degree in software engineering exemplifies one such framing, which is built from a mathematical and engineering perspective [2]. Based on a first year that rigorously introduces students to mathematical and engineering principles, subsequent years introduce a host of software engineering topics by rooting them in the underlying theory (while still addressing the practical side of the discipline, naturally). This kind of framing is not uncommon,

P. Inverardi and M. Jazayeri (Eds.): ICSE 2005 Education Track, LNCS 4309, pp. 147 – 165, 2006.

since many view software engineering as an intrinsic engineering discipline that must therefore share its principles with other engineering disciplines.

A second framing is provided by the ACM/IEEE curricular guidelines for software engineering education [3]. These guidelines break down software engineering into a set of closely-related fundamental knowledge areas, each refined into detailed topics to be addressed by a software engineering curriculum. The fundamental knowledge areas focus explicitly on the topic of software construction, covering both technical aspects of software design and implementation and managerial aspects of the broader process involved. Informally examining various software engineering degree programs seems to indicate that, compared to the mathematical and engineering approach described above, the ACM/IEEE guidelines are the more widely adopted model curriculum to date.

In this paper, we present a new, third framing of a software engineering curriculum, one that we have instituted at UC Irvine in a new four-year degree program, a Bachelor of Science in Informatics. What distinguishes our approach is a central focus on *the context in which software will eventually be situated*. That is, we root our approach in the personal, organizational, and societal realities of software. This broadens software engineering education from a focus on software only to a focus on software and on the information that the software manages, from development only to development and design, from technical issues only to technical and social issues, and, finally, from synthesis only to synthesis and analysis. The first factor of each of these four pairs (i.e., software, development, technical issues, and synthesis) tends to be the focus of existing software engineering programs. In our Informatics major, this focus is complemented by an equally strong focus on the other four factors: information, design, social issues, and analysis. The result is a broader kind of software engineering education that we put in the appropriate context of designing solutions, incorporating human and organizational needs, and taking a multi-disciplinary approach to the field.

The remainder of this paper is structured as follows. In Section 2, we further detail our vision of Informatics and its underlying principles as an alternative way to frame software engineering education. Section 3 presents our curriculum and Section 4 the various pedagogical issues involved in delivering the curriculum. Section 5 reflects upon our experiences to date and Section 6 presents some challenges we have encountered that, we believe, must be addressed by any effective SE curriculum. We conclude in Section 7 with our plans for future work and our hopes for the future of software engineering education.

2   Our Perspective and Principles

We begin the discussion of our perspective on software engineering education with a look at the ACM 2005 Computing Curricula document [1]. It attempts to provide perspective by partitioning the broad field of computing into several subdisciplines; we reproduce their result in Figure 1 and refer the reader to the CC 2005 document for their definitions of the subdiscipline boundaries. We note that software engineering has achieved a place, but we also note the lack of connection between software engineering and information technology. This gap may exist because computer science schools tend to offer the majors shown towards the left of the figure while business schools tend to offer those towards the right. One might even contend that this reflects an appropriate separation of concerns. However, we take the opposite view. We argue that the *context* in which the software will be situated profoundly affects the nature of software and of the processes we use to create it. Figure 1 exposes this gap; in Figure 2 we correct it, completing the picture and illuminating the core principle of our approach: explicit consideration of context is essential, both in the practice of software engineering and in the education of its practitioners.

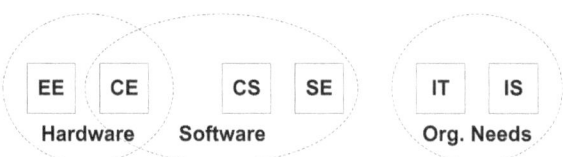

Fig. 1. Original Division of Disciplines from Computing Curricula 2005

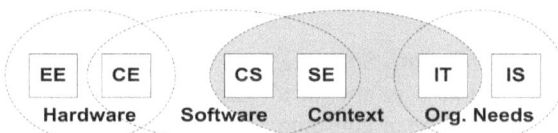

Fig. 2. Disciplines from Computing Curriculum 2005, Emphasizing the Context for Software Design and Development

Consideration of the surrounding context appears in more traditional CS and IT programs as well — for example, as an HCI course in a CS major or an organizational impacts course in IT. The way to read Figure 2, then, is that each of the ovals frames the degree programs contained in it. Hardware is the key framing for electrical engineering, as are organizational needs for information systems. For the degree programs "in the middle", multiple framing factors exist and must be taken into consideration. Typically, though, one of those factors dominates. For computer science, this dominating factor is software, and for information technology, it is organizational needs. For software engineering, it is the context in which the software will be deployed. After all, the success of software engineering is measured not by the software we develop, but by how well that software addresses the contextual problem at hand.

At UC Irvine, we have created and instituted a new degree program that focuses on context: our new B.S. in Informatics. We define Informatics as the study of the design, application, use, and impact of information technology. Not surprisingly, then, at its core Informatics resembles software engineering, but this is augmented by many additional courses that broaden the focus (see Section 3) and by a different pedagogy that roots the delivery of the software engineering topics in context (see Section 4). To put this in perspective, we return to the ACM 2005 Computing Curricula document. It presents a series of diagrams that show the various areas of concern for different degree programs and further describes their focus as more theoretical or more practice-oriented. In Figure 3, we have reproduced those diagrams and added one diagram that shows the focus of Informatics. (The field of Electrical Engineering does not appear here, or in the source document, as EE addresses topics such as circuit theory that are outside the computing disciplines.) Informatics appears at the appropriate location in the continuum from hardware to information. Compared to a traditional software engineering degree, we note that Informatics has an equivalently strong focus on application technologies and software development, a less strong focus on systems infrastructure, and a stronger focus on organizational and systems issues. In Section 3, we further detail this focus in terms of the courses that we offer in the Informatics curriculum.

With the position of Informatics established, we now return to our definition of Informatics as the study of the design, application, use, and impact of information technology and derive the four principles that guided us in constructing our degree program. Each principle balances a traditional software engineering topic with an appropriate focus on context. In particular, we relate software and information, development and design, technical issues and social issues, and synthesis and analysis.

1. **Software and information.** Software is never a goal in and of itself. Instead, the real goal of software is always to manage some kind of information (by "manage," we broadly mean consume, produce, transform, visualize, store, recall, and similar activities). As such, software always provides its services as part of a larger system. Often its design requires careful consideration of how the software's management of information will affect the real world—not only when it fails but also when it behaves as desired. *Our first principle is that software engineering education must always place software in the context of the information it manages.*

2. **Development and design.** Existing educational programs tend to focus strongly on teaching the overall software development process. The development process is an essential topic, but typical programs address each of the lifecycle phases equally. Furthermore, programs tend to frame design education in notations for documenting a design, typically with little design practice attached. This is shortsighted. At its core, software engineering is a design discipline, one in which the creative process of designing a solution is a central, yet very difficult, activity. The difficulty of design must be addressed explicitly by teaching of principles, learning from case studies, and extensive practice—not with notations alone. *Our second principle is that software engineering education must place development in the context of design; that is, it must treat software engineering as a design discipline.*

3. **Technical issues and social issues.** Software engineering is not just a technical discipline. While technical issues form a vital core, they should not be the only issues we consider. Software is always placed in social settings, and we must address those as an integral part of our teaching. This is not the same as just inserting a human-computer interaction course, though that is an important part of

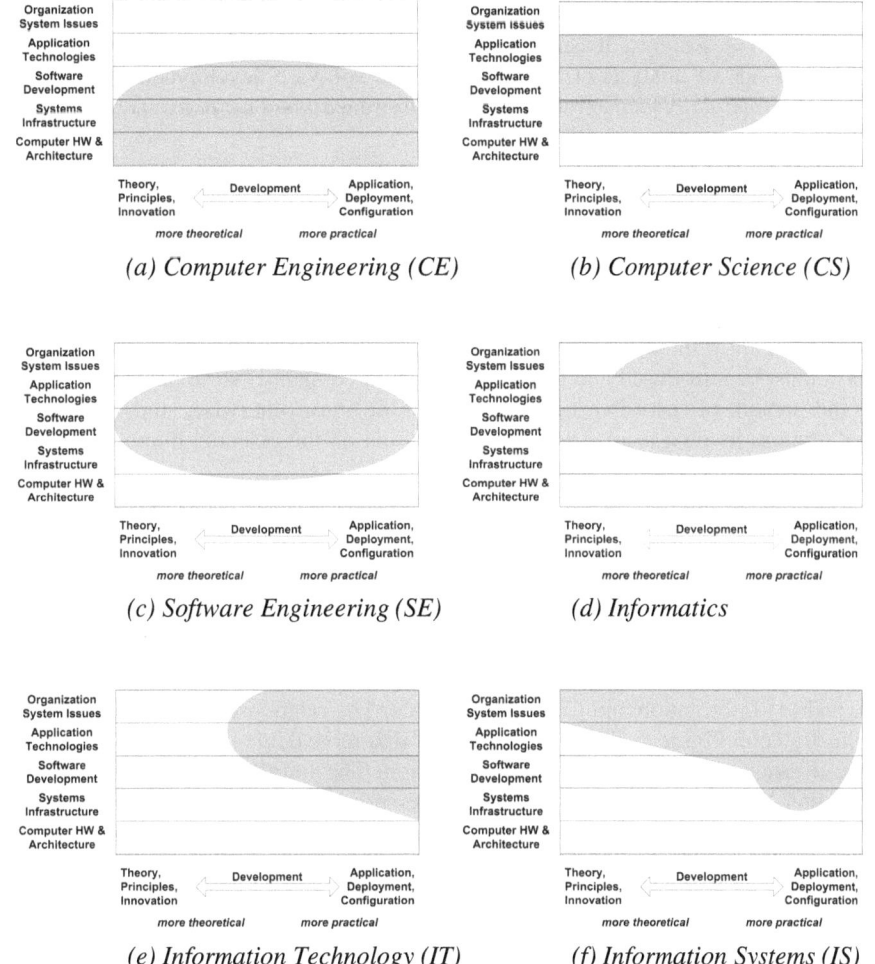

Fig. 3. Areas of Concern for Various Degree Programs

software engineering education. The need for educating students about social issues goes much farther and must include extensive treatment of topics such as organizational impact, cultural differences, and social responsibility (e.g., ethics, privacy, and security concerns). *Our third principle is that software engineering education must place technical solutions in the context of the social structures in which those solutions will operate.*

4. **Synthesis and analysis.** At the heart of software engineering lies our ability actually to construct software. Such construction, however, must be accompanied by careful analysis – both before and after construction. By this we do not mean

only algorithm analysis, requirements gathering, or testing; we also include organizational assessments, feasibility studies, cost analyses, user studies, and so on. These kinds of analysis critically inform the software development process. *Our fourth principle is that software engineering education must place its focus on synthesis in the context of analysis.*

Following these principles, we designed the Informatics curriculum as described below. The result is an education that provides much broader perspective than traditional software engineering alone. We further note that any degree program wishing to address these principles must address them from all eight perspectives—software, information, development, design, technical issues, social issues, synthesis, analysis—and employ those perspectives pervasively throughout the entire program. The topics must be introduced and taught in an integrated manner so students will appreciate the breadth of software engineering from the start; otherwise, students will treat each topic as its own insular domain, missing out on the essential interconnectedness in the discipline.

3   Our Curriculum

The Informatics major is one of four majors offered in the Donald Bren School of Information and Computer Sciences: (1) Computer Science and Engineering, jointly with the Henry Samueli School of Engineering, (2) Computer Science, (3) Informatics, and (4) Information and Computer Science. The relationship among these majors is illustrated in Figure 4. We observe that the first three degree programs adhere to the topic divisions laid out in the previous section. The fourth degree, Information and Computer Science, is the original degree offered by the school. The school continues to offer this highly configurable major, since it serves students who want to sample courses across the spectrum (although it sacrifices some depth for the breadth it affords).

The major in Informatics is a four-year undergraduate bachelor of science degree [4]. Courses at UC Irvine are offered in three ten-week quarters per academic year. (A summer session is also offered, but summer attendance is not required. Students typically use the summer to catch up with courses they missed or to push ahead if they are on an accelerated schedule.)

Table 1 shows the entire four-year Informatics curriculum at a glance. Unlabeled courses are offered by faculty in the Department of Informatics, which is the academic home for the major. Courses typically taught by faculty in the Computer Science Department, the sister department to the Department of Informatics, are designated (cs). Courses offered outside of the Bren School of Information and Computer Sciences are designated (o) or (b), depending on whether the course is specifically required for the Informatics major or a course that students can freely choose to satisfy UC Irvine's breadth (general education) requirements. Finally, as we will discuss below, light grey shading indicates courses with significant treatment of software's broader context.

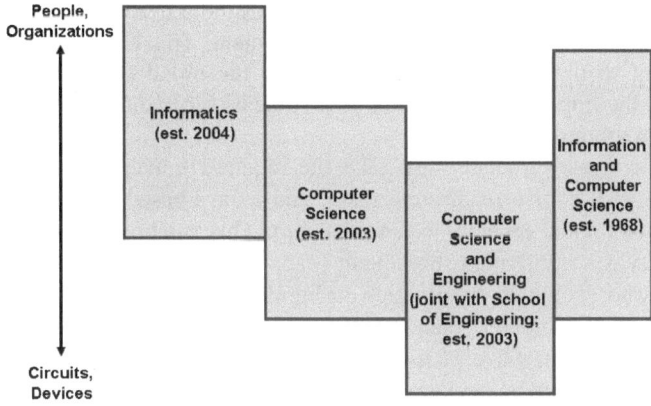

Fig. 4. Areas of Concern for UC Irvine Degree Programs in Computing

At the center of the first-year program is the year-long Informatics Core Course, a broad introduction to the field that carries a 50% higher unit load than the typical course at UC Irvine. The first two quarters introduce programming in Scheme and in Java[1] and include conventional first-year data structure and algorithms topics, but beyond that they also give students a background in the fundamentals of computing technology (the Internet and the Web, a functional overview of operating systems, exposure to machine-level instructions and programming, bit-level and higher-level data representation) and opportunities (particularly via case studies) to approach broader, contextual issues such as human-computer interaction and the social and organizational impact of computing. The third quarter of the Core Course is an introduction to software engineering with a strong emphasis on design alternatives. Also in the third quarter,

---

[1] Our choice of programming languages was driven by our overall goals for the programming portion of the year-long course. Beyond building students' programming skills, we want the material to be accessible to students without prior experience, to provide a design methodology rather than leaving students to flail at their code without direction, to emphasize high-level concepts like design and abstraction over low-level coding details (while still producing executable programs), and to foster students' appreciation for the variety of tools available and the criteria for selecting the most appropriate for a given task. We find that first-year students often feel swamped by the sheer volume of small details they must master. As novices, they have yet to develop any conceptual framework for organizing those details and deciding which are important in a given situation. When every asterisk, semicolon, or brace may carry crucial semantic information, confusion abounds. The syntactic and semantic simplicity of Scheme minimize this confusion, allowing an early concentration on data abstraction and program design (which in turn provides an excellent foundation for object-oriented programming and design). We also find that a two-language approach helps students distinguish between fundamental concepts and mere language artifacts, reduces their tendency to be uncritical fans of the first language they learn, and helps them avoid looking at every problem from the perspective of a single language's features and idioms. We cover Scheme in the first quarter and migrate to Java as a mainstream, industrial-strength language in the second quarter.

students take a half-course seminar that introduces them to the research interests and projects of the faculty in the Informatics Department. This comes relatively early in their program so they get an early exposure to the broad possibilities in the field (overcoming the impression some first-year students receive that computer science is only about programming).

In their first year, students also take the required university writing courses, a course in logic, a course in discrete math, and a Java-based course in intermediate data structures (at the level of balanced trees). This establishes some fundamental skills that they will build on in subsequent years.

Students who decide on Informatics during their first year, having enrolled in another introductory computer science course sequence, will generally be permitted to apply that sequence in place of the Informatics Core Course. While these students will not have the complete background we would prefer, we felt this was outweighed by the advantages of allowing a seamless transfer into the Informatics program.

The anchor of the second year is a three-quarter series in software engineering: a course in software methods and tools, one in requirements, and one in specification and quality engineering. Students also take a two-quarter sequence in programming languages (considering not only different programming paradigms and language implementation details but also domain-specific languages and scripting languages), a two-quarter sequence in human-computer interaction, a course in statistics, and the first quarter of a series on software design.

This year provides students with many practical tools and techniques, approaches they will use in their later work. But these courses emphasize the underlying concepts: what is the problem, what are the symptoms, what are the underlying issues, what is the spectrum of potential approaches to address the problem, what are the characteristics of those approaches, why might we choose one approach over another, and so on. Only after we introduce those concepts do we hone the practical skills with specific exercises using particular tools and methodologies. The result is that students, after the second year, have at their disposal a portfolio of foundational techniques and skills that further establish the discipline of Informatics.

The third year, aside from university breadth requirements and electives, includes a three-quarter series on the social and organizational impact of computing, culminating in a field-study project course. This series provides the broadest context, ranging from privacy and intellectual property through organizational issues and methodology for conducting field studies. The year also includes the second course on software design, a course on designing software architectures and distributed systems, and a first course on databases. This year is key to the curriculum in terms of design, examining it from two perspectives: social and technical. Each course introduces students to the issues involved from one perspective, but weaves in some from the other perspective to properly balance the presentation of the material.

The fourth year includes a three-quarter capstone course, a database project course, a project management course, a course on computer-supported collaborative work, and a pair of courses on information retrieval and visualization. The capstone course is a year-long senior design project in which student teams work with real clients to specify and implement a realistic system. Under the supervision of an interdisciplinary faculty team, students must bring together material from previous years (tools, skills, processes, ethnographic methods, design approaches, and many others) to complete their project successfully.

Returning to our principles, we have shaded in Table 1 the courses where context plays a significant role. Ideally, this would occur in every single course, but that would be unrealistic. Some courses are offered by another department, which does not always share our vision with respect to the importance of context, focusing instead on the traditional and theoretical aspects of computer science. Other courses present basic software

Table 1. Required Curriculum for the UC Irvine B.S. in Informatics

	Fall	*Winter*	*Spring*
First	Informatics Core	Informatics Core	Informatics Core
			Informatics Research Topics Seminar
	(o) Critical Reasoning	(o) Discrete Mathematics	(cs) Fundamental Data Structures
	(b) Writing	(b) Writing	(b) Writing
Second	(o) Statistics	Human-Computer Interaction	Project in Human-Computer Interaction and User Interfaces
	(cs) Concepts Programming Languages I	Concepts Programming Languages II	Software Design I
	Software Methods and Tools	Requirements Analysis & Engineering	Software Specification and Quality Engineering
	(b) Breadth	(b) Breadth	(b) Breadth
Third	Social Analysis of Computerization	Organizational Information Systems	Project Social and Organizational Impacts of Computing
	Software Design II	Software Architecture, Distributed Systems, and Interoperability	(cs) File and Database Management
	(b) Breadth	(b) Breadth	(b) Breadth
	(b) Breadth / Elective	(b) Breadth / Elective	(b) Breadth / Elective
Fourth	Senior Design Project	Senior Design Project	Senior Design Project
	(cs) Project in Database Management	(cs) Information Retrieval	Information Visualization
	Project Management	CSCW	(b) Breadth/ Elective
	(b) Breadth / Elective	(b) Breadth / Elective	(b) Breadth / Elective

engineering techniques; these courses are foundational and focus mainly on introducing the concepts behind the techniques and exemplifying their application. Nonetheless, most of our courses, from the first-year introductory course to the final capstone project, take a contextualized approach.

Examining our principles in more detail, we make the following observations:

1. **Software and information.** Information plays a critical role throughout the curriculum. It is the prime topic in the two-course database sequence and the information retrieval and visualization courses. But our coverage goes much beyond that. In the introductory course sequence, for example, we avoid the traditional programming-only approach in favor of one where projects are presented and addressed in terms of information needs (e.g., a project to enhance the design of a web store first involves considering the proper information flow and then examines the technical details of how this information flow is supported). The two software design courses are another example of courses in which information plays a critical role: The case studies and assignments focus on defining the information needs and then working those into software solutions.

2. **Development and design.** Some part of the curriculum has to introduce the development focus. We do this in the third course of the Informatics Core series and in the second-year software engineering series. Beyond that, however, design takes center stage throughout the curriculum. We paid particular attention to design in the introductory course. While students certainly are not asked to perform full-fledged design exercises, the materials are presented and exercised from a design point of view, which we deem critical to instill a sense of design right from the beginning of the major. A subtle but important example of how our design focus influences the courses and material we teach is the Concepts in Programming Languages II course. While a traditional course like this would focus on the construction and operation of compilers, our course is more about "little languages". By this we mean that quite often one is forced to incorporate some kind of mini-language in a design solution, whether directly exposed to the users or internally processed. Our course is about choosing the appropriate kind of language for a particular task, including situations where a solution requires some kind of mini-language designed and built for that task.

3. **Technical issues and social issues.** The three-quarter series on the social and organizational impact of computing, offered in the third year, is the primary place where students will learn about the social issues involved in software development. This series covers in detail topics such as privacy and intellectual property; social, ethical, and cultural differences and issues; and organizational issues and methodology for conducting field studies. That said, the material is truly put to the test in their senior design capstone course, where they will be designing and implementing actual systems that will have to pay attention to these factors. In addition, the first year Informatics Core course provides the students with a preview of these issues and the courses on human-computer interaction also pay attention to these factors even though these courses focus more on the actualities of user interface design.

4. **Synthesis and analysis.** Analysis returns in many forms throughout the curriculum, both with respect to the internal structure of a design or process and the externally visible properties of the software Analysis of the internal structure occurs, for example, in the design courses, which focus heavily on how to make informed tradeoffs. Analysis of the external manifestations of software occurs in the HCI course, where students learn how to perform user studies, and in the Social Analysis course, where students learn to recognize and analyze the effects of technology on individuals, organizations, and society.

Additionally, the Informatics program includes courses in logic, discrete mathematics, and statistics. The technical and mathematical underpinnings of the field form an essential component of the program; these skills are necessary for performing statistical analyses for user studies and certain tradeoff analyses of alternative design choices. Our choice, however, is not to promote additional math as a mechanism to raise "mathematical maturity" or to make the major "more rigorous". It is our belief that these more general benefits attributed to math can also be achieved in other ways, and in particular through building these skills in the domain in which they will be applied. In our case, this is through the study of the design, application, use, and impact of information technology. By framing software engineering through the consideration of context, the topic is sufficiently rich to challenge the students deeply and instill in them a strong sense of critical thinking.

4 Pedagogy

A program as diverse as Informatics must be taught in an interdisciplinary way by an interdisciplinary faculty. The Department of Informatics is composed of individual faculty members with diverse backgrounds, including law, programming languages, computer-supported cooperative work, human-computer interaction, psychology, anthropology, ubiquitous computing, and, indeed, software engineering. It is important to note that these faculty members not only engaged in the overall design of the major but also significantly shaped the pedagogical approach for delivering the individual courses.

We employ several best pedagogical practices throughout the curriculum, at varying levels of detail. At the highest level, we note that most of the curriculum is structured in course sequences rather than individual, disconnected courses. First, this brings continuity to the program, allowing us to treat important topics in depth while still supporting a gradual introduction to the more complex topics such as software design and information management. This is particularly important for those topics that require extensive practice complementing the lectures. With multiple courses, there is room to practice more and larger examples. A second reason for creating course sequences is that it allows us to integrate materials that should be taught together, particularly with respect to the principles we laid out in Section 2. Traditional courses are already typically full. Rather than simply creating a new, separate course to provide the additional context, we have combined, reorganized, and redistributed the traditional and newer material in an integrated manner over several courses. This is particularly evident in the Informatics Core series, which provides a balanced view of context that frames the traditional orientation of introductory computing courses around programming and data structures. It is present in the other course sequences as well. The first course in the software design sequence, for instance, first introduces students to general design process and principles (i.e., as involved in different kinds of disciplines) and only then makes the transition to apply this general knowledge to software. This is only possible because there are three courses in this sequence, allowing us to take a broader look at design before we address the specifics of notations, metrics, and such topics as architectural styles and design patterns.

A second high-level pedagogical practice we adopted pervasively was that of group work. Software engineering is not an individual activity; every software engineer interacts with people, whether it is peers (e.g., their software engineer colleagues) or others (e.g., customers, consultants, management). For this reason alone, it is necessary that students receive training in group work. But it is also a settled pedagogical principle that frequent group work provides a stimulating, engaging, supportive, and effective learning environment for students [5]. We begin in the first year with the use of pair programming, which we broaden in later years with projects involving larger groups of students. We ensure that students do not always work with the same set of other students, particularly in the first year. This helps provide them with a balanced experience and also promotes a sense of community as the students move through the program. We also note that we provide the students with the tools and approaches necessary to perform their work effectively in groups. The second year in particular provides them with methods and tools for configuration management, bug tracking, modeling, process management, requirements solicitation and management, and testing, analysis, and so on. The expectation is that they will use those in subsequent years as needed, particularly in the final year-long project course. We also note the project management course that is slotted at the beginning of the fourth year, but can be taken earlier in the program of study (as desired by individual students and depending on their progress).

Case studies are used frequently to seed the courses and provide students with real examples that set an appropriate context for the material being taught. The course on social analysis of computerization, for instance, uses quite a few examples of "computing gone wrong"; not in the traditional sense of a crashing program, but in the sense of mismatches between technology and its actual use. Similarly, the software design course sequence uses many real-life examples to illustrate designs, both good and bad, in terms of the code structure they prescribe. Some courses ask students to find their own case studies, for instance by asking them to choose a software application and perform a detailed analysis of how effective it is in use or how a particular user interface is perceived by a target group of users. When a full, realistic, detailed case study is not feasible, we attempt to provide alternative ways of approaching real-life situations as realistically as possible. For example, we use a tool that simulates the software process to allow students to visualize and practice different approaches to the software development life cycle (e.g., waterfall, incremental, XP) [6].

Each year ends with a capstone course that brings together the materials taught in that year. As mentioned previously, the senior year is anchored by a year-long capstone course, the Senior Design Project. In it, students work with real clients to specify, design, and implement a solution to a particular IT problem that the client faces. Past experience with a quarter-long project course shows that students do high-quality work and the students enthusiastically cite the course as one of the most influential in their future careers. The quarter-long course, however, is too hurried and does not offer much time for iteration and full delivery of the results. (Though we have seen some remarkable successes in which systems created by a student team are readily adopted and "go live" shortly after delivery, students must be able to sleep, too!) The year-long version brings stability in this regard and also allows us to tackle systems of larger scale and broader variety, especially because students will have been prepared much more thoroughly with the skills necessary to successfully undertake their projects. Moreover, it provides an opportunity to exercise requirements gathering (which is hardly done now in the one-quarter course) as well as UI design and evaluation, specification changes (which are inevitable over the course of nine months), final packaging, deployment, and installation.

Our overall approach and courses incorporate many different learning theories (learning by doing [7], situated learning [8], learning through failure [9], Keller's ARCS [10], and so on). This is an artifact of having been able to design many of the courses from scratch, a luxury we realize one does not always have. This also allowed us to insert, in the spring of year one, a seminar course in which the students meet each of the faculty members and hear about their research. This is important for building community and putting a face on the program, but it also better enables the students to approach the faculty later if they want to work on a research project. The program is designed to allow room for semi-independent research projects, a minor in another field, or free elective classes.

5 Reflection

The first students entered the Informatics program in Fall 2004; as of this writing, they are now sophomores (about 20 students) and a second cohort is completing its first year (about 30 students). We have instituted an ongoing, detailed, long-term evaluation process to determine the effectiveness, strengths, and weaknesses of our approach; clearly, just two years with students who have not yet completed the program is insufficient to draw firm conclusions. As part of this process, we are closely monitoring the performance of the Informatics students as compared to students in the other computing majors in the Bren School. We also gather information from a significant amount of informal contact. Here, we provide some of the data that we have collected, some of our anecdotal experiences, and our impressions of the program structure so far.

5.1 Student Performance

Table 2 presents the data we have collected to date on the GPA per quarter for students who entered any of the Bren School of ICS computing majors in Fall 2004 or Fall 2005.[2] This represents the two years that the Informatics major has been in existence. Overall, we note that the GPA of Informatics students is somewhat lower than that of students in the other majors, but that the best students in any of the majors are comparable. The lower GPA can be attributed to many factors and this comparison is like comparing apples and oranges. Students in different majors take different courses with different instructors; Informatics students in particular take some courses in their first and second years that are third- or fourth-year courses for the other students; students have different characteristics (see below); and so on. Monitoring students' performance also ensures that the major does not pose significant bottlenecks that impede students' progress.

Some of the courses that Informatics students take are shared with the other majors. In these courses (data not shown here) we see some polarization: the best Informatics students perform as well or even better than the other students, but other students are a bit worse in their performance. That is, the traditional normal distribution does not quite apply to our students in these shared courses. We have two hypotheses: (1) the shared courses are junior-level courses for the other students, so they have more practice and experience than the typical Informatics student in the same course, (2) more than students in the other majors, Informatics students fall into two distinct camps – those who like to program and those who do not. This last factor is interesting: the Informatics major attracts a higher percentage of students who do not wish to

---

[2] Data are collected only for students who have consented to be part of an official study that is sanctioned by the UC Irvine Institutional Review Board (IRB). Our reporting here is therefore constrained to just those students and limits itself to non-identifying data that can be shared under the current IRB guidelines.

become traditional computer scientists eventually but rather wish to enter careers in interaction design, game design, management, consulting, film production, and other careers that require very little hands-on production of code and instead require a deep understanding of overall design issues. These students tolerate the shared Programming Languages and Software Methods and Tools courses, and we believe that a solid grounding in the technical fundamentals is essential for those who will be managing or working closely with hands-on programmers, but they are seldom the students who excel in those courses. By the same token, we expect them to perform well in courses that are oriented towards design issues.

Table 2. GPA per Quarter for Students in each of the Four Computing Majors of the Bren School of ICS

Major	Qtr	Mean	Median	SD	Min	Max
CS	F05	2.95	3.09	0.95	0.00	4.00
	F04	3.40	3.57	0.55	1.91	4.00
	W05	3.14	3.33	0.59	1.86	4.00
	S05	3.18	3.30	0.56	1.78	4.00
CS&E	F05	2.85	3.05	0.91	0.00	3.77
	F04	3.15	3.42	0.73	1.48	3.98
	W05	3.13	3.09	0.46	2.45	3.92
	S05	2.92	2.95	0.64	1.75	3.76
ICS	F05	2.84	2.98	0.83	0.33	4.00
	F04	3.03	3.10	0.76	1.33	4.00
	W05	3.04	3.11	0.71	0.83	4.00
	S05	3.01	3.11	0.79	0.00	4.00
Informatics	F05	2.88	3.07	0.96	0.26	4.00
	F04	3.22	3.51	0.66	1.91	3.91
	W05	2.93	3.13	0.86	0.29	3.93
	S05	2.74	3.33	1.22	0.00	3.91

We also note that the gender distribution is quite different for the different majors. Informatics attracts a significantly higher percentage of female students than the other majors. At present, about 25% of the Informatics students are female, a percentage about twice as high as the other three majors. We attribute the difference to the focus of Informatics. Because of its integral treatment of context—particularly people and organizations—and because of they way we have structured even the introductory courses to integrate this focus on context, the major is more accessible, has a clearer structure, and has much more grounding in realistic situations. These are precisely the factors that have been identified as critical for achieving and maintaining a gender balance in computing degrees [11].

5.2 Anecdotal Experience

Our anecdotal experience reveals great enthusiasm among the current Informatics students. They enjoy the challenge of participating in a new program that is at the frontier of computer science education and they spread the word to students in the other majors. They have even organized an Informatics Student Association with the mission of spreading awareness and information about Informatics, both on campus and off, to high school students and industry.

We have made some adjustments to the program as circumstances warranted. In the first year of the program, we noticed that more students than expected left the program. We attributed this in part to a mismatch in expectations; our initial recruiting materials and presentations, in emphasizing the context to distinguish Informatics from the more traditional degrees, may have left the impression that the Informatics program did not involve a significant amount of programming. But it does, as we have described above, and we have edited our materials to reflect this more accurately with the result that our second-year attrition rate to date is lower. Another factor contributing to attrition is that each Informatics course is offered exactly once a year, while courses in the other, larger majors are typically offered more often. A student who does not pass a required Informatics course may need to wait an entire year to repeat it and to take other courses for which it is a prerequisite. Some students in this situation have switched to the Information and Computer Science major when they failed one of the critical courses. We hope that, in the future, the size of the program and of our faculty will grow, enabling us to offer these critical courses more frequently.

We have also observed a high degree of interest in Informatics from juniors and seniors in other computing majors, higher than from first- and second-year students. We hypothesize here that "younger" students have a more limited view of the alternative ways to study computing and tend to opt for the majors with the more conventional, familiar names. As they progress through those programs, they learn more about their preferences and potential future careers. At that point they often recognize the value of Informatics. This parallels our recruiting experiences with local high schools: prospective students know the Computer Science name and don't look any further. On the other hand, when a prospective student's parents are in the computing industry themselves, often they appreciate the value of the Informatics approach. As a School, we are updating our promotional materials to describe and distinguish the majors and to help students with their choice.

5.3 Program Structure

Although the Informatics program is still quite young, we re-evaluate it periodically. At this point, we are contemplating a few changes to the ordering of the courses:

- *Move the database course series one year earlier in the program.* With the prevalence of databases and their likely inclusion in many of the senior design projects, we feel that an earlier exposure will be helpful.
- *Move the project management course into the junior year.* Learning this material before starting the senior design project should help students carry out their project more effectively.

- *Delay the software design course sequence by one quarter.* Besides making room for the changes listed above, this rearrangement will allow students to consider database issues in their study of design.

Continued experience in teaching the program undoubtedly will bring additional fine-tuning, but we are confident that the Informatics program, especially with these changes, presents a well-balanced education in the design, application, use, and impact of information technology.

6   Challenges

In creating our Informatics curriculum and continuing our efforts to improve it, it is clear that the field of software engineering still faces many challenges on the way to becoming a mature discipline. Here, we discuss the four that have the greatest impact on our curriculum; we believe they apply to other software engineering degrees as well, regardless of how they are framed.

1. *How to balance teaching to students who like programming and students who do not.* Our discipline must nurture students of both varieties; not every software engineer will be a coder. In fact, with the growth of outsourcing, we should examine our curricula carefully to ensure that we do not educate "just programmers". While most software engineering degree programs do offer some kind of broader perspective, perhaps it is time to engage in the discussion of how broad this perspective should be and how large a role programming should play. One could argue that programming is a fundamental principle underlying all of software engineering, but one could equally argue that we should be able to train designers (in the broadest sense of the word) without their having to be master coders (since, for example, building architects are not necessarily trained, or even competent, in the masonry or carpentry necessary to construct their designs). This discussion is merely beginning right now, and our Informatics degree simply occupies one spot in the space of possible solutions. We have not abandoned or curtailed programming, but we have placed a much heavier emphasis on design and context to balance programming with other skills.

2. *How to teach design.* To date, our focus as a discipline has centered mainly on notations for capturing designs. While these notations are tremendously useful, their focus on the end product limits their usefulness during the creative, exploratory, iterative design process, which we want our students to learn. For our Informatics degree, we have created a course series that introduces a novel theoretical perspective on design in general before focusing on software design. This helps set the appropriate expectations, brings the treatment of software design in line with other disciplines, and changes the focus from notations to theory, examples, case studies, and extensive practice. A theoretical framework by itself is not sufficient, however. We must invest significant effort in collecting examples of good and bad designs, creating new design environments that focus on supporting the creative process rather than the documentation process, and collectively figuring

out ways to understand what works and does not work in design education.

3. *How to incorporate context in the educational experience.* Our Informat-
    ics major has chosen to interpret software's context in terms of informa-
    tion, design, social issues, and analysis; it addresses the context with
    specific courses and a concerted effort to provide a broadly balanced
    view throughout. This represents but one approach to incorporating con-
    text. The Informatics major at Indiana University provides another exam-
    ple through the use of focused plans of study in other domains, to balance
    the more technical material related to computer science [12]. The introduc-
    tory courses at Georgia Tech use media computation (graphics and audio) to
    provide a more contextualized approach to the introductory topics in the ma-
    jor [13]. Many approaches and experiences are emerging; an examination
    and discussion of their relative merits is much needed.

4. *How to develop students' appreciation for issues of complexity and scale.* It
    is well known that the projects one can feasibly undertake in an educational
    setting are significantly smaller in scope than those undertaken in industry.
    Issues that crop up in these larger projects may not arise in the smaller pro-
    jects. We must find ways to expose students to such issues nonetheless. The
    literature mentions many techniques for addressing these issues (e.g., 20
    dirty tricks [14], maintenance projects that continue from year to year [15],
    purposely handing out unclear requirements [16]), but these tend to focus on
    specific symptoms. They illustrate one or two visible results of what may go
    wrong, but do not comprehensively discuss and explore issues of scale. The
    Informatics major includes a year-long design project in which students un-
    dertake a project for a real customer. It also uses project simulation software
    for "hands-on" practice with larger, hypothetical situations in a safe, virtual
    setting [6]. We view all of these as beginning to address complexity and
    scale, but we believe that much more work is needed to create many more
    educational approaches that do so in a principled way.

Answers to these questions are at the heart of a high-quality SE education. The lessons we learn as we answer them will benefit the community at large and the sooner
the community sorts them out, the better.

7 Conclusions

We have presented the new Informatics major at UC Irvine, the result of our attempt
to create a new way of framing software engineering education,. What distinguishes
our approach is a framing in context: we integrate coverage of software and information, development and design, technical issues and social issues, and synthesis and
analysis. We believe that in this way, we will train well-rounded software engineers
who have flexibility in their careers and a deep understanding of the issues involved
in creating new information technology.

As technology advances and our knowledge increases, a complete education
in computing no longer fits into a single four-year degree program. Software engineering is a leading candidate for "splitting off" into a separate degree (much as

mechanical, electrical, and other engineering disciplines became programs separate from general engineering). Software engineering is criticized in some quarters as being more vocationally oriented than the usual academic discipline. An Informatics approach, integrating software creation with context drawn from many traditional academic fields, may go a long way towards answering these critics and developing software engineering as a mature discipline.

We are not alone in attempting to revamp software engineering education. Jazayeri describes a similar effort at the University of Lugano [17]. Earlier we mentioned the Informatics program at Indiana University [12]; other similar efforts are underway [18,19,20,21,22]. As software engineering educators, we face many challenges — not only the pedagogical ones listed above but also the challenges of rapid technological change, global increase in demand for information technology, and the development of a global IT workforce. To prepare our students for productive careers, we need more support, experimentation, evaluation, and discussion of alternatives such as these.

Acknowledgments

The Informatics major at UCI is sponsored in part by the Fund for the Improvement of Postsecondary Education (FIPSE), U.S. Department of Education.

References

1. ACM, AIS, and IEEE-CS Joint Task Force for Computing Curricula 2005, Computing Curricula 2005, http://www.acm.org/education/curricula.html
2. McMaster University, Department of Computing and Software, http://www.cas.mcmaster.ca/cas/
3. IEEE-CS and ACM Joint Task Force on Computing Curricula, Software Engineering 2004: Curriculum Guidelines for Undergraduate Degree Programs in Software Engineering (A Volume of the Computing Curricula Series), 2004, http://sites.computer.org/ccse/
4. University of California, Irvine, Department of Informatics, http://www.ics.uci.edu/informatics/ugrad/
5. Smith, *Teamwork and Project Management*, McGraw-Hill, 2004.
6. Oh Navarro and van der Hoek, *Design and Evaluation of an Educational Software Process Simulation Environment and Associated Model*, Eighteenth Conference on Software Engineering Education & Training, February 2005, pages 25–32
7. Schank and Cleary, *Engines for Education*. 1995, Hillsdale, NJ, USA: Lawrence Erlbaum Associates, Inc.
8. Brown, Collins, and Duguid, *Situated Cognition and the Culture of Learning*. Educational Researcher, 1989. 18(1): pages 32–42
9. Schank, *Virtual Learning*. 1997, New York, NY, USA: McGraw-Hill
10. Keller, and Suzuki, *Use of the ARCS Motivation Model in Courseware Design*, in *Instructional Designs for Microcomputer Courseware*, D.H. Jonassen, Editor. 1988, Lawrence Erlbaum: Hillsdale, NJ, USA
11. Margolis and Fischer, *Unlocking the Clubhouse: Women in Computing*, Cambridge, MIT Press, 2001
12. Indiana University, School of Informatics, http://www.informatics.indiana.edu

13. Guzdial, *Introduction to computing and programming with Python: A Multimedia Approach*, Prentice-Hall, 2004

14. Gehrke, et al., *Reporting about Industrial Strength Software Engineering Courses for Undergraduates*, Proceedings of the 24th International Conference on Software Engineering. 2002, pages 395–405

15. Sebern, *The Software Development Laboratory: Incorporating Industrial Practice in an Academic Environment*, Proceedings of the 15th Conference on Software Engineering and Training, 2002, pages 118–127

16. Daniels, Faulkner, and Newman, *Open Ended Group Projects, Motivating Students and Preparing them for the 'Real World'*, Proceedings of the Fifteenth Conference on Software Engineering Education and Training, 2002, pages 115–126

17. Jazayeri, *Education of a Software Engineer*, keynote at the Automated Software Engineering Conference, 2004

18. University of Washington, Information School, http://www.ischool.washington.edu

19. York College of Pennsylvania, http://www.ycp.edu/academics

20. Montclair State University, Department of Computer Science, http://cs.montclair.edu/undergraduate.html

21. Rochester Institute for Technology, Department of Software Engineering, http://www.se.rit.edu/degrees.html

22. Milwaukee School of Engineering, B.S. in Software Engineering, http://www.msoe.edu/eecs/se/

Software Engineering Education in the Era of Outsourcing, Distributed Development, and Open Source Software: Challenges and Opportunities

Matthew J. Hawthorne[1] and Dewayne E. Perry[2]

Empirical Software Engineering Lab (ESEL),
Dept. of Electrical and Computer Engineering,
The University of Texas at Austin,
Austin, Texas, USA
{hawthorn, perry}@ece.utexas.edu
http://www.ece.utexas.edu/~hawthorn,
http://www.ece.utexas.edu/~perry

Abstract. As software development becomes increasingly globally distributed, and more software functions are delegated to common open source software (OSS) and commercial off-the-shelf (COTS) components, practicing software engineers face significant challenges for which current software engineering curricula may leave them inadequately prepared. A new multi-faceted distributed development model is emerging that effectively commoditizes many development activities once considered integral to software engineering, while simultaneously requiring practitioners to apply engineering principles in new and often unfamiliar contexts. We discuss the challenges that software engineers face as a direct result of outsourcing and other distributed development approaches that are increasingly being utilized by industry, and some of the key ways we need to evolve software engineering curricula to address these challenges.

1 Introduction

Driven by a critical combination of technological and economic forces brought on by ongoing developments in technology and economic pressures caused by globalization, software engineering is changing in fundamental ways. We must rethink many of the assumptions that have provided the basis for software engineering education in the past, and make fundamental changes to the way we educate software engineers in order 1) to prepare them to navigate the increasingly dynamic environment that software engineering has become, and 2) to equip them with the perspectives and skills they will need to thrive in the midst of the even greater challenges they will face throughout their professional lives. In the remainder of this section, we highlight three basic trends that are changing the way organizations develop software: third party components, integration platforms, and globalization. These trends are already changing the practice of software engineering, and we believe they will continue to impact the practice of software engineering for the foreseeable future.

P. Inverardi and M. Jazayeri (Eds.): ICSE 2005 Education Track, LNCS 4309, pp. 166–185, 2006.

1.1 Third-Party Components

The first trend is the increasing reliance on *third-party components* for core system functionality, including open source software (OSS) [13] and commercial off-the-shelf (COTS) components. The impact that delegating significant functionality to OSS or COTS components has on software development projects is similar in many respects to that of outsourcing: more system functionality is being developed by third parties, potentially reducing the amount of software that organizations develop internally, but at the same time, making integration technologies, architectures and frameworks, and software engineering competencies related to integration, of paramount importance to software development organizations. Project planning and engineering need to expand beyond traditional technical concerns to encompass methods for locating and evaluating candidate third-party components, and selecting the optimal set of components for a given project by evaluating and balancing tradeoffs between such diverse concerns as functionality, licensing terms and fees, integration costs, and technical support, etc. This trend toward increasing use of third-party components is also bringing about basic changes in software development organizational structures and processes. Requirements engineering assumes a more significant driving role in developing software systems. Quality and evolution issues are complicated and exacerbated because of the lack of control over component problems and evolution. Integration is hindered by architectural mismatch, etc.

1.2 Integration Platforms

The second trend is the growth and maturation of integration platforms and architectural frameworks such as J2EE, .NET, web services, and service-oriented architectures (SOA), as well as problem domain model-oriented abstraction approaches to system design such as model-driven architecture (MDA) and the semantically richer intent-based system abstraction technologies of the near future. These approaches are providing new tools, architectural platforms and system abstractions to integrate the diverse set of components that inevitably results when development organizations build products that incorporate a large number of third-party components. Since current technologies and standards are likely to continue evolving rapidly, emphasizing a thorough understanding of the principles behind these approaches and their applicability for solving software engineering problems will be more useful over the long term than complete mastery of the minute details at a given point of time. However, using appropriate platforms and standards as teaching tools is an excellent way to illustrate and reinforce architectural styles, patterns, techniques and principles related to integration.

1.3 Globalization

The third trend that is changing software engineering is the *globalization* of software development, often referred to as "outsourcing". We make no distinction in this paper between literal outsourcing, in which one organization pays one or more other organizations or individuals to develop software components or systems, and "internal outsourcing", where an organization distributes development projects to one or more of its own development teams located in different countries. The overall impact on software engineering is similar in either case: organizations are transitioning from primarily local models of software development to globally distributed models. This transition is motivated by two basic issues: cost and time. In the first case, lower labor costs in other countries has had the same effect on the software industry as it has had in other industries – namely, significant parts of the work are done either by external contracts or by opening international facilities using local talent. In the second case, the possibility of *round the clock* development has the attraction of significantly shortening the lapse time required for software products.

This trend towards globalization brings with it its own set of problems and further complicates and exacerbates existing software development problems.

- *Cultural differences.* With different countries come different social interaction assumptions and rules. There are differences in expected and acceptable behaviors and interactions. For example, a simple request may be perceived as a significant social obligation. Moreover, different languages may result in radically different interpretations from what is expected. For example, the word "envy" has both positive meanings in English, Italian and French. However, there is no positive meaning of "envy" in German.
- *Legal differences.* One significant legal difference may be that involving the laws about working overtime. What is permitted in one country may be prohibited in another. Doing business in a specific country may require a certain percentage of the workers to be local to that country. And there may be different rules and regulations about the domain of the software systems involved. For example, there are significantly different rules and regulations about telecommunications system in different countries that must be accommodated by the systems.
- *Interaction differences.* A significant amount of problem solving while developing software systems is done informally at the coffee machine, over lunch, etc. With geographical and temporal separation, these informal modes of interaction are virtually impossible. Given that roughly 75 minutes per day in one project were spent in short (3 minutes or under) unplanned interactions informally solving problem [15], the removal of these informal channels of interaction seriously affects project interactions.

1.4 Challenges and Opportunities

The increasingly distributed nature of development and the ubiquitous use of third-party components, along with new integration platforms and tools, have created a dynamic software development environment in which organizations continue to search for ways to reduce the cost of software development through outsourcing and other means. This process is compounded by the fact that 1) new OSS and COTS components, 2) development tools are continually being introduced and existing ones extended, and 3) there is lack of local control over improvements and problems fixed. Software engineers need to be prepared to deal with unprecedented levels of diversity and change, not only in the technologies and components they will be working with, but also in the nature of the development teams and organizations with whom they will need to interact on a regular basis, and even in the very roles and responsibilities they will need assume as development processes and organizations continue to evolve. The new integration platforms and technologies represent further movement away from the system development processes and architectural styles of the past, which tended to be much more monolithic, toward more loosely coupled integration models that will better enable systems to be composed of components from diverse sources.

The impact of these trends on software engineering projects, processes and practitioners means that the mix of competencies required to practice successfully software engineering now includes much more than just software development skills. In today's competitive global environment, short-term market opportunities and financial concerns increasingly impact software development projects, often causing project requirements and priorities to change on short notice, while simultaneously increasing the pressure to produce software at the lowest possible cost in the shortest possible time. At the same time, the increasing commoditization and distribution of hands-on software development via outsourcing and the use of third-party components is causing the demand for traditional software development skills in many areas to be eclipsed by new opportunities available to software engineers who possess certain kinds of enhanced software *engineering* expertise.

To enable engineers to take advantage of these opportunities, we need to augment traditional software engineering strengths in requirements engineering [11], software architecture [14], design, and development processes with new techniques that will enable software engineers to *apply engineering principles* in larger organizational and project management contexts. We need to produce software engineers who are just as comfortable practicing engineering in environments where the "tools" are distributed project teams and third-party components as they are designing and implementing complete systems themselves. We also need to equip engineers with architecture, design, and development approaches that facilitate third-party component integration, and the simultaneous evolution of product family architectures and external components. Given the right set of knowledge, skills and perspectives, we see this trend toward distributed and third-party development as an excellent opportunity to build on the unique strengths of software *engineering* as a distinct discipline, by equipping software *engineers* to play a central role in ensuring the success of development organizations as they explore these new development models.

In the next section we briefly discuss several new "core competencies" -- attitudes, perspectives, and skills that are not usually considered core aspects of software engineering education, but that we believe will serve new software engineers well as they navigate the increasingly dynamic development environment, and help equip them to flourish throughout their careers as they face whatever unforeseen challenges may arise in our profession in the future. In the following several sections, we discuss several areas of competency that we believe will be among the most valuable for software engineers, and hence require additional curricula to support. These include *organization and process engineering, system and product family architectures, integration techniques and technologies, product and product line management,* and *distributed project management.* Finally, we briefly discuss several important aspects of ethics as they relate to software engineering education and practice.

2 Non-technical "Core Competencies"

Non-technical skills and characteristics such as verbal and written communication, social sensitivity, adaptability and creativity have always been important factors contributing to the success of many of the most successful software engineers. The pervasive changes software engineering is undergoing are making it more critical than ever that we prepare future engineers to be excellent communicators (e.g., so they will be able to communicate effectively with diverse groups of stakeholders and developers who may be globally distributed). Further, engineers of the future must be prepared to be extremely adaptable, and to consider solutions that may be "outside of the box" of previous software engineering experience, including their own. And they must be sensitive to the cultural and linguistic contexts in which these projects take place. This section discusses several of these non-technical competencies and characteristics that we believe will be crucial to the success of future software engineers, and that software engineering programs will need to address if we are to prepare our students to leverage the new opportunities that change will inevitably bring to our profession. Since any specific tools, technologies or programming languages we teach student software engineers today are almost certain to be obsolete long before the end of their engineering careers, it is imperative that we also give them the tools and perspectives that will enable them to adapt to whatever the future holds for our profession.

2.1 Targeted Communication

Interpersonal communication has always been an integral part of software engineering, since most software projects involve some kind of team interaction, and even engineers working on single-person projects must still communicate with users, managers and other stakeholders at some point. But communication is increasingly critical to the success of software engineering projects, especially given the increased reliance on third-party components. Communications with distributed development team members, project stakeholders, managers and other members of the extended development team should be undertaken as deliberately as any other critical-path engineering task. Software engineers need to learn and practice purposeful or *targeted communication*, directed toward achieving specific results. This requires engineers to understand how software development projects and organizations work, and how the different roles that individuals may assume within projects and organizations relate to their own projects. It also requires them to have a clear understanding of what and with whom they need to communicate to accomplish a given purpose, what specific effect they wish their communication to have, and how best to accomplish the desired effect.

While traditional technically oriented engineering communications such as requirements documents, UML diagrams, etc. will continue to be important skills, engineers also need to learn to be comfortable and confident communicating in other contexts such as marketing and business planning meetings, as well as meetings with customers and other non-technical stakeholders. And as software engineering becomes more distributed and project-oriented, the "target" or goal of targeted communication by engineers increasingly will include areas that were previously the domain of business managers, especially in the area of obtaining and justifying the resources necessary to complete projects successfully. Project planning and design activities increasingly will incorporate P&L (profit & loss) projections. Whether P&L models remain the province of business managers in a given organization or not, engineers will be under intense pressure to minimize costs by maximizing the use of third-party developers and components. In such an environment of intense competition for project resources, business advocacy and persuasion skills, or at least a basic understanding of business drivers combined with strong communication skills, increasingly will become important for many engineers if they hope to compete successfully for resources for their own projects, much less reengineer and optimize the processes and engineering organizations to which they belong.

Along with traditional and extended engineering skills, engineering training should emphasize communicating engineering models, evaluations, plans and other engineering results both to technical and non-technical stakeholders, especially business managers and user representatives. Engineers have traditionally excelled at presenting technical facts. Targeted communication goes far beyond imparting technical knowledge, and is geared toward communicating in a way that will achieve desired results. This means that the engineer must understand 1) what they want to say, 2) what result or results their project requires that the communication should achieve and 3) how to communicate what they want to say to the target audience so that the communication achieves those desired results. This is why we sometimes refer to targeted communication as goal- or result-oriented, or engineered, communication. What this really means is that engineers need to stop imagining that everybody who reads their documentation or listens to their presentations is also an engineer. To function effectively in modern development organizations, engineers need to understand how to communicate effectively with diverse members of the "extended engineering team", including business management, sales and marketing, users and user domain experts, customer support, and others. Finally, as engineers, we should point out that the ultimate "target" or desired result, of targeted communication is always to enhance the success of the engineering projects with which we are involved.

2.2 Professional Habits and Traits

The increasingly dynamic nature of software engineering means that to maximize their chances for success in this environment, future software engineers will need to practice professional behaviors and habits such as adaptability and creative problem-solving in addition to mastering the appropriate tools, technologies and processes. Although such personal habits or traits are widely held to be inborn traits that people "naturally" possess to a greater or lesser extent, when we talk about characteristics such as flexibility or inquisitiveness, we are really referring to related sets of behavioral traits that, if habitually practiced in the context of software engineering projects, will greatly contribute to their success over the long term. Since we are essentially talking about behavioral habits that can be learned, or at least enhanced with practice, for the purposes of software engineering education and practice, it doesn't really matter whether these characteristics are more the result of "nature" or "nurture". Merely adopting these behaviors is sufficient. For example, if we can convince software engineers who are "naturally" inflexible, or who are not particularly inquisitive by nature, of the benefits of making flexible or inquisitive behavior an integral part of their software engineering practice, their projects and careers will still reap the same benefits, regardless of whether they feel "naturally" inclined to exhibit those behaviors.

- *Adaptability*. Software engineering will continue to change, whether software engineers are prepared to deal with change or not, and the most successful software engineers will be those who are the most able to adapt. Indeed, for the foreseeable future at least, the rate of change appears to be accelerating, and we don't see anything on the horizon that is likely to change this significantly anytime soon. Adaptability is really an application of one of the engineering discipline's greatest strengths – the "filter" of practicality. Good engineers adopt the best tools available for a given task at the time, and engineering tools always change over time, even if they did so at a less dizzying pace in the past. Adaptable software engineers grow professionally primarily by abstracting essential principles from past experience, while staying open to new models, paradigms, technologies and methodologies. This allows them to benefit from past experience, but at the same time, never to allow that experience to limit their perspective.

- *Intellectual curiosity*. Along with adaptability, practicing intellectual curiosity is a valuable skill for software engineers. While adaptability is practicing openness and flexibility toward new ways of practicing software engineering, intellectual curious or inquisitive software engineers are always proactively looking for better ways to practice their profession, including new tools, technologies, architectures and processes. And when new models and paradigms are developed, inquisitive engineers will be the first to notice and adopt them, if indeed they are not the ones who developed the new models and paradigms in the first place.

- *Creative problem-solving*. Another important skill that will enhance the success of software engineers in a dynamically changing environment is creative problem-solving. By definition, ongoing and future change implies uncertainty, since no matter how forward-looking we may be, the future we envision will inevitably include unexpected developments (indeed, the world would be a dull place if this were not the case!). While practicing adaptability and intellectual curiosity will help software engineers stay open to new things, greatly helping them to avoid ever "missing the boat" by not noticing or embracing new developments in software engineering, the creative problem-solvers will be the engineers who are driving future change in our profession. Since engineering always concerns solving some problem or set of problems, creativity in engineering is mainly the ability to conceive of solutions that are "outside the box" of normal theory and practice.

- *Knowledge assimilation and categorization*. Finally, to complement adaptability, intellectual curiosity and creative problem-solving, software engineers of the future will need to be very adept at rapidly assessing, assimilating and adopting new knowledge. This knowledge may be in the form of new development models, tools and technologies, or it may be involve new abstractions and paradigms for which we currently lack even the concepts and language to discuss. But the important thing is that whatever form it may take, there are always going to be new models, theories and technologies that a software engineer will need to evaluate to determine first of all, whether they are applicable to the set of problems they are trying to solve, and then, whether they are the best solution available. Since there is no way we can teach new software engineers all the technical knowledge they will need over the course of their careers, we must at least give them the tools and perspective they will need to assimilate new technologies rapidly.

3   Requirements Management and Engineering

In recent years, there has been a trend in many software development organizations for software engineers to focus almost exclusively on software development, with marketing representatives or other "domain experts" increasingly taking responsibility for defining, analyzing and managing system requirements, sometimes even including aspects of system design (e.g., human-computer interface (HCI) design, use case engineering, etc.). Although business-related drivers related to outsourcing have motivated much of this change, a tendency among software developers to avoid being limited to a single application domain or industry by focusing on implementation technologies like programming languages, tools and techniques, while deemphasizing problem domain analysis and expertise, has also contributed to this trend. While the need to involve domain experts actively during requirements gathering and prioritization is a well-established principle in software engineering, ongoing industry trends and upcoming developments in software engineering theory and practice make it more critical than ever that software engineers refocus on requirements analysis and engineering to counter the recent trend toward non-engineers "owning" or managing many aspects of system requirements.

One basic reason software engineers need to refocus on requirements is because requirements are arguably the most fundamental software engineering concern. The functional requirements of the system (often referred to as "goals"), along with the non-functional requirements (often referred to as "constraints") together form the basis for the architecture and design of the system. While non-engineering domain specialists may have some idea about the overall problem domain functionality of the system, without the system, product line, and architectural perspectives of software engineering, they are unlikely to be able to produce the kind of coherent set of system requirements that can form a robust basis for the system architecture. Since current requirements engineering practices (RE) [11] include analyzing, refining and rationalizing the requirements, all of which involve changing the requirements because of *engineering* concerns, it is critical that software engineers fully understand the central role of requirements in the software development process, and learn the requirements elucidation, analysis and engineering skills that will enable them to play an active leadership role in managing the requirements for the systems they design and implement.

Requirements are becoming even more fundamental to designing system architectures as a result of new architectural design paradigms that are being developed, e.g., rationale and intent-based architectures [5] [4] [1] [2] [8]. Building on recent developments in RE, problem domain modeling [9], and decision-based architectural models [3] [10], under these new approaches, models of the functional intent of the system as expressed in the requirements form the basis for the system architecture. In many respects, under these new system abstractions, the requirements will *be* the system architecture, allowing models based on the functional requirements of the system to function essentially in much the same way as we currently use architectural designs. With requirements poised to become, if not the actual system architecture, at least the integrally connected wellspring and literal basis for the system design, it is all the more imperative that we prepare software engineers to take the lead in requirements analysis and engineering. They must also be willing to "dirty their hands" by embracing application domain expertise and communicating with actual system users and other stakeholders, so they will be able to elicit, analyze and engineer models of system requirements that will enable the system design to fulfill the desired functional intent of the system. Requirements are the ultimate wellspring of system architecture and design.

Also, whenever business unit proxies for actual system users are inserted into the development process as designated domain experts, they can serve to isolate the system architects and developers from meaningful contact with users. While this kind of arrangement may be useful from the standpoint of condensing divergent user requests into a coherent set of requirements and buffering the development staff from being "bothered" by users, unless the user proxy is exceptionally good at requirements elicitation and analysis, the quality of the system may suffer from inadequate requirements analysis. Furthermore, each additional indirection and communication link that requirements must traverse to reach the implementation team increases the potential that requirements may be misinterpreted or misunderstood somewhere along the way.

A final reason we need to reemphasize requirements is related to the "business-related drivers" to which we previously alluded. Transitioning requirements gathering and analysis from software engineering teams to business groups has contributed to the marginalization of internal software development organizations, effectively causing all software development, including in-house development, to be done "to order", according to specifications developed by the business group. This kind of ubiquitous outsourcing model of product development has been particularly attractive to organizations that are actively exploring or practicing significant software development outsourcing. While it is beyond the scope of this paper to argue the relative benefits and drawbacks of outsourcing in general, attempting to outsource software development without retaining a software engineering perspective in the system requirements specification and architectural design loops is a sure recipe for disaster, including shortcomings in system architecture and design, as well as product line integration problems, among others.

4 Processes and Organizations

As software development becomes more globally distributed, we envision software engineers increasingly utilizing their expertise in architecture, design, and process engineering to take ownership of *engineering-in-the-large*, moving beyond implementation engineering to reengineer the very organizational processes and teams that are involved in conceiving, designing, developing and deploying software solutions. Organizational and process modeling are critical from multiple standpoints. During system design and development, business modeling and simulation techniques are important means of understanding target user organizations and how they will use a software system. Further, they are especially useful for developing, refining and validating system functional requirements. Business and process modeling also are becoming increasingly critical aspects of system architecture and high-level design, as system designs increasingly make use of problem-domain-based architectural abstractions.

In addition to utilizing organization and process models as an integral part of design and development, software engineers must also possess strong organizational and process modeling and optimization skills, techniques and perspectives if they are to reengineer and to optimize their own software development organizations and processes. Pervasive pressure to reduce software development costs, combined with increasing third-party development options, means that software development organizations and processes are continually being "reengineered", whether actual engineers are involved in the process or not. While it is not our intention here to focus on any potential career benefits that may result from being personally involved in managing organizational change, at least relative to the alternative (i.e., being affected by such processes without a seat at the table), as a practical matter, an engineering perspective is critical to ensure that cost-driven reengineering of software development projects, organizations and processes ultimately produces successful results.

Organization and process engineering to optimize software development includes determining the optimal organization of distributed projects that may include a mixture of internal resources and outsourcing, as well as third-party (COTS and OSS) components. *Project allocation, estimation and control* present special challenges in this kind of mixed-mode distributed project, and depend on stringent *requirements specification*. Besides new approaches to software development itself, software engineers should understand the entire range of roles in the extended software engineering organization, including business management (e.g., *cost and. risk analysis*), sales and marketing (e.g., *requirements gathering and prioritization*), customer support (e.g., *usability and supportability*), and others. An understanding of the *intellectual property ownership* and *security* issues involved with incorporating external project teams and components is also critical.

5 System Architectures

The increasing use of distributed and outsourced development, and the resulting need to incorporate third-party components within existing and newly developed systems, makes it more critical than ever that software engineers understand how to design and use system abstractions and architectural models that support the integration of components from diverse sources. Incorporating third-party components from diverse sources also compounds and complicates security and dependability concerns. Techniques and technologies that will enable engineers to design architectures that integrate diverse sets of components into systems that fulfill the functional and non-functional goals and constraints of the system include *product family architectures*,

integration styles and patterns, *system abstractions* derived from functional requirements, and application *integration frameworks*.

- *Product family architectures*. Incorporating diverse sets of third-party components into existing or newly developed products will require that software engineers understand how to design, develop and extend *product family architectures* [16] that are robust and comprehensive enough to encompass all these
  disparate elements, and organize them into a consistent architectural view.
- *Integration styles and patterns*. To enable integration at a finer level of architectural design granularity, engineers will also need to be very familiar with
  integration styles and patterns such as *connectors*, *adapters* and *wrappers* so
  they can use them as building blocks to create architectures that effectively
  manage the complexity induced by components designed and developed in
  parallel by diverse teams. These and similar styles and patterns that encapsulate functionality and component interactions within consistent interfaces are
  also important techniques for simplifying the incorporation of security concerns into complex systems by allowing security functionality to be centralized
  within the design of the encapsulating framework entities (i.e., the connectors,
  adapters, wrappers, etc.).
- *System abstractions*. System abstractions that enable implementation architectures to be derived more directly from abstractions of the problem domain,
  such as *goal- or prescription-based architectures* [2] and *intent-based architectures* [5], will also be important techniques to reduce complexity and enhance architectural consistency.
- *Integration frameworks*. Industry application frameworks such as J2EE [7]
  and .NET [12], and platform-independent integration frameworks such as web
  services and service-oriented architectures (SOA), are extremely useful technical skills for software engineers.

In general, system abstractions, architectural styles and design processes that enhance
the ability of software engineers to design flexible software architectures with enhanced support for architectural evolution to accommodate changing functional specifications and integration requirements will become increasingly critical competencies
for software engineers as system evolution and integration, along with related security
concerns, increasingly come to dominate the set of architectural concerns that engineers must balance.

6 Product and Project Management

Software development is rapidly moving away from the traditional model [17], which
primarily involved designing and building systems entirely within a given organization, increasingly utilizing a range of mixed development models incorporating varying levels of third-party (OSS and/or COTS) components and outsourcing, and
increasingly including projects that are primarily, or even completely, outsourced.
Mixing outsourced component development, where the paying organization retains at
least some level of management input into the design and implementation of the con-
tracted deliverables, with OSS and COTS components, where the paying organization

may have little or no input into design and implementation, adds to the challenges faced by the software engineer/architect who must somehow integrate these diverse components into a working system.

6.1 Managing Versus Contributing Organizations and Projects

One result of outsourced development in particular is that a dichotomy is emerging between the role of a software engineer in the *managing* organization for a project (i.e., the organization managing and ultimately paying for a given development project), and that of a software engineer or developer in a third-party *contributing* organization (i.e., an organization that is developing components that will be incorporated into the managing organization's product). The situation is further complicated by the fact that a given organization may be simultaneously managing some software projects and contributing to others. While the emerging trends we highlight in this paper can and do affect both kinds of projects, over the near term, contributing projects will continue to include more traditional hands-on software implementation, while managing projects will move more rapidly toward requiring the kinds of extended software engineering competencies we emphasize in this paper.

6.2 Product Management

Product management, or managing the direction and functionality of software products and product families, including many aspects of *requirements engineering (RE)*, is increasingly performed by marketing professionals. Software engineers may only become involved in software development projects at implementation time, after the domain and marketing experts have specified the requirements (and often, the resource budget and project schedule), without considering engineering concerns like reusability and product family architectures. We need to prepare software engineers to be fully engaged in projects from the outset, when important decisions about project feasibility are made. As approaches like goal-driven prescriptive architectures and intent-driven implementations become more prevalent, requirements analysis and engineering will become the most critical part of the software engineer's job. Software engineers will need to become *problem domain experts* and experts in *requirements elicitation and analysis* to engineer the implementation domain. This will require engineers to work more closely with customers, business managers and other stakeholders, and to be flexible enough to reason about software design and usage from diverse points of view.

6.3 Project Management

Project management will also become an increasingly important concern of software engineering as development projects become more globally distributed. Software engineers will increasingly find themselves working on projects where their ability to deliver their product directly depends on third-party development teams delivering components on time and according to agreed-upon functional specifications. Managing software project resources and schedules is notoriously difficult even under the best of circumstances. Adding distributed development teams to the mix will require software engineers to become much better at *planning and estimation*, using advanced techniques for accurately estimating the time it will take the various internal and external teams to complete their parts of the project, including integration and quality assurance (QA). This will also require much better *interpersonal communication skills* than many software engineers currently possess to communicate project requirements effectively to distributed and outsourced team members, and verify that the requirements are satisfied. Software engineers also need a theoretical and practical background in *"agile" methods* such as XP. Agile methodologies challenge traditional design-centric models of software engineering by using test code, user representatives and other relatively lightweight methods to represent the functional intent of the system, as well as changing many aspects of project planning and estimation.

7 Ethics

While professional ethics may not appear to be related to outsourcing and the other developments in the software engineering profession we have been discussing, they bear mentioning here, both because the technical and business environment changes brought about by these developments are related to certain aspects of professional ethics, and also because professional ethics training in general appears to be lacking in many software engineering curricula. While we only discuss several aspects of professional ethics that we believe are most pertinent to navigating the current professional environment, more thorough treatments are available (e.g., in [6]).

The general ethical principle we should impart to our students is to practice *integrity* and *excellence* [18] in every aspect of their software engineering practice. While integrity and excellence are excellent guidelines for life in general, in the practice of software engineering this includes honesty and openness, good stewardship of time and resources, and excellence in the application of software engineering principles. In the rest of this section, we discuss ways to apply these in software engineering education and practice.

7.1 Communication Integrity

Communication integrity includes openness and honesty. In software engineering, this includes being proactively honest and open when reporting project status, not only when the project is on schedule, but especially when problems are anticipated or realized. Software projects are almost never done in a vacuum; any technical, design, or schedule problems are very likely to impact other members of the development team, or even the success of the development project as a whole. In addition, project managers need to know about any problems as soon as possible to implement mitigation strategies, manage customer expectations, etc. That is why software engineers need to be trained to not only be honest (i.e., give an honest answer when asked), but also to be proactive and take initiative in communicating any information that is important to the success of their project.

Another area where communication integrity is important for software engineers is when they are called upon to provide an engineering evaluation or estimate, particularly when the honest answer is not what the listener (e.g., management) wants to

hear. Examples include how long it will take to design or implement a given compo
nent or product, whether a proposed design or solution should be adopted, etc. More
subtle, but equally common, are situations where someone asks the engineer "casu-
ally" or "off the record" whether something is possible, can be done within a certain
time, etc. Since any statement, no matter how casual, may be repeated or otherwise
used in unintended ways, software engineers should treat all project-related communication as an engineering communication for which integrity is imperative. It is
important to emphasize to student engineers that communication integrity always
leads to better results in the long term. For example, if as a software engineer they go
along with a management schedule expectation that their own estimates show to be
unrealistic, they will either end up working excessive hours under tremendous stress
trying to meet the schedule expectation they failed to challenge, or else they will miss
the target delivery date altogether and earn the wrath, however unjustified it may
seem, of management.

7.2 Ethical Use of Time and Resources

Another ethical area that should be emphasized in software engineering education is
good stewardship of time and resources. While the Internet is undoubtedly the most
useful research and communication tool ever invented, it is also arguably the most
efficient way ever devised to waste time. Software engineers need to be taught (or it
needs to be reemphasized) that unless they are being paid as a contractor on a per-
deliverable basis, any normal employer-employee relationship includes an implicit, if
not explicit, contractual understanding that they will spend at least a certain number
of numbers per week performing the agreed-upon function (the actual number of
hours varies by company and by country). For software engineers, this means that
they have a professional ethical obligation to spend at least the designated amount of
time actually practicing software engineering. Since software engineering schedules
often include "slack time", e.g., times when an engineer is temporarily waiting for
another part of the project to be finished, or when an engineer finishes his or her part
of the project sooner than expected, integrity and discipline is necessary to avoid
wasting time, and find something to do that actually contributes to the project. Engineers can also be creative; if they feel burned out or need to do something else for
awhile besides staring at the computer, they can always spend some "slack" time
helping or mentoring more junior engineers, helping other engineers brainstorm about
the design of some aspect of the system, etc. Integrity does not need to be boring; it
just needs to be practiced.

7.3 Personal Responsibility

Another ethical issue related to integrity is personal ownership and responsibility.
Software engineering students should be taught always to take ownership of, and
responsibility for, their own actions. This includes the results of their actions, including any projects they work on, software they design or implement, etc. Any blaming
of others, or attempting to shift blame, is unethical. It is also counterproductive, because it poisons the software development team environment, and in the worst case,
can degrade or destroy the ability of a team to function. The behavioral aspects of

personal responsibility, taking responsibility for one's own actions, are included in communication integrity. What we are addressing here is really more of an ethical attitude of personal responsibility that will serve to motivate ethical behavior under any circumstance, than a set of behaviors *per se*.

7.4 Engineering Practices

While software engineering education does often emphasize engineering practices like good system design, the principle of integrity should be extended to cover all software engineering activities. The general principle here is to practice engineering at all times. For example, students should be taught never to make any unjustified (or undocumented) shortcuts, claims, promises, etc. All of these should be based on evidence. And valid evidence is always ultimately based on some kind of model, even if it is only a mental model based on experience. We need to equip students with the models they need now and the skills they will need to extend current software design and development models, and create new models, to meet unforeseen future software engineering needs. Technically, what we need to give engineering students is good software engineering domain meta-models, including useful entities, relationships and organizational principles they can use to create and adapt their own models in particular project and organizational contexts. Examples of software engineering domain models include application domain models, requirements analysis and requirements engineering models, architectural models, design patterns and other design models, project planning and scheduling models, testing and verification models, and even models for more esoteric aspects of software engineering like team interaction and communication. Students should be taught to refine these core software engineering models continually as they gain experience and encounter new circumstances or challenges, and ultimately, to recognize new domains as they arise in the future, and create appropriate models for them.

7.5 Intellectual Property

Finally, no discussion of software engineering ethics would be complete without talking about intellectual property. For the purposes of this discussion, we consider intellectual property in the broader context as potentially including any information a software engineer gains while working for a company that may harm the company if it is disclosed. We do not include areas such as disclosure of illegal activity at the company to the proper authorities, where there may be an ethical or legal obligation to disclose information that does prove to be harmful to the company. But even leaving out such cases leaves a wide area where behaving ethically is not only a professional imperative, but may also save a software engineer from legal problems. For example, every software engineer knows, or ought to know, that it is illegal and unethical to steal or take source code from a company without permission.

Where software engineers have sometimes run into problems is cases like using proprietary knowledge (also known as trade secrets) they obtained while working for a company in their own business or while working at another company. Such proprietary knowledge can include details of system functionality and design, customer lists, knowledge of implementation plans and schedules, or any other private company information, whether it is explicitly protected by patent or copyright, or not.

In addition, the nature of software engineering is such that software engineers often have access to personal information, especially if they are involved with building or maintaining databases that contain personal information (e.g., human resources or financial data systems), or if for whatever reason they have root or administrator privileges on any system where personal information is stored. While it should be apparent, software engineers have an absolute ethical obligation not to use or divulge any personal information to which they may gain access. And while this also should be obvious, it is unethical for a software engineer to gain access deliberately to any database, directory, system, etc., in which they have no legitimate project-related business (i.e., all forms of "hacking" are unethical).

8 Discussion

To prepare software engineers to thrive in an increasingly distributed and outsourced environment, we recommend starting software engineering programs with an enhanced introduction to software engineering principles, including material that explicitly addresses outsourcing and distributed development, before any core technical coursework is attempted. A basic understanding of *software as a service* will provide important conceptual, technical and practical perspective for applying the technical material in real-world situations. The goal is to give students both the tools and the perspective needed to become software *engineers* who design *solutions*, rather than programmers who write programs. Starting with engineering principles gives students a firm foundation in software engineering, avoiding the need to "retrofit" them with this knowledge later on, and also enables the technical course materials, assignments, and projects to reinforce and expand upon these principles. Industry practitioners and managers should also be brought in regularly to provide perspective on how software engineering principles are used in industry.

8.1 Software Development Process Curricula

Software development process curricula should emphasize *requirements engineering (RE)*, including *requirements management*, i.e., methods and techniques for managing the expectations of customers, managers and other stakeholders. While much of requirements gathering and prioritization is currently done by marketing professionals, software engineers should be prepared to take a leadership role in RE, taking market concerns into account, and working closely with market researchers and other stakeholders. While software as a service utilizes technical means such as service-oriented architectures (SOA), a complete understanding of the *service* aspects of modern software development and delivery also impacts all aspects of the software development process. Software engineering students need to be acutely aware that they serve a "higher purpose", in that their technical knowledge will only be useful to the extent that they learn to use it to contribute practically to providing a needed service. Curricula should also teach students when and how to adopt aspects of "agile" methodologies and other *iterative approaches* to software development projects. Process education should include *organization engineering*, i.e., methods and techniques engineers at all levels can use to reengineer their organizations to optimize the success of development projects.

8.2 Architecture and System Design Curricula

Architecture and system design curricula should emphasize *distributed system architectures*, and *component-connector architectures*, both of which make it easier to incorporate components developed by third parties, whether outsourced, OSS, or COTS. The trend toward providing and utilizing *software as a service* is impacting the way software-based systems are designed and deployed. Architecture curricula should include styles that support software as a service, particularly distributed service provider network architectures, such as *service-oriented architecture*. However, the service-oriented software approach also requires software architects and designers to approach basic system design in entirely new ways. Curricula should teach engineers to provide specifically needed services by developing service provider components, and architects to design applications and systems primarily by composing sets of these services, which may have been developed globally by disparate organizations. Architecture curricula should also include *product family architectures*, to give engineers tools to develop frameworks that bring order and consistency to systems developed by diverse distributed teams. Application frameworks such as J2EE, .NET, or similar platforms, should be used as practical training tools in their own right, as well as to illustrate, e.g., the difference between a common component model and a product family architecture. And finally, *prescription-based architectural approaches* [2] [5], in which the system architecture is directly derived from the requirements, will give software engineers important techniques to help ensure that systems they design fulfill the specified functional goals and constraints. Specific attention should also be given to *domain-specific* software engineering techniques, methods and tools.

8.3 Expanded Project Management Training

Project management education should be expanded to include *program management*, including such business-related concerns as cost/benefit analysis and market analysis, among others. Project management education should emphasize *cost and time planning and estimation for distributed projects*, including projects that utilize *internal and external outsourcing*. Software engineers need to think of themselves as manager-integrators who are comfortable engineering systems using outsourced teams and third-party components, while avoiding inefficient practices like unnecessary hands-on development. Outsourcing often includes international teams, so the effects of *cultural and linguistic issues* on team communication, expectations, etc., should also be addressed. And since the success of software projects largely depends on resource availability (time, engineers, equipment, tools, etc.), project management education would not be complete without addressing *advocacy and resource management* for development projects. Software engineers must be able to determine as early as possible whether the resources allocated to their project are sufficient to enable the

project to be successful, so they can reengineer teams and processes, manage re
quirements and expectations, and do whatever else is necessary to ensure success.

8.4 Change Management

Although we have mentioned the need for software engineers to manage change in
different software engineering contexts throughout this discussion, we believe this is
an important enough topic to merit special mention here. All core software engineering curricula should emphasize the dynamic nature of software engineering. For
example, in the real world, projects must often be completed under different organizing principles, using a different set of development team members than the ones who
were available when the project began. And requirements often change many times
before the project is finished, sometimes invalidating the fundamental assumptions
underlying the original architecture and design. This intrinsic need for system evolution is further complicated by the increasing reliance on components developed and
separately maintained by distributed teams from different organizations or open
source communities, since these disparate components usually also continue to evolve
in parallel. In general, software engineering curricula needs to stop acting as though
software development occurs in some kind of a vacuum where a developer or team
can use a given set of requirements to derive an architectural design and implementation, without the need to accommodate changes from various sources at inopportune
times throughout the process. Some ideas for incorporating change management
training into software engineering curricula include changing the requirements for
design and implementation projects at different project phases, changing the individual roles and membership of project teams during class projects, and making change
management concerns an integral part of all software engineering process and design
curricula.

8.5 Practical Ethics Education for Engineers

Software engineering curricula should include a course in software engineering ethics,
and all core software engineering curricula should encourage students to practice
software engineering in an ethical manner by highlighting the practical ethical concerns related to utilizing the technologies and methodologies being taught. However,
curricula should avoid presenting software engineering ethics as merely a set of rules,
which students might be tempted to dismiss as irrelevant. All software engineering
ethical principles and guidelines have very practical benefits, which may include
preventing interpersonal or legal problems, or enhancing other aspects of software
engineering practice. Preventative benefits of ethical behavior range from preventing
various practical or team-related problems, to in extreme cases, perhaps protecting
software engineers from lawsuits or other legal penalties. Most of the ethical software engineering behavior we have discussed also yields practical benefits that either
directly contribute to the success of software engineering projects (e.g., communication integrity and engineering practice integrity), or at least help prevent practical
problems later on. So software engineering core curricula should include the appropriate professional ethical context, and in turn, the ethical discussion should be
grounded within a framework that includes practical benefits.

9 Conclusions

For our profession to remain relevant, we need to prepare software engineers to assume leadership roles in engineering system requirements, building solutions using internal and third-party components and distributed development resources, and integrating software elements from these diverse sources into coherent product families using optimal component and connector architectures. To develop systems successfully using distributed resources, engineers will need to learn better product and project management, organization and process engineering, and interpersonal and cross-cultural communication skills. We see these challenges as an excellent opportunity for properly prepared software engineers to play a central role in ensuring the success of software projects and product families, by applying enhanced engineering principles to manage the architectural and process complexity induced by the current drive toward distributed and third-party development models.

References

[1] Bosch, J.: Software Architecture: The Next Step. In Proceedings of the First European Workshop on Software Architecture (EWSA 2004) (2004) 194-199
[2] Brandozzi, M., Perry, D.: Architectural Prescriptions for Dependable Systems. ICSE 2002 Workshop on Architecting Dependable Systems (WADS 2002) (2002)
[3] Dueñas, J., Capilla, R.: The Decision View of Software Architecture. In Proceedings of the 2nd European Workshop on Software Architecture (EWSA 2005) (2005) 222-230
[4] Grunbacher, P., Egyed, A., Medvidovic, N.: Reconciling Software Requirements and Architectures with Intermediate Models. Software and Systems Modeling, Vol. 3 No. 3 (2004) 235-253
[5] Hawthorne, M., Perry, D.: Exploiting Architectural Prescriptions for Self-Managing, Self-Adaptive Systems: A Position Paper. ACM SIGSOFT 2004 Workshop on Self-Managed Systems (WOSS '04) (2004)
[6] IEEE Computer Society/ACM Joint Task Force on Computing Curricula: Software Engineering 2004: Curriculum Guidelines for Undergraduate Degree Programs in Software Engineering, http://sites.computer.org/ccse/SE2004Volume.pdf (2004)
[7] Sun Developer Network Products and Technologies: Java Platform, Enterprise Edition (Java EE), http://java.sun.com/javaee/index.jsp (2006)
[8] Divya Jani, Damien Vanderveken and Dewayne E Perry: "Deriving Architectural Specifications from KAOS Specifications: A Research Case Study", European Workshop on Software Architecture 2005, Pisa Italy, June 2005
[9] Hall, J., Jackson, M., Laney, R., Nuseibeh, B., Rapanotti, L.: Relating Software Requirements and Architectures Using Problem Frames. In Proceedings of the IEEE Joint International Requirements Engineering Conference (RE'02) (2002) 9-13
[10] Jansen, A., Bosch, J.: Software Architecture as a Set of Architectural Design Decisions. 5th Working IEEE/IFIP Conference on Software Architecture (WICSA 2005 (2005)
[11] van Lamsweerde, A.: Requirements Engineering in the Year 00: A Research Perspective. In Proceedings of the 22nd International Conference on Software Engineering (ICSE'00), Invited Paper, ACM Press (2000) 5-19
[12] Microsoft Developers Network (MSDN): Microsoft .NET Framework Developer Center, http://msdn.microsoft.com/netframework/ (2006)
[13] The Open Source Initiative (OSI), http://www.opensource.org (2006)

[14] Perry, D., Wolf, A.: Foundations for the Study of Software Architecture. ACM SIGSOFT Software Engineering Notes, 17(4):40 (1992)

[15] Perry, D., Staudenmayer, N., Votta, L.: People, Organizations, and Process Improvement. IEEE Software (1994)

[16] Perry, D.: Generic Descriptions for Product Line Architectures. ARES II Product Line Architecture Workshop (1998)

[17] SWEBOK: Guide to the Software Engineering Body of Knowledge. www.swebok.org

[18] The Tau Beta Pi Engineering Honor Society, http://www.tbp.org (2006)

On the Education of Future Software Engineers

Andrea Bolognesi, Paolo Ciancarini, and Rocco Moretti

Dipartimento di Scienze dell'Informazione
University of Bologna, Italy
{abologne, ciancarini, moretti}@cs.unibo.it

Abstract. The education of software engineering students more and more addresses enterprise-oriented organizational and management issues, like for instance modeling the business structure and environment of the enterprise which will receive a new software system. The teaching of business modeling technologies based on standards like UML and the Rational Unified Process raises novel questions that need to be addressed. Business modeling consists in modeling organizations and their workflows; in several cases the modeling can be complemented by business simulation. This paper presents as a case study some Agent-Based Simulation tools for modeling the enterprise dynamics, and shows how we exploited them to teach an Organizational Software Engineering laboratory course, providing students with Software Engineering skills along with Agent-Based Simulation principles.

1 Introduction

Less than a decade ago, SE courses were intended to provide students with conceptual principles as well as experienced skills in designing and developing a large software project. However, the conceptual basis of software design has broadened, for instance with notions of Business Process Modeling (BPM), which is necessary in those cases where the new software system modifies the internal behavior of an enterprise.

The scope of business management has changed over these years as well, as economists become more and more acquainted with the role of software from an economic perspective [5]. Until few years ago, BPM aimed mainly to manage the workflows within a company. Today it addresses complex intra- and inter-enterprise interactions, including the possibility of integration and orchestration of the processes of different enterprises.

This paper deals with teaching a laboratory course in what we call Organizational Software Engineering (OSE). We are especially interested in how business-oriented modeling is involved in SE evolution in conjunction with BPM. In particular we will discuss the role of enterprise simulations during the analysis phase of a project.

Business simulations are created by iterating business processes through a sound model of a given organization, which in a way strengthens the BPM analysis by adding concretely the concept of time to the process modeling. Such

P. Inverardi and M. Jazayeri (Eds.): ICSE 2005 Education Track, LNCS 4309, pp. 186–205, 2006.

addition of a time dimension allows us to see the progress of the activities and analyze the consequences of a process as it evolves.

Agent-Based Simulation (ABS) offers novel tools for representing, imitating, and understanding real world and human interaction behaviors, that were not accessible through classical analytic methods [1]. ABS is being transposed to business-oriented topics and found an exciting reply from organizational economics. Within this subject, enterprise modeling is a promising field of research, which focuses on a company's business processes and their inner organizations.

In our classes we recently started using UML and RUP for teaching OSE, that for a student means

a) to learn to model the behavior of an organization in order to analyze and eventually reengineer its workflows and services, and
b) to learn to simulate the behavior of the same organization, in order to analyze its perfomance when producing some manufacts.

The former activity usually consists of shaping a top down view of an organization, centered upon its workflows [27]; the latter activity shapes a bottom up view, that can be constructed for example using agent-based abstractions [28].

For this purpose a first natural question arises about how SE teaching changes for those undergraduate students, whose classes match Computer Science with Management Science.

Our primary objectives were to teach students some OSE skills using UML and RUP as principal vehicles for explaining some core concepts and providing the students with practical experiences while they learned to model computer programs.

In order to prepare students for organizational processes analysis, improving their abstraction expertise, we must draw attention to both the software development process, assisted by modeling and designing tool, and the organizational processes forming and evolution.

The need of business-oriented SE is a first consequence of the great economic support yielded by suitable software development, which considerably increased software worth for modern corporations. For software to be useful, it must directly support the business, leading to models which are sound, and give the possibility of exploring different improvement choices as avoiding inefficiencies or superfluous operations and adopting automatic schedules for unvaried tasks.

The design of a novel piece of software is more and more a matter of (re)designing the structure of the organizazion exploiting that software, rather than just an exercise in documenting a development process. For instance, the Rational Unified Process (RUP) has included among its core workflows one specialized in business modeling, that is intended to model the organization which has to receive the software system being designed with other, more technical, workflows.

Hence future software engineers cannot neglect the analysis of business dynamics and how a given software affects business processes and must address organizational and management issues, like, for instance, modeling the business structure and environment which will receive a new software system.

Moreover the students we teach are not normal Computer Science students, because they attend a novel curriculum where we match Computer Science with Management Science. This interdiscipinary cultural background is very challenging when teaching a lab in SE, because the students try to apply the principles that they study in their courses in Organizational Economics. This course was given indeed in conjunction with another class where students were improving their understanding on simulation models of complex systems, business-oriented management and organizational systems.

For pure Social and Economic science students, of course, the weight of software development could reveal to be a difficult barrier to be broken. A way to reduce such an obstacle consist in supply students with well known agent-based development tools, unburdening them from learning a programming language and leaving them to concentrate exclusively on the content of the simulation rather then its implementation. In this sense, a good compromise could be found by employing tools based on the OO paradigm, which offer libraries of functions and graphic plotters, accepting the subtle differences between the concept of agent in Computer Science and Social Sciences [20].

For Computer and Management science students teaching requirement changes, because undergraduate students need to develop and improve their ability on SE along with the expertise for modeling a business organization.

With this main aim, in spring 2004 and 2005 we set up a laboratory in SE and ABS applied on business modeling and complex system analysis in the economic field. With this respect we lay a particular stress on the very important and promising field of modeling enterprise simulation. The simulation of a firm depends on the understanding of its operations and rules, covering the process productions, the resources, which may be seen as machines, humans and materials, and the interaction between processes and resources. Traditionally enterprises are seen as systems, which becomes complex systems when considering the high number of elements which constitute it.

An enterprise's functioning can be suitably represented by modeling the interactions of such elements. A tool called Java Enterprise Simulator (jES), developed at the University of Turin by Pietro Terna [25], has been adopted for this task. Being a good example of agent-based abstraction and simulation tool of enterprises it has been chosen as the hub of the laboratory activity, as we will describe in depth in Section 5.

The science of complexity brought the scientific community to pay attention to a new way of interpreting the natural phenomena. To a certain extent it reunites the contrast between social and physical sciences, being intrinsic properties of complex systems dealt with principles from both the sides. As stated in [19], a multi-level and multi-domain research method is required by complex systems investigations which give importance to detailed models to better account for correct natural world representations. Micro simulation becomes therefore a suitable approach to deal with phenomena typified by the interaction of many individuals, where a crucial role is assumed by artificial simulations, owing to the increased power of modern computers. Consequently, computers are today accepted as decisive scientific tools from a wide range of researchers.

Business-oriented fieldwork along with Social Sciences aims at understanding how individuals behave and interact with each other and how such a reciprocal influence leads to large-scale outcomes. The researchers' objectives consist in identifying emergent properties which arise from the interactions of the individuals and cannot be obtained simply by adding together the individuals behaviors.

Dealing with systems and individuals leads directly to the insight of formalizing a complex systems in terms of Agent-Based Modeling (ABM), which is indeed well suited for the Social Science purpose as well as for organizational management. First of all, ABM represent systems in terms of individuals, or agents, which interact with each other, secondly an agent-based system exhibits emergent properties. When the agents behavior and interaction essentially depends on their past experiences, mathematical analysis is typically insufficient to describe the dynamic outcomes. In this case, ABM might be the only practical method of analysis. Normally the procedure starts from assumptions about agents and their interactions and proceeds with computer simulations in order to produce data which may reveal the dynamic consequences of such assumptions. Multi agent technology has been then successfully used to model and simulate social systems, which requires recognizing the unique role of simulation as a third method of doing science, in contrast to both induction and deduction. ABS can be then a powerful and convincing apparatus for discovering unexpected effects from simple assumptions [1]. Thus, when an analytic solution to a problem doesn't exist without simplifications which devalues the problem itself, it is useful to use ABM systems which can be seen as alternative to purely analytic approaches and can be collocated between analytical models and empirical observations. Examples of such case study are dynamic models of Social Sciences, instability of financial markets, surveys on consumers satisfaction, models of oligopolistic competition and human resources management.

Computer-Management scientists have interdisciplinary skills which must cope with the growing field of business simulation and ABM techniques. Destined to deal with both software development and software employing as a means of accomplishing a purpose, our students must learn both principles of SE and social modeling. Teaching modeling languages plays therefore a very important role, intended to improve their capacity for abstraction and representing their knowledge of a system. Hence, UML and RUP can be adopted both for modeling software systems and modeling business organizations through simulation models.

Section 2 describes simulation frameworks for ABS, which we used for OSE modeling. Section 3 introduces the reader to a metaphor-based approach to model organizational business system and presents an ABM enterprise simulator, developed at University of Turin [25], along with its connection with BPM. Section 4 deals with the choice of what Computer-Aided Software Engineering (CASE) tool to choose suitable for teaching purposes. Section 5 discusses how OSE materials applied to company analysis have been introduced into undergraduate-level courses over the past two years and analyzes some educational related technical issues.

2   ABS Frameworks and Support Libraries

In this Section we introduce the reader to ABS frameworks and libraries which are of particular significance in developing business and social simulations. In order to run a computer simulation a specific software for time progress control, casual events creation by random numbers generators and statistical and progress representation plots, must be developed. Some ready-made tools simplify the model implementation, reduces the effort for programming and improves the code reliability.

We focus on a well accepted framework for ABS, called Swarm [15], which is an experimental multi-agent simulation framework designed to facilitate the creation and the study of agent based models [13,14]. Originally developed at the Santa Fe Institute, Swarm is a package well known among the researchers on Natural and Social Sciences and Complex Systems analysis. Its first aim was to allow researchers to develop their own simulations in an easy way, without spending too much time on technical problems, arising from a specific programming language or from the exchange of simulation data.

Swarm offers a collection of libraries that can be used for writing Objective-C or Java programs to create ABM simulations. These libraries are distributed under GNU licensing terms and are intended to work on a very wide range of computer platforms.

With this framework, it is possible to easily define models which include a multitude of concurrently interacting agents and it is quite easy to model different agent-based scenarios. The term 'swarm' metaphorically indicates a group of agents and a schedule of activity which rules them according to a particular behavior.

The combined actions of the agents in a complex system may stimulate changes and affect the environment, therefore in order to analyse the whole system a steady dynamic representation of the environment itself must be built. Examples of the connection between agents and their environment are easy to be found out, for instance biological cells influence and are influenced by metabolism, or economy which is based on consumers' behavior but in the meantime affect consumers' choices. Actually, any element of an ABM could be though as being an agent, where usually with the term agent one intends some component with a particular task, but sometimes also special elements of the system, such as the environment, could be addressed as agents. The subtle difference between agents and objects from the OO paradigm and their strict connection let us exploiting and reuse modeling languages with the intent of representing the complex system and its scenarios. Agents have an internal data representation, which could be seen as their memory or state, along with perceptions, that are means for changing it, and with behaviors, that are means to interact with their environment. We can then depict agents as objects, their state as instance variables, their perceptions and behaviors as methods. Figure 1 shows an example of abstraction reification into the OO paradigm.

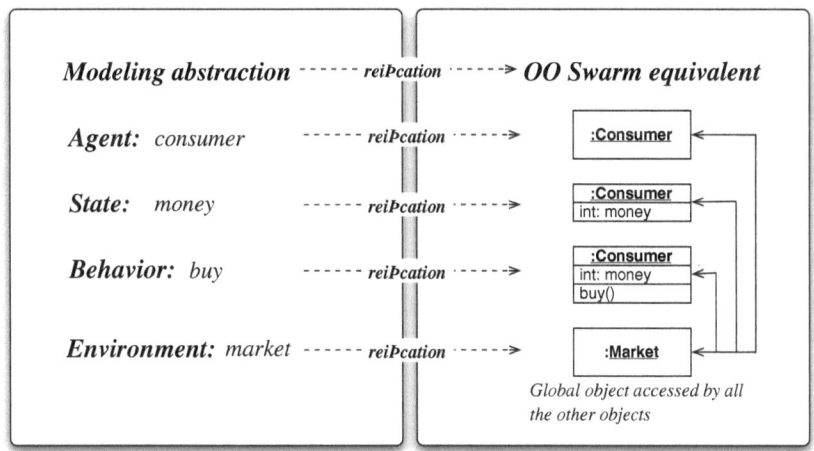

Fig. 1. Modeling abstraction reified into OO equivalent

The fundamental insight exploited by Swarm designers considers OO programming a suitable approach for defining agent-based models [14,21]. Instead of defining a domain specific language, a set of ready-made classes and libraries is offered to developers in order to easily build agent-based simulations and make a better use of their time, by concentrating exclusively on modeling.

The Swarm architecture defines a special object, called *observer*, whose primary task consists in probing, hence observing, other agents via a specific interface, called the *probe interface*. This approach enacts a metaphor where events happen and the researchers analyze them from the outside without affecting their evolution. Model agents send to the observer real-time data which will be stored for later analysis. The observer objects can be considered agents as well, and it is possible to define different observers. These compose an actual *agent swarm* which combines with the model to form a complete experimental framework for agent-based simulations.

3   Enterprise Modeling

This Section introduces a simulation framework developed to analyze how enterprises work and interact, hence to better understand the mechanisms behind firms and company and, of course, how to improve their functioning. This Swarm based simulation framework, called jES (Java Enterprise Simulator), was originally developed by Pietro Terna, at the University of Turin [25], and it aims to reproduce in detail the inner mechanisms of enterprises. The fields of application of this tool range from real enterprises simulation to theoretical models construction, in order to concrete optimize actual situations or just investigate possible problems.

Being such a task closely related to the understanding of human choices, it is difficult to formulate an universal scheme to comprehend, explain, and improve organization activities. From the decision-making process side things can get quite complex, lacking an effective theory with which supporting our analysis.

The simulation approach in this field is useful. Following Terna's argumentation, we state that the approach is invariant with respect to the complexity of the system which is going to be modeled and simulated, and requires us to just specify some parameters and behavioral definitions, without assuming anything a priori.

Many different kinds of investigation can be performed with simulation, as for instance checking correctness of our hypothesis, exploring new ideas and considerations, helping us formalizing and solving problems. With this insight in mind we use simulation as a means for reproducing in detail the inner mechanisms of a firm [22,23].

A significant strain under with researchers may find themselves is due to the transposition of the observed properties of a given system into a computer language, even if an OO approach can easily create agent based models and simulations. A formal method, called Metaphors Based Modeling, is proposed in [16] and [17] in order to overcome such difficulty. This consists in using effective metaphors with which translating real situation into software models. Following this indication we transpose real observed systems into computer models, then the program simulator can be executed and the simulated results can be transferred back by means of a counter-metahpore into the real scenario, suggesting expectation results about the real systems. Clearly this method is successful when the counter-metaphor is easily obtained from the metaphor initially used. In this case it is easy to validate a model as representative for the reality we observed and want to simulate.

A simple example of metaphor is proposed in jES, based on the concept of 'recipe', implemented through an array of integers, to model the products manufactured by the simulated enterprise. An *order* is defined as the item to be produced, containing accounting and technical information. A recipe is represented as a sequence of steps to be executed to produce some good, that is, metaphorically speaking, the set of instructions for preparing the given order, disguised as a list of the ingredients required.

jES recipes can represent parallel production paths and batch activities, leading to the possibility of simulating and testing procurement processes. Figure 2 shows a simplified view of the modeling of an enterprise done within the jES formalism. A recipe, in this representation, is a list of natural numbers, representing the components, to be executed in a certain order. The agents which can produce orders are called *production units*, each of which is associated with one or more steps of the recipes.

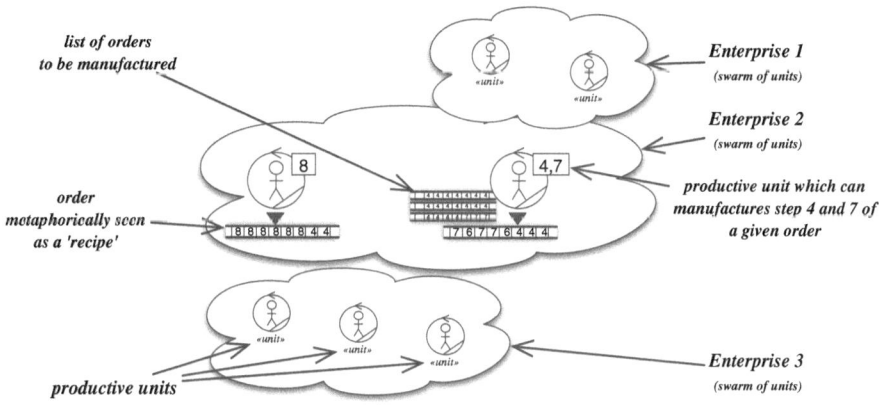

Fig. 2. Simplified view of an enterprise modeling using jES

In this particular example, when a concrete task (here represented by step number 8) in a recipe is found, then the order will be processed by a unit which can handle that particular task, which may indicate for example an "assemble product" task. This unit will take the time needed to complete the work and then it will send the order to the unit corresponding to the next step in the list. Note that within this formalism all the necessary information to achieve the order completion is listed into the recipe: when the activity of a production unit is concluded then the next step to be executed is read from the order. Then a search among production agents is carried out asking to all the units whether they can manufacture that step and, in the affirmative, the product is added to the waiting list of the consenting units. With this scheme it is possible to represent different organizational structures, for example an assembly line can be simulated by predetermining the recipes and by assigning production units with unique steps.

Thus enterprises can be represented by a set of production units, composing swarm of units which interact with each other. This representation format can be applied mainly to the industrial sector and to firms that produce physical goods, but could be adapted to more general structures representation [24]. As we have seen in Section 2, the use of a 'swarm' is a powerful metaphor well known and used among ABM researchers.

Because of jES strict relation with BPM, we exploit here the RUP traceability feature for connecting business representation to jES models through trace-abstractions relations. In this way the standard-conform use of UML is enabled for jES domain also, and the seamless integration of different methods is encouraged.

Within the jES simulator, the main abstraction consists in understanding the world which is going to be simulated in term of orders to be executed and structures that are able to execute them, which are formalized in terms of production units, as we have already seen in Figure 2. Following this way of representing the enterprise we may note that the principal intent is to describe the firm as exactly as the available data are.

Figure 3 depicts the jES elements notation. The jES productive units notation traces the Business Case Worker, which is a special Business Worker that interacts directly with actors outside the firm system, by simply adding its production information, represented by natural numbers. This choice is due to the fact that units are the constitutive elements of an enterprise and receive orders to be executed. As we discussed before, orders are represented by means of recipe metaphors, hence they trace Business Entities, being passive elements which represents important pieces of information that are manipulated by Business Actors and Business Workers. The notation of orders is, as already seen in Figure 2, depicted as tape of 'ingredients' required to complete the good.

Some swarm of agents, in particular of productive units, trace Business Systems, being these elements joined together by the responsibility to fulfill a specific task. Other jES elements will simply be described with stereotypes from the standard UML elements for BPM.

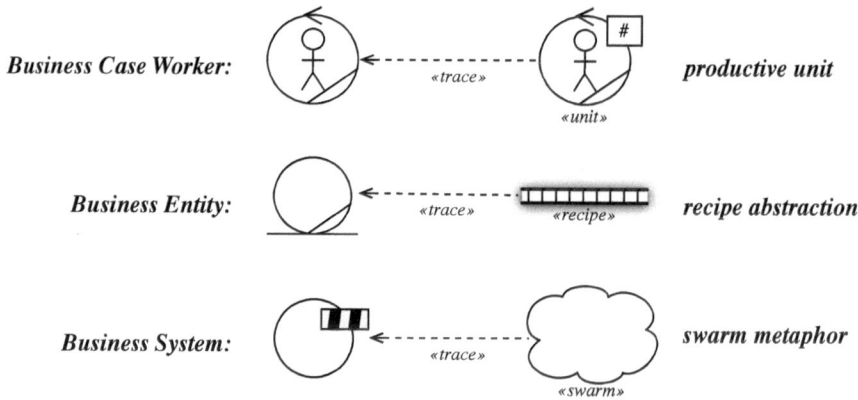

Fig. 3. Traceability from the business model elements to jES model elements

The figure 4 shows the workflow representing the life cycle of a simulated day in jES, on the basis of some input simulation data. The productive units manufacture a step in the recipe of the first order in their waiting list, then new orders are inserted into the simulation and are assigned to those productive units able to perform the next task in the respective orders recipes. A way of communicating the new orders added and advising other units of the next steps to be accomplished is represented by the 'news' metaphors in order to send working information. These can be seen as the act of reserving a future production in order to speed up the performance of manufacturing, hence with analogy to emails or phone calls [24].

A more detailed view of a jES simulated day is proposed with the collaboration diagram depicted in Figure 5. Here the gear-shaped element represent the inner mechanism of simulation, we will refer as the simulation model or just

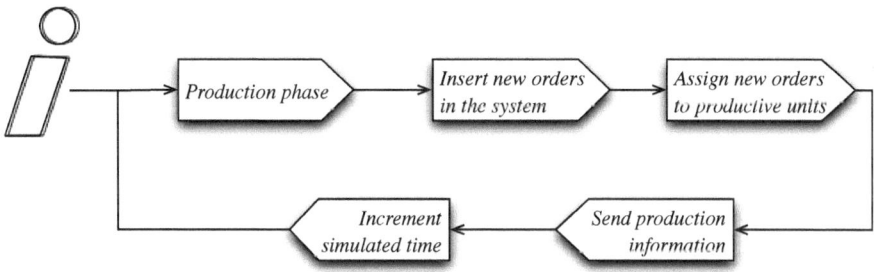

Fig. 4. Workflow for the cycle of life of a simulated day in jES

simulator. This represent the core from which all the actions of the simulation are started. We can then imagine that when a swarm receives a signal from the simulator it pushes all of its agents to simultaneously do the requested operation. The production phase is initiated by sending to the productive units swarm the command of processing locally waiting orders. The insertion of new orders in the system is then obtained by means of a Business Actor, indicated with the stereotype ≪reader≫, which concretely reads the simulation data, but represents the role of participants outside of the scope of the enterprise. The orders assigning operation is triggered by a particular worker, called ≪distributor≫, whose task is to sort orders to the right productive units. Depending on the kind of model we are dealing with, the role of such agent can be seen either as a internal object of the whole simulation mechanism and so not interesting from the business-oriented side, or as an active element in the enterprise modeling. Again the exchange of information is started from the simulator which sends to productive units the specific command to propagate news information.

Figure 6 shows an activity diagram proposed by our students which describes in a detail how the Java Enterprise Simulator works. On the left side the swimlane for the simulator model abstraction is depicted: there are two cycles, where the nested one represents the operation repeated during a day of simulation and the other one performs the passage to a new day. The variable *timeUnit* represents how long a simulation day must be, while the variable *tick* is simply a counter. For each *tick* the model sends messages to all agents of the simulation. Actual agents are the productive units of the system, whose operation at the receipt of messages from the model are depicted in the middle swim-lane.

Orders are implemented as objects, but it is difficult to see them as agents, being just a vehicle of information which represents the step to be accomplished for completion. For example, when units receive the signal to produce, they check if their own production list contains an order and in the affirmative they execute a step in the order. When the signal to proceed is received, units control if the order has been completed and, if not, they send the order object to a special agent, the Order distributor, which has the task of finding the right productive units for the order according to the next step in the order. Whether such a unit is found, the order is added to its production list. Another special participant

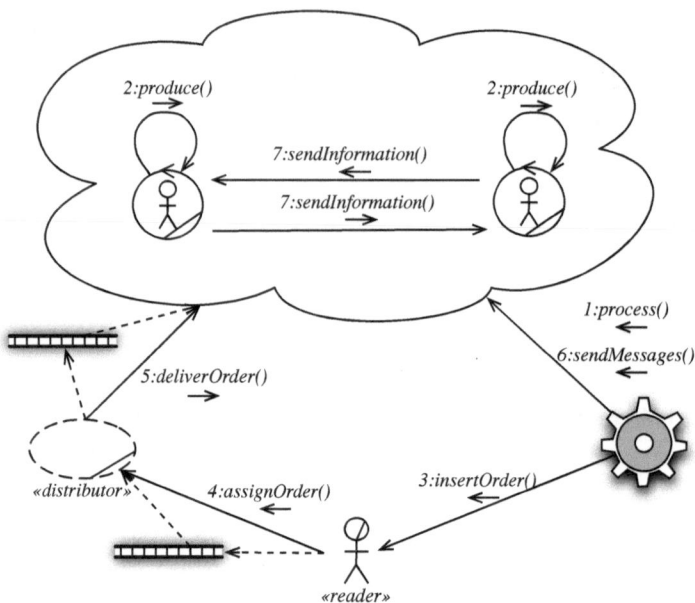

Fig. 5. Collaboration diagram of a simulated day in jES

depicted in this action diagram is the object Reader, which simply reads from input files the information needed to the creation of orders and proceeds in distributing them through the Order distributor.

In the next Section we will place emphasis on the choice of modeling tools in order to assist students during the laboratory activity and let them easily work with core concept as abstraction and devising correct models to better understand the problems they are dealing with. In particular in Section 4 we will discuss about what CASE tool and development environment to adopt during lectures and laboratory activities. In Section 5 we will focus on activities organized during the courses in 2004 and 2005.

4   What CASE Tool to Choose?

A crucial decision that must be taken to help students in their efforts to practice principles they learned in class is the suggestion of what modeling tools to use. We were looking for a specific tool which would help students in modeling software along with implementing it. The desired programming language was Java. Our striving for choosing a professional tool for modeling and software developing suitable for educational purposes was fulfilled when Eclipse [8], a new professional and complete development environment, appeared on the scene. This is part of an open source project, sponsored in November 2001 by an association of several companies such as IBM, Borland, Merant, Qnx Software, Rational Software, Red Hat, Suse, Togethersoft and Webgain. It is an integrated

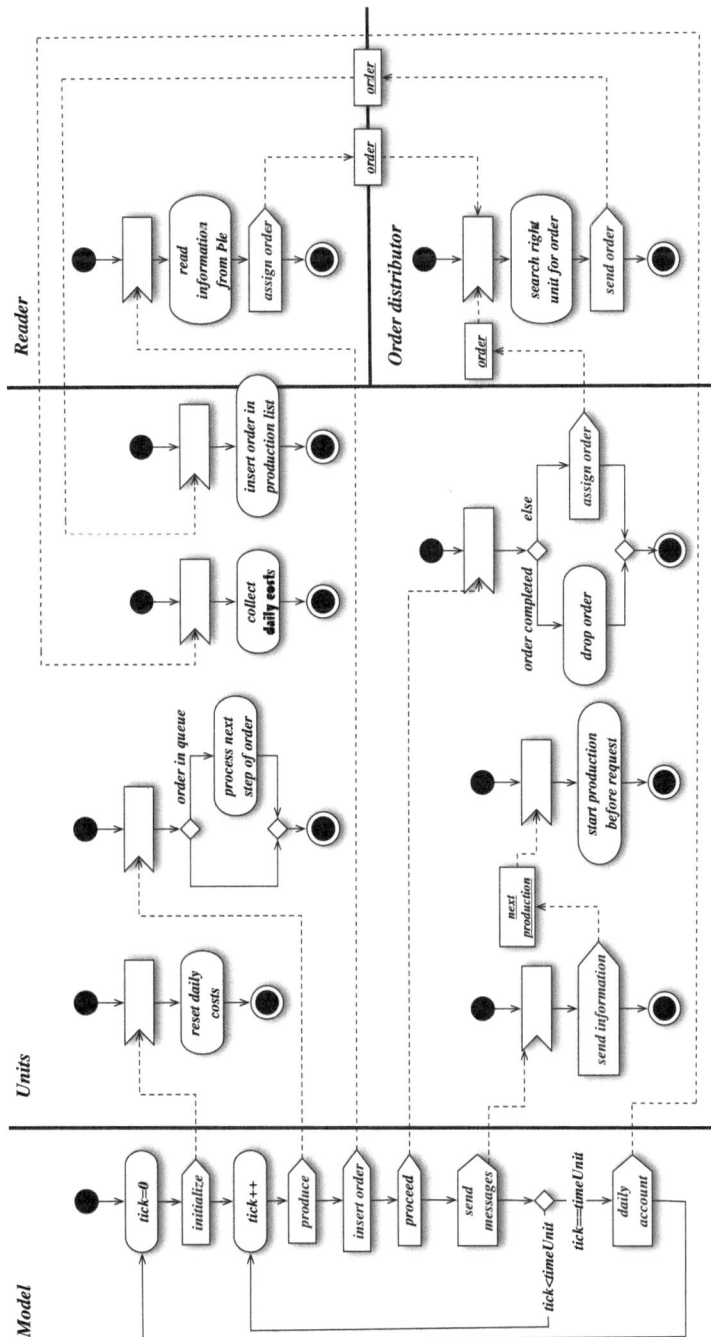

Fig. 6. Activity diagram describing the base model of jES

platform which let developers to handle the entire software generation process for enterprise application.

Being regularly used by developers all over the world, Eclipse is characterized by quality and productiveness attributes. Moreover, it is strongly platform independent and can be installed on the major OS platforms.

Eclipse can be used as an Integrated Development Environment (IDE), offering the manipulation of various content types, hence it can be used for writing code. But it could be used also as a product base, supported through plug-in architecture and customizations. When it is used as an IDE, Eclipse provides a set of workbench plug-ins for manipulating Java code. The Java compiler is built in and is therefore used for checking errors on the fly, during the production of the code, by means of special markers when the compilation fails. When it is used as a product base, it can be employed as a finite product framework, exploiting its flexible plug-in architecture.

In this direction, a useful and popular plug-in for teaching UML and software modeling available in Eclipse is Omondo EclipseUML [26]. It is a visual modeling tool, natively integrated with Eclipse, among the most successful Eclipse plug-ins.

The plug-in based architecture fostered many software companies to develop their own plug-in designed for particular purposes, in order to improve Eclipse as a base product. Following this way in the last years some products have been presented for BPM and business management based on UML notation. Unfortunately, none of them were freely distributed and we were not able to use them in our classes.

However, EclipseUML can be easily adopted even during lectures allowing, for gradual generation of rather complex models and modeling activities, being changes easily expedited. The resulting UML diagrams are depicted clearly and let students focus on the content of the model maintaining a neat memory about the sequence of adjustment during the modeling process.

To sum up, we feel like saying that the choice of Eclipse has been a success: students appreciated the development environment and how it facilitates them in finding and resolving programming errors. User interface, with the addition of UML plug-in, give a clear representation of OO structures, which are graphically depicted and then easier to understand.

However, in order to not confuse or distract inexperienced students which face SE studies for the first time, we must hide some functionality of the system, even if expressly asked by some students, deferring further widening to a thorough lecture. For example some students may want to understand in depth how the debugging mechanisms works, in that case our suggestion is to postpone such investigations to an optional detailed discussion with interested students.

With these considerations in mind many recent works aim to develop plug-in to adapt Eclipse for teaching purposes confirming that Eclipse has proved to be a suited platform for a teaching environment. The reader which is interested in this aspect of Eclipse may give a look to the Eclipse Community Education Project (ECESIS) [7], which aims the development of educational technologies, such as tools or plug-ins that help people learn about Eclipse or use Eclipse for educational purposes. Among several research project in this field are, for instance, Eclipse Training Perspective (ETP), a framework for hosting courses, and Penumbra, a plug-in that makes Eclipse more suitable for use in an undergraduate teaching environment.

Finally, it is worth to write some information on another tool, called Dia [6], devised to draw a very large range of different diagrams and freely distributed under the GPL license. This program assist the modeler in designing visual models, from entity relationship to UML diagrams, including flowcharts and general graph-based models. It offers the possibility of exporting diagrams in a wide selection of format, among which we can choose vector-based formats such as EPS, which turn out to be very useful for students when writing the LaTeX documentation to the project laboratory. Being a very easy of use tool, it could be adopted from the beginning of the course, for example to model the different kinds of UML diagrams directly during lectures. It could comfortably act as a launching pad for more sophisticated software-integrated tools, as Eclipse is.

5   Laboratory Activities

This Section discusses how OSE materials applied to company analysis have been introduced into our undergraduate-level courses over the past two years.

5.1   A Reverse Engineering Experience

In the spring of 2004 we organized a project activity for students, which were divided into groups of 3 or 4 members. The aim was to provide students with OO modeling principles along with abstraction skills needed in modeling an AB simulation. They already had some notions of Java programming, but they had never faced a software engineering approach. Therefore, we gave around 20 lectures dealing with UML and ABM.

The requested project was then stated as the reverse engineering of the Java Enterprise Simulator, jES, starting from its code to a detailed description of its architecture backed by a UML representation.

This experience was challenging but it had also some disadvantages which we needed to carefully weight and we will discuss about in this Section. The exercise consisted in studying the simulator way to use from the input data representation to the analysis of output information. Afterwards they had to analyze more in depth the framework architecture, reading directly the source code and starting drawing sketch of models which, step by step, became more appropriate. The outcome was then composed by a report containing the models rightly depicted by means of UML specifics through Eclipse drawing tools, which were though to be useful during the reverse engineering, having some features explicitly created for this intent, as an effective and correct creation of class diagrams from source code.

The project was indeed difficult for two main reasons:

- learning abstraction, and
- explaining one's understanding with simple and effective diagrams.

There were no requests for code production and the only central aim was to push students practicing and going beyond their abstracting and explaining difficulties. What to model and how to express the model were obviously a great stumbling block for students.

The major difficulties were probably due to the lack of code generation, which frightened students as if they were loosing an important point of reference.

The jES source code was complex and it was a difficult task to understand specific parts of it before having understood the whole framework.

Some students gave a justification for their poor modeling activity ascribing it to the strain for understanding the code and the whole software. Such has been their exertion on discovering how was implemented the entire mechanism of the simulator that they neglected to focus on how to model their understanding by means of UML.

Let us give an example of the obstacles that they have encountered.

The agent-oriented recipe metaphor we have seen, which describes the steps to be accomplished to achieve an order production, is actually described in the implementation with three different formats, namely an external, an intermediate, and an internal representation.

In order to translate the external user defined alpha-numeric list into the internal purely numeric vector, a scheme of transformation steps has been worked out. Thinking in Java, there is no need to formulate such a variety of formats. Besides the translation between these three formats could reveal to be particularly complicated, being recipes able to represent complex typologies of orders, such as batch production and procurement from warehouses.

Clearly, this implementation choice does not affect the whole sense of the software definition, hence a high level modeling of how the simulator works it is not difficult to be pointed out. But doing a reverse engineering operation change the perspective and a cryptic source code may lead to a very awkward job. A lot of students made their own comments and suggestions about jES implementation presenting how they would have changed it. For instance, about the recipe formats example seen before, the majority of students proposed to merge all the representations for recipes, maintaining a unique format and exploiting Java powerful string management.

This kind of comments and feedbacks has been a reliable indicator for us to understand how the laboratory activity improved students abstraction and modeling skills.

In conclusion, starting from an unknown software and doing a reverse engineering operation is for sure an exciting and effective exercise to learn SE principles and techniques, but it it could be quite difficult and required a particular dedication. Modeling a software in conjunction with the generation of programming code enabled our students to experiment a concrete design activity and fostered them to apply the theory learned during the class.

The following year, we assigned a different project, which will be discussed in Section 5.2, joining both the reverse engineering and the source code production requirements.

5.2   Developing an Enterprise Simulator

In the Spring of 2005 we planned a project activity with another simulator. We adopted a simulation tool alternative to Swarm, called JAS, which is less known, but in some ways more suitable for educational proposes. The Java Agent-based Simulation library (JAS) [18] is an open-source Swarm clone simulation toolkit, but, differently form Swarm, which requires a lot of efforts to be installed, is written completely in Java and is quite reliably platform-indipendent. We thought that it could be worth choosing JAS for teaching OSE to novices, looking for an effective simulation framework with which little time is required to familiarize students. Moreover, for helping students understanding the functioning of Terna's enterprise simulator, a simplified version, called jES-light, was developed at University of Turin. This soft version has been ported from Swarm framework to JAS toolkit, but the whole jES system was not. The natural consequence of these considerations was to require students to do a reverse engineering of jES-light, straightly unburdening them from a too much onerous offline analysis of the whole architecture.

Besides the analysis of jES architecture, students were asked to develop an extension of the simple jES-light, improving its features and building a more useful tool for simulating an enterprise. Such a new tool was called 'jES-light plus', to characterize the aim of obtaining a boosted version of the simpler jES-light.

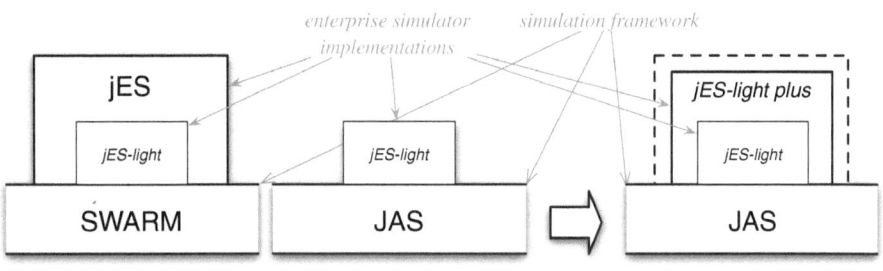

State of the art before laboratory activity   *Laboratory activity requirements*

Fig. 7. State of the art of jES and project requirements

For each extension implemented, the reason and the justification for the choice had to be motivated along with the explanation of the needs which led to propose such extension. A suitable analysis and modeling during the development of the code was required as well.

In order to foster students to concentrate on modeling before programming code, we divided the project delivery into two different deadlines. The first one demanded a detailed account of what was implemented with a right UML description, the second one requested for the source code.

The figure 7 shows the state of the art of jES implementations before the laboratory activity, on the left, and the project requirements on the right. It was a challenging proposal which theoretically could have led to an almost complete implementation of the whole enterprise simulator for JAS. The dashed line depicted in figure stays to indicate how jES-light plus was placed between the enterprise simulator soft and advanced version.

This second experience was more effective in involving students in the laboratory activity, according to the projects results and the feedbacks we received. We believe that the code production requirement played a crucial role in attracting students' attention and responsibility.

6   Conclusions

The advent of the Internet reshaped both the way we design software systems and teach how to build them. Apparently, the educational impact has been high on both the processes we teach and the products we exercise to build in our Software Engineering classes. However, the nature of software has not been really modified: a proof of this is that most languages and tools we use today derive directly from pre-Internet processes and tools. For instance, the Internet language par excellence, Java, is directly derived from C++, eliminating some quirk mechanisms, like direct pointers. Another proof is that most Software Engineering introductory books written in the pre-Internet era are still in business, in their most recent versions "adapted" to the Internet simply adding some chapters about Web based Software Engineering.

Last but not least, in the current version of the SWEBOK (2004), there is almost no trace of the "Internet revolution", and no impact on the related curricula [3].

We observe that the current perception of software as a product widespread in the society is quite different from the pre-Internet days, because of its impact on the economy at large. For several years the richest people in the world have been those made rich by inventing or marketing some piece of software; Microsoft is currently the company with higher value in the US Stock Exchange; the IPO on Google has been big news on international media.

Thus, the great economic value of software increased its importance for modern organizations, which directly or indirectly are being deeply influenced by software-intensive technologies.

From an educational viewpoint, the most important novelty of the last decade in the discipline of Software Engineering has been probably the end of the "methodology war" resulted after the definition of the UML as an industrial standard by the Object Management Group. In a globalized economy, modern organizations are clearly interested in product and process standards. UML-based technologies offer standards for developing and documenting software products, thus they gained rapidly a prominent position in the industry. Moreover, the very same technologies offer a clear basis to educators to create Software Engineering courses. Thus, UML has become a common topic in several Computer Science courses.

For instance, our CS students in Bologna get a number of courses in which some UML is taught; a non-comprehensive list includes: introduction to programming, comparative programming paradigms, software engineering laboratory, design of information systems. Although UML is very useful in a variety of educational situations, when it is used for teaching how to design software systems some students raise a number of questions which are quite difficult to answer. For instance, these are typical questions: Which is the rationale behind UML? Why it includes "those" diagrams and not others? How UML can be used to design "good" software systems and architectures? How do we reconciliate the lack of formal semantics for UML, with the fact that it is used to create programs in languages whose formal semantics is well known? Some of these questions are familiar to software engineering scholars, who probably know some very good answers to them. For instance, UML basics are rooted in object oriented analysis and design and this transpires in UML reference documents and in papers that address the UML evolution [10,2,11]. In the last years, however, especially since organizations traditionally producing software like IBM and Microsoft started transforming themselves into organizations offering business services, a novel set of difficult questions can be raised by students during a software engineering course specifically using UML for business modeling. This is a sample of this second type of questions: How can we use UML for describing, analyzing, and reengineering organizations? How can we reconciliate (top down) business analysis with (bottom up) business simulation? Is UML suitable for non-OO modeling, for instance for agent oriented modeling or for ontology-based modeling? How can we use UML to evaluate the cost of a piece of software or the business plan for a service? How do we reshape and enact the RUP for a specific organization, especially one that is strongly used to the waterfall process model [12]?

The shift of focus from designing a piece of software to analyze and reason upon its role inside an organization is important and quite difficult to appreciate. We found for instance that the students have difficulties in appreciating the distinction between using UML for modeling a software system and using UML for modeling a business organization [9]. Also difficult to appreciate is that to build a software intensive service means to measure and (re)design the organization that will offer or exploit that service [4]. We believe that studying the foundations of Organizational Software Engineering is an important point for the education of future software engineers.

Acknowledgements. We thanks the support of the Italian Ministry of University, project FIRB2005-TOCAI.

References

1. Robert Axelrod. Advancing the Art of Simulation in the Social Sciences. *Complexity*, 3(2), 1997.
2. Morgan Bjorkander and Cris Kobryn. Architecting Systems with UML 2.0. *IEEE Software*, 20(4):57–61, 2003.

3. Pierre Bourque, Francois Robert, JeanMarc Lavoie, Ansk Lee, Sylvie Trudel, and Timothy Lethbridge. Guide to the Software Engineering Body of Knowledge (SWE-BOK) and the Software Engineering Education Knowledge (SEEK) - A Preliminary Mapping. In *Proc. 10th Int. Workshop on Software Technology and Engineering Practice (STEP)*, pages 8–23. IEEE CS Press, 2002.

4. Fabio Casati, Eric Shan, Umeshwar Dayal, and MingChien Shan. Business-Oriented Management of Web Services. *Communications of the ACM*, 46(10):55–60, 2003.

5. Michael Cusumano. *The Business of Software*. Free Press, 2003.

6. Dia. gtk+ based diagram creation program http://www.gnome.org/projects/dia/.

7. ECESIS. Eclipse Community Education Project. An Eclipse Technology Research Subproject http://www.eclipse.org/ecesis/.

8. Eclipse. http://www.eclipse.org/.

9. Simon Johnston. Rational UML Profile for business modeling. Technical Report White paper, IBM, 2004.

10. Cris Kobryn. UML 2001: a Standardization Odyssey. *Communications of the ACM*, 42(10):29–37, 1999.

11. Cris Kobryn. UML 3.0 and the Future of Modeling. *Software System Modeling*, 3:4–8, 2004.

12. Craig Larman, Philippe Kruchten, and Kurt Bittner. How to Fail with the Rational Unified Process: Seven Steps to Pain and Suffering. Technical Report White paper, Valtech and Rational, 2002.

13. Francesco Luna and Alessandro Perrone, editors. *Agent-based methods in Economics and Finance: Simulations in Swarm*, volume 17 of *Advances in Computational Economics*. Kluwer, 2002.

14. Francesco Luna and Benedikt Stefansson, editors. *Economic Simulations in Swarm: Agent Based Modelling and Object Oriented Programming*, volume 14 of *Advances in Computational Economics*. Kluwer, 2000.

15. Nelson Minar, Roger Burkhart, Chris Langton, and Manor Askenazi. The Swarm Simulation Sistem: a Toolkit for Building Multi-agent Simulations. Technical Report www.santafe.edu/projects/swarm, SantaFe Institute, 1996.

16. Marco Remondino. Agent Based Process Simulation and Metaphors Based Approach for Enterprise and Social Modeling. In *Procs. 4th Int. Conf on Agent Based Simulation*, pages 93–97. SCS European Publishing House, 2003.

17. Marco Remondino. *Analysis of Agent Based Paradigms for Complex Social Systems Simulation*. PhD thesis, University of Turin, 2004.

18. Michele Sonnessa. JAS: Java Agent-Based Simulation Library, an Open Framework for Algorithm-Intensive Simulations. In B. Contini, R. Leombruni, and M. Richiardi, editors, *Industry and Labor Dynamics: The Agent-Based Computational Economics Approach; Proceedings of the Wild@Ace 2003 Workshop*. World Scientific, Singapore, 2003.

19. Michele Sonnessa. *Modelling and simulation of complex systems*. PhD thesis, University of Turin, 2004.

20. Pietro Terna. Simulation Tools for Social Scientists: Building Agent Based Models with SWARM. *Journal of Artificial Societies and Social Simulation*, 1(2), 1998.

21. Pietro Terna. Cognitive agents behaving in a simple stock market structure. In Francesco Luna and Alessandro Perrone, editors, *Agent-based methods in Economics and Finance: Simulations in Swarm*, volume 17 of *Advances in Computational Economics*, pages 187–227. Kluwer, 2002.

22. Pietro Terna. Simulazione ad agenti in contesti di impresa. In *Sistemi intelligenti*, volume 1, XVI,, pages 33–51, 2002.

23. Pietro Terna. La simulazione come strumento di indagine per l'economia. In *Sistemi intelligenti*, volume 2, XV, pages 347–376, 2003.
24. Pietro Terna. How to Use the Java Enterprise Simulator (jES) Program. http://web.econ.unito.it/terna/jes/how_to_use_jes.pdf, August 2004.
25. Pietro Terna. The Quest for the Enterprise: jES, a Java Enterprise Simulator. Dipartimento di Scienze economiche e finanziarie G.Prato, Università di Torino, August 2003.
26. Omondo UML. http://www.eclipseuml.com/.
27. Wil van der Aalst, Arthur Hofstede, and Mathias Weske. Business Process Management: A Survey. In *Proc. Int. Conf. on Business Process Management*, volume 2678 of *Lecture Notes in Computer Science*, pages 1–12. Springer, 2003.
28. Gerd Wagner and Florin Tulba. Agent-Oriented Modeling and Agent-Based Simulation. In Manfred Jeusfeld and Oscar Pastor, editors, *Conceptual Modeling for Novel Application Domains*, volume 2814 of *Lecture Notes in Computer Science*, pages 205 – 216. Springer, 2003.

Author Index

Lecture Notes in Computer Science

For information about Vols. 1–4242

please contact your bookseller or Springer